Abstracts *from* Newspapers *of* Wilmington, North Carolina
- 1798 -1800 -

(Volume #2)

(New Hanover County)

Compiled by:
Raymond Parker Fouts

Southern Historical Press, Inc.
Greenville, South Carolina

This volume was reproduced
from a personal copy located in
the Publishers private library

Please direct all correspondence and book orders to:
SOUTHERN HISTORICAL PRESS, Inc.
PO Box 1267
Greenville, SC   29602-1267

Copyright 1984 by: Raymond Parker Fouts
Copyright Transferred 2023 to:
        Southern Historical Press, Inc.
ISBN #978-1-63914-211-8
Printed in the United States of America

PREFACE

These abstracts were made from microfilm of the original newspapers, obtained from the North Carolina State Archives at Raleigh, North Carolina.

Information concerning dates available, and location of the originals, is included at the beginning of each year. All issues located are noted, though nothing may have been abstracted from them.

Advertisements are recorded only from the first issue in which they appear in legible form. Each item has been assigned a number, within parentheses. The name index and location index refer to these numbers.

When used as initials, the letters "I" and "J" are indistinguishable in the original.

TABLE OF CONTENTS

	Pages
1798 - HALL'S WILMINGTON GAZETTE	1-20
1799 - THE WILMINGTON GAZETTE	20-44
1800 - THE WILMINGTON GAZETTE	44-89
Index	91-108
Location Index	109-112

ABSTRACTS FROM NEWSPAPERS OF WILMINGTON,

NORTH CAROLINA

1798-1800

VOLUME II

1798 - All issues missing except for the following from Harvard University Library-February 8, 22; March 8; April 12; May 31; June 21; October 11; November 15. From American Antiquarian Society-March 29; August 30, November 29.

HALL'S WILMINGTON GAZETTE.
(No. 58.) Thursday, February 8, 1798. (Vol. II.)

(1) Providence, Jan. 9. Mr. Wm. MARGEE, who arrived from Canton in the ship Grand Turk..informs, that on their homeward bound passage, in the Straits of Banca, they spoke the ship Eliza, of this port, late commander capt. Wm. PAGE. Capt. CARR (the commander) informed him that on the 17th of April last, in the Straits of Java, they discovered a prow with Malays on board; supposing her a trading vessel, the Capt. dispatched a boat to her, on which she came along side. The Linguist asked if they were Traders, they answered in the affirmative, upon which he, with the Capt., Thomas PAGE, and another Seamen, went on board. Capt. PAGE, observing nine Weapons, requested the Malay Chief to give him one, which he did, on seeing some others of a more curious shorkmanship, he asked for one of them; on his stooping to examine them, a Malay thrust a knife into his body. Capt. P. on receiving the wound sprang for his own vessel..he lived about 40 minutes. On the Captain's being wounded, the action began general. Thomas PAGE and the Linguist were killed on the Prow, the Malay Chief and 10 of his crew killed.. Few men have been more beloved than capt. PAGE;.. To the public his loss is great, but to his family..it is irreparable.

(2) Wilmington, February 8. The President of the United States, by and with the advice and consent of the Senate, has appointed Fisher AMES, Bushrod WASHINGTON, and Alfred MOORE, Esquires, commissioners for holding a treaty with the Cherokee Indians, for the extinguishment of the Indian titles to certain lands in the state of Tennessee.

(3) On Wednesday the 14th instant, Will be Sold, on the spot, The Lot with improvements thereon, in NUTT's alley occupied by Mr. CREVILLIER. The house has lately had some improvements, as also the bake house with a large new oven... William NUTT. Wilmington, Feb. 5.

(4) The following Lands and Town Property Are for Sale, for ready Pay in Cash or Produce. About 500 acres in New-Hanover county, on the New-Inlet, commonly called Federal Point. About 1600 acres in Cumberland county, within two miles of Fayette-

(4) (Cont.) ville, called Spring-Hill. Several parcels of Land on Black River. The House and Lot in Wilmington, at present occupied by Mr. Wm. NUTT, opposite to Mrs. DUBOIS's. 160 acres of Land on Masonboro' sound. Several Water Lots in the south part of Wilmington. Geo. HOOPER. February 1.

(5) For Sale, cheap for Cash. A Likely young Negro Fellow..by the month of April next will have finished his apprenticeship with Mr. John NUTT of this place..to learn the business of cabinet work, and Windsor chair making.. Enquire of the Printer.

(6) For Sale, About 100 bushels Black Ey'd Peas. John BURGWIN.

(7) Notice. All those indebted to the estate of Mary M'ALLISTER, dec. are requested to make payment on or before the first day of March next... Benjamin MILLS, Ex'r. Wilmington, February 1.

(8) For Sale, 3,840 acres of Land, lying in the state of Tennessee south of the river Ohio, in the county of Davidson, on the waters of Mill-Creek and Bigg-Harpoth, within a few miles of the town of Nashville, surveyed in February, 1785..recorded in the Secretary's office of the state of North Carolina patented by his Excellency Richard CASWELL, then Governor of said state.. Enquire of the Printer of this paper.

(9) Notice. The Copartnership of Jonathan AVERY and Co. is this day dissolved by the mutual consent of all parties concerned... Daniel INGALLS; Sam. I. THURSTON, Jonathan AVERY. Wilmington, January 4.

(10) Passports and Rolls of Equipage, agreeable to the 25th and 27th articles of the treaty between France & the United States, made the 6th of February, 1778, for sale at the Printing-Office. Wilmington, Jan. 18.

(11) To Be Sold, On Wednesday the 7th day of March next, at the Court House in Wilmington the following Lands, Or as much as may be necessary to satisfy the taxes due thereon, viz. 56,640 acres, entered by Daniel WHEATON and I. CARRAWAY, on the south side of Holly Shelter creek, joining a Tract of Land entered by James HOWARD, now the property of John HOWARD bounded southwardly on lands belonging to Robert SAGE eastwardly and northwardly on the lines of the counties of New Hanover and Onslow. The sale to begin with the first survey of 640 acres. Also, The following Tracts, as the property of George BLYTH, deceased. Patent No. 200, 40 acres on the east side of Cape-Fear river, beginning at a Cypress CLARK's lower line, and joining the lines of Samuel BLYTH and Henry YOUNG. No. 201. 100 acres on the east side of MOORE's creek, beginning at a pine in LEWIS's line, near the White Oak Swamp, and joining the line of Nathaniel M'GUFFORD. No. 202. 200 acres on the west side of the North-East river, and north side of Long creek, beginning at a pine on or near Samuel BUNTING's line, bounded on the west by Long creek. No. 203. 120 acres on Stump Sound, beginning at a cedar at the head of a cove, Amos LOVE's corner. No. 204. 200 acres on the east side of the North-East river, beginning at John Ablen CAMPBELL's corner, and joining lands of John COSTON. No. 205. 100 acres on the east side of Cape-Fear river near the forks of EVAN's road, Henry BOOK's corner and joining Lands of Jas. TATE. No. 557. 350 acres between Wilmington and the Sound.. No. 558. 300 acres on the north east side of the road from Wilmington to Brunswick, lying between two surveys of Land granted to Samuel SWANN. No. 596. 100 acres..near Brunswick road, and joining Lands of Roger MOORE. No. 788. 300 acres..joining No. 558. No. 789. 320 acres..joining No. 788. N. B. Mr. WHEATON disclaims any title to the above lands, he having transfered them to persons unknown. Thomas WRIGHT, Sheriff.

(12) List of Letters remaining in the Post Office at Wilmington, N. Carolina. Ben-

(12) (Cont.) Jamin AYDELOT, 2; Andrew ADAMS, Cetoyen AUBINAUD. J. B. BROWARD, Herral BLACKMORE, Jas. BROWN, Joseph BRECK, Isaac BURR, William BROWN, 2. William CAMPBEL, Wm. CUTLAR, Thomas CROSS, John CAMOCK, Thomas CARLIE, Alexander CAMPBELL, care of Duncan? LIVINGSTON; John COOK, Wm. CHADWICK, Thomas CONNOLY, Doctor CLAYPOOLE. Joseph DEAN, Mrs. Milly DEALE, Richard DOUD, Monsieur DE LAMOTHE, Ralph DODSWORTH, Jeremiah DANAVON. Richard GREEN. Henry HALSEY, James HARPER, Gershom HOMER, John HALL, Mr. HOLT, Rebecca HARTSON?, Jacob HARTMAN, Capt. Thomas HEATLY. Dilson JORDAN, 2; Charles JORDAN, Wm. JONES, 2; Edward JONES, Esq., Thomas JOHNSON, Esquire; Mr. JOHNSON, tavern keeper. Daniel LEWIS, Sam. LEE, B. LASPEYRES, Docteur LAROQUE, Mrs. Sarah LILLINGTON. Daniel M'KINZIE, George M'KINZIE, Esquire; Thomas M'CULLOCK, Benjamin M___ Esquire; John MILLINGTON, Messrs. M'COMB and TILSON, Hugh MULHLAND, Duncan MORISON, to the care of John M'RAY; Archibald M'LEOD, care of Collin CAMPBELL; William MUNN, care of Mr. GIBBS; Capt. William M'CONDRAY, James M'CAULY, George M'DONALD, John B. MOORE, Esquire; Samuel MASON. John O'NEIL. William PATTERSON, 2; William POLK, Esquire, Supervisor of the Revenue, care of James READ, Esq. Collector. Mrs. QUINCE. George READ, Samuel RUSSELL, Richard ROWELL, James RODGER, Moses RITTER, John RICH, Captain Joseph ROBINSON, Edward ROBINSON. Isaac SIMS, Daniel SLOAN, Henry STOLEY, John SCURLOCK, George STEELE, Robert SAGE, Samuel STOCKING, Jonathan SNOW. Charles THOMSON, Onslow county-Caleb THOMAS. Captain William WILLIAMS, Michael WALSH, Mr. WISS, Capt. Joseph WHITFIELD, Mrs. Mag Mary WALKER, James WALKER, Hays G. WHITE. R. BRADLEY, A. P. M.

(13) For Sale, At the subscriber's Store, French Brandy, New-York Porter, Irish Linens, Nails... F. FONTAINE & Co. Dec. 21.

(14) Notice. All persons indebted to the estate of the late Richard QUINCE, dec'd. by bond, note, or otherwise, are requested to make immediate payment to the Administrators... A. D. MOORE, George DAVIS, Adm'rs. January 25.

(15) Just Imported From New-York, And for Sale, by R. BRADLEY (Dry Goods).. With an Assortment of Hard Ware & Iron Mongery.

(16) Ran away on the 9th inst. from the subscriber, in Sampson county, a Negro fellow by name of IRELAND, formerly the property of Col. John SAMPSON, deceased... Thomas SEWELL. Sampson county, Dec. 18.

(17) Will Be Sold, On Saturday the 13 h instant, A S rawberry Plantation, Rocky Point, All the perishable property of the late Mr. Thomas MOORE, consisting of Household Furniture, Horses, &c. At the same time a number of valuable Negroes will be hired till the first of January 1799.. Th_mas HOWE, R_bert HOWE, Ex'rs. February 8.

(18) Pursuant to a Decree of the Court of Equity, Will Be Sold At Public Auction, On Saturday the 21st day of April next. All that Lot of Land in Wilmington, (including the wharf) formerly the property of Charles JEWKES, deceased, and lately occupied by WARD and LANGDON.. Also, A Water Lot..with the tar shed &c..adjoining the house and lot now occupied by Samuel R. JOCELYN. Also, That Lot and Store in Wilmington, now in the occupation of MACLELLEN and LORD. Also, That valuable Plantation called PORTER's Neck, situate in Bladen county, on the west side of the North-west river, near to General BROWN's, containing about 640 acres... Sam. R. JOCELYN, C. & M. E. Wilmington, Jan. 11.

(19) The subscriber informs his friends and customers, that he continues his store at the old stand, and has on hand a general Assortment of European and West-India Goods, suitable to the season... Jonathan AVERY. Wilmington, January 4.

(20) Five Dollars Reward. Ran away from the subscriber, the 29th of January, a Negro Wench named SALLY, about 30 years of age..has a husband belonging to Mrs. Ann QUINCE of Wilmington, named VIRGIL.. Whoever will secure the said wench..or deliver her to the subscriber at Moorfields, shall receive the above reward... Richard QUINCE. February 8.

(21) State of North-Carolina. In the House of Commons, Dec. 22. The committee to whom was referred the Governor's message of the 18th inst. further report-That since the partial report already made..every hour's progress produced additional instances of frauds committed in the obtaining of military land warrants and grants-forged certificates and forged assignments of warrants.. They further find, that to effect the detection desired, to remedy the evils suffered..that it will be expedient to pass into an act, the bill "to repeal all acts heretofore passed, authorising and requiring the Secretary of State to issue Warrants to any officer or soldier of the late continental line of this state, for military services..for a limited time." ..researches made..leave the committee without doubt that the Secretary of State has.. been unmindful of his duty.. But the committee are fully of opinion, that..the Secretary should immediately be suspended from office..

Your committee are fully of opinion that undue means have been used to obtain the signatures of Major NELSON and Captain PHILIPS, to certificates of a very great number..the certificates were in many instances filled up with fictitious names..the committee have not doubted that Wm. TYRREL, first charged, has been materially concerned in the frauds, and procured them to be done. In the course of the enquiry the committee also found, that Stokeley DONALDSON, Redmund D. BARRY, John MADEARAS, were also materially concerned in the same. They also find that Sterling BREWER, Allen BREWER, John CONROY, John MANN, Wm. LYTLE, Robert YOUNG and Joseph ADAMS..appear to have been the instruments of the said TYRRELL, BARRY and DONALDSON... Capt. G. BRADLEY and Col. Wm. POLK, the committee suppose to be material witnesses, and recommend that they be bound over to give testimony.

Your committee cannot conclude this report, without earnestly recommending that the office of Martin ARMSTRONG be closed... John SKINNER, Chairman. Raleigh, Dec. 22, 1797. Resolution No. I, relative to the suspension of the Secretary, was not adopted. Resolution No. II. Resolved, That William HINTON, Esquire, be requested to bind in sufficient recognizance, William TYRRELL, Stokeley DONALDSON, Redmund D. BARRY, John MADEARAS; Sterling BREWER, Allen BREWER, John MANN, William LYTLE, Robert YOUNG, Joseph ADAMS and John CONROY, to appear and answer such prosecutions as may be preferred against them at the superior court..for the district of Hillsborough, at April term next.. (A Copy) J. HUNT, Clerk H. C. In Senate, Dec. 23, 1797. Read, amended and concurred with as amended, the resolution No. 1, excepted as by the House of Commons. Benj. SMITH, Speaker. By order, S. HAYWOOD, C. S.

(No. 60.) Thursday, February 22, 1798. (Vol. II.)

(22) Congress. House of Representatives. Tuesday, Jan. 23. ..Mr. Dwight FOSTER, from the committee of claims, made an unfavorable report on the petitions of John NELSON and widow RUSSEL, who prayed to be allowed to locate certain lands before the session had been made by the Indians.. The house again resolved itself into a committee of the whole on the bill providing means of foreign intercourse; when Mr. NICHOLAS's amendment being under consideration, Mr. FINDLEY spoke in favor of it, and Mr. Isaac PARKER against it. Mr. GALLATIN presented the petition of Gustavus and Hugh COLHOUN, of this city, praying for certain redress on account of 121 cases of claret, which were seized and sold for not being included in the manifest of the cargo..from Charleston, though the duty had been secured by Hugh COLHOUN, in Charleston, before

(22) (Cont.) he sent them off..which..was unknown to Gustavus COLHOUN at the time of the seizure.. On motion of Mr. W. C. CLAIBORNE, the unfinished business of yesterday was postponed.. Tuesday, Jan. 30. .. "Resolved, that in the ballot for managers on the part of this house, of the impeachment against William BLOUNT, a majority of the whole number of members present shall make a choice.." Wednesday, Jan. 31. .. The house being cleared, Mr. SEWALL stated, that he had been informed.. that in the presence of the house, whilst sitting, Matthew LYON, a member from the State of Vermont, did this day commit a violent attack and gross indecency upon the person of Roger GRISWOLD, another member of this house.. Resolved, that Matthew LYON..be, for this disorderly behaviour, expelled therefrom...

(23) Wilmington, Feb. 22. William MILLER, jun. is appointed Commissioner of the Revenue of the United States, vice Tench COXE.

(24) To Be Sold, As Escheated Property, On the 20th day of March next, An undivided Moiety of that House and Lot in Market-street, formerly possessed by Mr. Charles JORDAN, now occupied by Mr. SPAULDING... Jos. G. WRIGHT, Att'y. February 22.

(25) Wanted To Purchase, Two or Three strong young Plough Horses. A liberal price will be given by William H. HILL. February 22.

(26) Notice. The subscriber informs..that the success he has met with in his Lottery, will enable him to draw it the latter end of next week... D. LAMBERTOZ. Wilmington, February 15.

(27) Great Bargains For Cash. On the 19th day of March next, Being the second day of New-Hanover Court, will be exposed to Public Auction, At the Court House in Wilmington, The Following Valuable Lands: ..formerly the property of John ROWAN, Esquire, deceased: viz. situate In Brunswick County. 2120 acres on & near WOOD's creek, called the Mill Lands..near Wilmington..296 acres on the Northwest river, being the Plantation whereon the late Mr. John HOWELL lived, called Westmoreland, and lying between Point Repose and Rowan Plantation.. 400 acres on the Northwest river and WOOD's creek, running back to Indian creek.. In Bladen County. 1251 acres on both sides of the Northwest river..bounded above by lands formerly the property of Goodwin ELLETSON, deceased; and below by those of John Porter? GRANGE, or John HALL, Esquire.. Also..Town Houses, viz. One in QUINCE's alley, which has been long occupied by James JENNET, and in use as a well frequented Tavern.. The other..on the north side of Market street, between Front street and the river..carefully built of the best brick and materials, Two rooms on the ground floor and part of the cellar being subject to Mrs. JAMES's dower.. And in like manner Will be Rented out In Four Lots, The Three Apartments of the Ware-House Opposite DORSEY's Hotel.. Further information..by applying to Benjamin SMITH. Belvedere, February 14.

(28) Sheriff's Sales. Pursuant to a Writ of Execution, issued from the Court of Brunswick County, and directed to me, bearing test the 30th of January last past, Will Be Sold, on Thursday the 12th day of April next; at Ashton Barn, in Bladen County, late the residence of George WEARE, Esquire, now deceased, and now in the hands of the Trustees of the University of North-Carolina by Escheat, or so much of the same as will be necessary to satisfy said Execution; that is to say, Ashton Barn, That valuable improved Plantation, whereon the said Geo. WARE sometimes resided..on the south side of the Northwest river, between the Lands call Newfields and Mr. Peter GOUTIER's Plantation, containing by estimation 700 acres more or less. Two Tracts of Land of 640 acres each, adjoining or near to Colley Swamp, in said county, Patented by Joseph HOWARD. Also, one Tract containing 640 acres..near South river, and adjoining Lands now or latterly the property of Joseph REEVES, Patented to C.

(28) (Cont.) SUTTON. T. W. HARVEY, Sheriff. Bladen County, N. Carolina, 14th February, 1798.

(29) After the above, will be offered for Sale, The valuable Lands of Dr. James CLITHERALL, situate in Bladen county as follows, viz. 100 acres by deed from Warren BALDWIN, dated 2d January, 1735-6, then joining the Lands of John ASHE, to the westward and eastward, on Lands of Mr. Joseph WATTERS, whereon the said BALDWIN lived the day before mentioned, known by the name of the White Marsh. 640 acres by patent granted 20th February 1735, to Hugh CAMPBELL, lying on the most westwardly branch of HAMMOND's creek, and joining Lands of Francis THOMAS. 320 acres on both sides of HAMMOND's creek, whereon Neil SHAW lived, granted to Francis THOMAS, and by him sold to Hugh CAMPBELL. 640 acres on HAMMOND's creek, by patent granted to William FLAVELL, conveyed to David ROACH, and by said ROACH to Magdalen CAMPBELL, joining Lands then belonging to HOWE and SINGLETARY, viz. 24th November 1738. 150 acres granted to Magdalen CLITHERALL, 24th Nov. 1738, lying on Plumb branch, being a branch of HAMMON's creek, between the lines of Land then belonging to Robert HAMILTON and David ROACH. 640 acres granted to Magdalen CAMPBELL, 9th March 1736-7, lying on the head of WHITE's creek, a branch of Waccamaw river, four miles from the head of HAMMOND's creek, and the plantation of the then late Hugh CAMPBELL. 320 acres on a branch of HAMMOND's creek, granted to Hugh CAMPBELL 17th June 1736... Benjamin SMITH. Belvedere, Feb.14.

(30) State of the Frigates, taken from the report of the secretary of war.. Constitution. The Constitution was launched at Boston on the 21st of October last.. Constellation. The Constellation was launched at Baltimore on the 7th September, and has been so far completed as to be now ready to leave the Patapsco to receive her stores, officers and crew; she may therefore be sent to sea at a very short notice.

(No. 62.) Thursday, March 8, 1798. (Vol. II.)

(31) Agnes MACKINLAY, Midwife, From Glasgow, Respectfully offers her services to the Ladies of Wilmington, and its vicinity, and begs leave to solicit their favors in the line of her business. She has been in this town since July last, but indisposition precluded her making a tender of her services to the public till now..she subjoins the following certificate: Glasgow College, 12th May, 1796. These are to certify that Mrs. Agnes MACKINLAY has regularly attended my Course of Lectures in Midwifery, for one session of the College, and has undergone all the usual Examinations with approbation; and further, that the said Mrs. Agnes MACKINLAY has pursued the knowledge and practice of Midwifery under my direction at the Lying-in Hospital, where she had opportunities of assisting at a variety of Labours.-In testimony whereof, this certificate is subscribed by me, James TOWERS, A. O. P. Wilmington, February 15.

(32) Wilmington, March 8. On the 16th ult. in the House of Representatives of the United States, Mr. DAVIS presented the following resolution: "Resolved, That Roger GRISWOLD and Matthew LYON, members of this house, for their riotous and disorderly behaviour, committed in the house, be expelled therefrom." It was seconded by Mr. PARKER from Virginia, and upon motion referred to the committee of privileges, to whom has been referred the resolution for expelling Matthew LYON.. It was afterwards moved by Mr. OTIS that Roger GRISWOLD and Matthew LYON be requested separately to pledge their words to the Speaker, that they will not enter into any personal contest during the present session of this house..both entered into the engagement required.

(33) All persons indebted to the subscriber, by bond, note, or open account, are requested to make immediate payment, otherwise suits will be commenced indiscriminately. George DUNCAN. Wilmington, March 3.

(34) Wanted As an Overseer, a sober industrious man who understands farming. Apply to M. SAMPSON. March 8.

(35) Public Auction. This Day at 12 o'clock, Will Be Sold,..A variety of Dry Goods ... Thomas FITZGERALD, V. M. Wilmington, March 8.

(36) Thirty Dollars Reward. Ran away from the subscriber, a young Negro Fellow named NED, about 5 feet 8 or 9 inches high... William Watts JONES. March 8.

(37) For Sale, A Family Of Negroes, consisting of a Man, a Woman, and two Children ..seven..and..four... Alexander D. MOORE. March 8.

(38) For Sale. 45M feet Lumber. Apply to William NUTT. Wilmington, March 1.

(39) To be Let or Hired Out, For Two, Three, or Five Years, And possession given on the first day of January next, The Plantations and Land following, with about Thirty Working Negroes, Viz...Plantation called Castle-Haynes..about 1500 acres ___ Land between Prince George's creek and the North East branch of Cape-Fear River..the whole lying within eight or nine miles of Wilmington.. The owner being far advanced in years and in an infirm state of health, is the only reason for his hiring out these Negroes and Lands.. Also, To Be Let, And entered upon in June next, That Elegant and Pleasant Villa, called The Hermitage..-Prince George's Creek running between this plantation & Castle-Haynes..the proprietor intending next May to retire either to the back country or to the northward, for the recovery of his health..enquire of John BURGWIN. Hermitage, 23d Feb. 1798.

(40) Extract of a letter from George WARNER, Esq. Member of the House of Assembly for the city of New-York, to Doctor PERKINS on the subject of his Metallic Points...

(41) Portsmouth, N. H. Jan. 20. Crescent Frigate. On Thursday morning about sunrise a gun was discharged from the Crescent frigate, as a signal of getting under way.. Our best wishes follow Capt. NEWMAN, his officers and men; may they arrive in safety at..their destination, and present to the Dey of Algiers, one of the finest specimens of elegant naval architecture, which was ever borne on Piscataqua's waters. The Crescent is a present from the United States to the Dey, as a compensation for delay in not in__iling out Treaty stipulations in proper time. Richard O'BRIAN, Esq. who was ten years a prisoner at Algiers, took passage in the above Frigate, and is to reside at Algiers as Consul General of the United States, to all the Barbary States.

(42) Ten Dollars Reward. Ran away from my Plantation on Saturday morning last, a young Negro Fellow named JEM, about 22 years old, five feet 8 inches high..he has a Negro wench for his wife, belonging to Mrs. M___ J___... John BURGWIN. Hermitage.

(No. 65.) Thursday, March 29, 1798. (Vol. II.)

(43) Congress. House of Representatives. Wednesday, March 7. Mr. J. PARKER stated, that (owing to his late indisposition) he was not in the house when the bill for erecting a Light House on EATON's Neck was passed; but as he had received instructions from the merchants of Norfolk, to endeavour to get a Light House erected on Old Point Consort, in Virginia, he should propose a resolution..to enquire into the expediency of erecting such Light House. War-Office, Feb. 27, 1798. Sir, The committee to whom was referred "so much of the President's speech as relates to the protection of commerce and the defence of the country," desire to know the amount of the monies expended since the last session of Congress... James M'HENRY. Sam. SEWALL, Esq. Chairman.

(44) Charleston, March 20. Yesterday morning, between the hours of 3 and 4 o'clock, a fire broke out in this city, in a back-building in Federal-street, near the corner of King-street, occupied by Dr. FLOYD.. The sufferers in King-street are-Mr. BROKWAY..Mr. WESSINGER, the baker..Messrs. I. and C. BULOW..Mr. Hart LEVY..Messrs. ROBINSON & PENDALL.. In Federal-street-Mr. John Frederick KERN lost two excellent three-story houses, tenanted by Dr. KIRKLAND and Mr. Alexander PETRIE..and a house belonging to Doctor POINSETT, occupied by Mr. Thomas BARON, was also destroyed.. A small house, belonging to a Mrs. SCOTTOW, a widow who has several small children, and supports herself and them by keeping a school, was pulled down, to prevent the fire spreading.. At this fire, the new patent engine lately imported from London, and made by Mr. BRAMAH?, had the first opportunity of being fairly tried...

(45) Wilmington, March 29. Died on the 1st inst. at his plantation on South-River Mr. Matthew PRIDGEON, aged 105 years.-Some time ago, Mr. John SYKES, aged 95; and Mr. Thomas DEVANE, aged 110. There are several persons now living on said River upwards of 100 years of age, and many from 70 to 90.

(46) Notice. The subscribers having obtained letters of administration on the estate of the late Charles JORDAN, request all persons indebted thereto to make speedy payments... Dominick JORDAN, Sen., Dillon JORDAN, Adm'rs. Wilmington, March 29.

(47) Came to my house on the 26th instant, a Negro Wench named MONIMEN, and her child named JACOB; which Negroes I Formerly sold to Richard DOWD of Chatham county. Said DOWD is requested to come and take them away, by paying the expence of this advertisement. Margaret MURTAUGH. March 29.

(48) To Be Sold, On Friday the 30th instant, at the plantation of William NICHOLS, deceased, on the Sound, called Poplar Grove, All the perishable estate of said William NICHOLS, on said plantation. Also, on the plantation on Island creek, on Monday the second day of April next. Thomas WRIGHT, Sheriff. March 22.

(49) Dancing School. Mr. LOYSEL most respectfully informs..that he has arrived from Newbern, and purposes opening a Dancing-School at Mr. NICHOLS's Long-Room, for the instruction of youth and grown persons, in the newest fashion of that genteel accomplishment... March 21.

(50) Wanted an Apprentice to the Pump and Block-Making Business, apply to William SMEETON. March 29.

(51) For Hire, Two good Black Carpenters; one of them is a prime Cooper as well as Carpenter. Apply to T. HILL. Forceput, March 22.

(52) The subscriber gives thanks to the Ladies and Gentlemen of this town and its vicinity, for their past favors and encouragement. He informs them that he will depart from thence to Newbern, for two or three weeks, and perhaps not return until the fall of the year... Francis RABINEAU. Wilmington, March 22.

(53) By Legislative Authority. A Lottery For the benefit of the Pittsburgh Academy. Whereas the Trustees of the Academy aforesiad, hath represented to this General Assembly, that raising the sum of 700 dollars would be of great benefit to said institution.. That the Trustees of the Academy aforesaid, shall have leave to raise by way of Lottery the sum aforesaid; and that John RAMSEY, James TAYLOR, Charles CHALMERS, John HENDERSON, William WARDEN, James BRADLEY and John DABNEY..are hereby appointed Commissioners for the purpose of opening and completing a scheme of a Lottery ..Tickets in the above Lottery may be had of Mr. Richard BRADLEY, merchant, of this town. Wilmington, March 15.

(No. 67.) Thursday, April 12, 1798. (Vol. II.)

(54) Salem, March 16. Latest from France. Captain James HAY, of the schooner Violent, arrived at Gloucester, on Tuesday night, from Rochelle, which he left the 8th of February.. BUONAPARTE was said to be still at Paris and 100,000 troops devoted to him, in its environs...

(55) Notice. Those who have any demands against Mr. John BARCLAY, are requested, in his absence, to apply for payment to POTTS & GIBBS. Wilmington, April 2.

(56) The subscribers take this method of informing their friends, that they have commenced business under the firm of WILLKINGS & SCOTT; and have on hand a general Assortment of Goods..for Cash only... M. R. WILLKINGS, John SCOTT. April 4.

(57) Boston, March 17. From Glocester, March 15. "Capt. HAYES has arrived here this day from Rochelle.. He gives a report that was current in France when he sailed, that the Executive Directory had proposed to the Council of Five Hundred to pass a law making all American vessels good prize which should have on board papers signed by John ADAMS, as they view him as an emissary of PITT..."

(58) New-York, March 24. Yesterday morning, between 12 and one o'clock, a furious and destructive fire broke out in Maiden-lane:..consumed the store lately occupied by William WILMERDING & Co. and the dwelling house of E. DUNSCOMB, Esq...

(59) Georgia Lands. Important Decision. Messrs. William PAINE, Nathaniel PRIME, Comfort SANDS, and others gave to Messrs. Samuel SEWALL, Samuel, DEXTER and Geo. LANE, a bond, in the penalty of 300,000 dollars, conditioned, with a given time, to procure and deliver to them authentic documents of title to one million acres of Georgia lands; in consideration of which Messrs. SEWALL, DEXTER and LANE, and their associates, delivered to them their notes for 220,000 dollars, payable in instalments. An action was brought on the bond against Mr. PAINE; and after a full hearing in Chancery on the Bond, the Supreme Judicial Court on Wednesday gave judgment for the plaintiffs in the full sum of 22,000 dollars with the interest on the notes which had been due...

(60) Wilmington, April 12. Owing to an alteration in the arrival of the Northern Mail, this Gazette will in future be published on Thursday evening.

(61) To the Printer of the Wilmington Gazette. Philadelphia, March 23. Dear Sir, .. It only remains for me to assure you and those I have the honor to represent, that I view the present state of our political connections as fraught with events of the last importance to the peace, prosperity, and..the very existence of our happy system of government.... I am Sir, yours, James GILLESPIE.

(62) Port of Wilmington.. On the 9th inst. about 3 leagues to the Northward of Cape Fear Bar, Captain GARDNER spoke the Schooner Sophia, John ROYSE, from Burmuda bound to Newbern, 44 days out, and supplied him with provisions and water.

(63) Further Notice. The subscriber having some time ago notified his intention of leaving this place, is sorry to observe, that little or no attention hath been paid to the same, by those indebted to him;..requests payment before the 1st day of June next. All accounts not settled at that time will be put into the hands of his Attorney. Marshall R. WILLKINGS. Wilmington, April 9.

(64) For Sale About 100 Acres of Tide Swamp Land, on the North East River, about

(64) (Cont.) two miles above Wilmington... T. HILL... Forceput, April 5.

(65) Portsmouth, Feb. 17. United States Navy; N. Hampshire. It is worthy of remark, that the first Frigate launced in the then United Colonies; the first frigate built under the authority of the Federal government, and the only seventy four equiped in the United States were either launched or built and launched in New-Hampshire. The same builder colonel James HACKET, was employed in the construction of both frigates and the same superintendant Col. Thomas THOMPSON, conducted their building and equipment. About 30 of the carpenters, who worked on the Raleigh in 1776-77 were employed on the Crescent in 1796 and 97-The Raleigh was built and launched in 63 working days.

(66) Richmond, March 23. (The following letter from Mr. KING Minister Plenipotentiary from the United States, at the Court of London, to the Mayor of this city, was received by last night's mail.) London, Dec. 18, 1797. Sir, ... Rufus KING.

(67) Fifty Dollars Reward. A Mulatto fellow belonging to me, named ALLSTON, ran away last week from Mr. Gorton CHACE, to whom I had hired him for one year-he is tall, well made, about the age of 23 years, and remarkably expert as a workman in the shoemaker's trade... W. H. HILL. April 5.

(No. 74.) Thursday, May 31, 1798. (Vol. II.)

(68) Message of the President of the United States, To Both Houses of Congress. May 4th, 1798... I Now transmit to Congress copies of all the communications from our Envoys Extraordinary, received since their arrival in Paris.. John ADAMS. United States. May 4th, 1798. (No. 6) Paris, February 7th, 1798. Dear Sir,... We have the honor to be, with great respect, your most obedient humble servants, Charles C. PINCKNEY, J. MARSHALL, E. GERRY. (To) Col. PICKERING, Secretary of the United States.

(69) Savannah, May 24. The following is an extract of a letter from Thomas KING, Esq. to James SEAGROVE, Esq. now at Louisville, dated St. Mary's, 4th May 1798...

(70) Charleston, May 17. The British frigate Thetis, capt. COCHRAN,..yesterday brought to almost every inward bound vessel. The following vessels have been captured by the Thetis: The Hamburgh brig Frederica..the property of Mr. C. C. SCHN?TT .. The schooner Ranger,..the property of Mr. Ben BOOTH...

(71) Wilmington, May 31. Married, on Wednesday the 23d inst. Monsieur John POISON, to Miss Ann QUINCE.

(72) To the Electors of the Town of Wilmington. At the request of a number of my friends, I offer myself..as a Candidate for the Honor of representing you in the next General Assembly... Jos. G. WRIGHT. May 31.

(73) Whereas the Heirs of WIMBLE originally had, and still have in possession, a large proportion of the southern or lower part of the town of Wilmington-and whereas some of the Lots..are said to be claimed by others; the subscribers..give public Notice, that they are in possession of full Power, in regard to the premises, from the Heirs of William WIMBLE, deceased, who was Son and Heir at Law of James WIMBLE, deceased; and that a final decision of the Right of Lots in Dispute, will shortly be attempted.. The Claimants and Occupants of the aforesaid Lots, are hereby also informed, that the Heirs of WIMBLE come all within the savery clauses of the Statute Limitations, being Infants of Fome Coverts... Joshua POTTS, Att'y in fact. Ed. JONES, Att'y in Law... Wilmington, May 28.

(74) Wanted To Purchase, Twenty large Oxen or Stears, and 100 Head large Hogs... apply to POTTS & GIBBS. Wilmington, May 22.

(75) Will Be Sold On the 20th day of June next, at Wilmington, in pursuance of a Decree of the District Court for the North Carolina District, Nine Tierces and Two Barrels of Brown Sugar. Michael PAYNE, Marshal. May 24.

(76) Windsor Chairs. H. VOSBURGH returns thanks to his friends in Wilmington..and begs leave to inform..that in future the business of Chair-making will be conducted under the firm of VOSBURG and DUNBIBIN... Wilmington, May 23.

(77) Notice. The subscribers having qualified as Executors to the last will and testament of Thomas MOORE, dec. request all persons indebted to the estate of said dec. to make speedy payments... Thomas HOWE, Robert HOWE. Cedar Grove, April 23.

(78) James CARR Informs his friends..he has removed into Capt. HOSKINS's front house, in Market Street, where he has opened a public house.. He will also accomodate six or eight gentlemen as boarders. Wilmington, April 26.

(79) To the Electors of the Town of Wilmington. Gentlemen,..I..offer myself a Candidate to represent you in the ensuing General Assembly... James WALKER, Nephew of John. Wilmington, 28th May.

(80) To the Inhabitants of Wilmington District, and of the county of Sampson. The subscriber believing the most important interests of the United States to be troubled and likely to be still more perplexed with difficulties, thinks it his duty to make an offer of himself to serve as a Member of Congress... Alfred MOORE. Wilmington, 8th May, 1798.

(81) To the Freemen of the Counties of Brunswick, Bladen, Sampson, Duplin, Onslow, New-Hanover, and of the Town of Wilmington. Fellow Citizens,..I again became a Candidate for the honor of representing you in the House of Representatives of the United States... W. H. HILL. Wilmington, 10th May, 1798.

(82) The subscriber takes this method of informing..that he has just commenced business in the Painting line. He paints in Miniature..and also in Hair, natural or dissolved. Fred. J. JOCELYN. No likeness-no pay. Wilmington, May 31.

(83) To the Electors of the County of New-Hanover. Fellow Citizens, My troubling you with this address is merely to do away a rumour that prevails, of my having declined offering as a Candidate at the ensuing Election... A. Duncan MOORE. 19th May, 1798.

(84) Being informed by Mr. MOORE that a report was in circulation, calculated to injure him with many persons, viz. that on my being announced at the last Election as the successful Candidate, he (Mr. MOORE) congratulated me thereon, declaring his satisfaction that Mr. BLOODWORTH was left out.. It is then only necessary to state one fact..that before Noon on the Day of the Election in Wilmington, I was violently attacked with a Fever which confined me to my bed immediately and for many weeks after.. I did not commune with Mr. MOORE for a week after, of consequence the greetings that was said to have taken place on that occasion, never existed. The conclusion is inevitable. John HILL. Wilmington, May 24.

(85) Henry MELVILLE, Watch and Clock-maker, From London, Makes use of this method to inform the inhabitants of Wilmington..that he carries on the above mentioned

(85) (Cont.) occupation in the shop of Mr. D. LAMBERTOZ in Dock-street... Wilmington, May 24.

(86) Ran away from my Overseer, at Castle Haynes Plantation, an old Negro Woman named NANCY, & her son named HARRY, about 18 years old. They are the wife and son of old CUPID, in Wilmington, by whom it is supposed they are harboured; or perhaps they may be about Old Town, harboured by some of Mr. CARSON's negroes.. Five Dollars for the Woman and 20 Dollars for HARRY. If the said Negro Woman surrenders herself within a month..a faithful servant, she will be forgiven.. And as I am convinced..that CUPID has been the cause of the elopement, I will give to any person Two Dollars, who will deliver..CUPID to me at the Hermitage. John BURGWIN... April 26 1798.

(87) I Am still desirous of selling the House in MANSDEN's? Ally, occupied by Mr. Miles KNIGHT; also that in Market-street, next above Mr. RICHARD's.. For further particulars enquire at Wilmington of Henry TOOMER, Esq. or at Belvedere of Benjamin SMITH.

(No. 77.) Thursday, June 21, 1798. (Vol. II.)

(88) For Sale, The Ship Warren, Burthen 280 tons as she came from sea, being just arrived and now lying in the River-for terms apply to Richard LANGDON. June 21.

(89) Notice. Whereas it has been too much the custom to apply to my negroe apprentices to repair riding Chairs or other work, which tends to my injury particularly as the materials to complete such jobbs must be purloined from me by said apprentices. Notice is hereby given that I will prosecute any person..who may hire..any of my apprentices without my permission. John NUTT. Wilmington, June 21, 1798.

(90) The Subscribers give Notice, that they are appointed Patroles for the County... A. B. TOOMER, A. CUTLAR, B. BLANEY, W. BUNTON, Tho's FITZGERALD. New-Hanover, June Term, 1798.

(91) For Liverpool, and to return immediately for this Port, The Brig Cecero... George CAMERON. Wilmington, June 5.

(92) The subscriber returns his most sincere thanks to his employers for past favors ... Asa BOWDISH, Mason. Wilmington, June 7.

(93) Advertisement. Notwithstanding the repeated notices given of the subscribers having dissolved their Copartnership under the firm of TELFAIR and KEDDY..often been requested..all those indebted..should make speedy payment..no attention has been given... John TELFAIR. William KEDDY. Wilmington, June 7.

(94) Notice. The subscribers having qualified as Executrix and Executor to the last will and testament of Frederick JONES, Esq. deceased, request all persons indebted to the estate..to make speedy payment... Jane JONES. John SWAN. June 7.

(95) Philip WILLIAMS Intends opening School in Smithville about the 18th inst.. Teaching Arithmatic..Navigation..Surveying..Gauging, Mensuration, &c...Algebra..Geometry... June 3.

(96) Notice. Pursuant to a Decree of the Court of Equity, Will Be Sold, On Friday the 10th day of August next, at Public Auction, in Wilmington, The Following Lots, Lands, and Tenements, To Wit. All that Lot of Ground in Wilmington, on the north side of Dock-street and east side of Front-street.. Also that Lot..on the south side

(96)(Cont.) of Dock street, between Front street and the river.. Also that Plantation on Cabbage-Inlet Sound, containing 550 acres more or less. Also that moiety or undivided half part of 70 acres of Land on the Island, held jointly with Thomas OWENS, Esquire. Also that moiety or undivided half part of a Tract of Land held jointly with Thomas ROBESON, junior, on the Great Swamp in Bladen county, containing 640 acres. Also that half Lot in the town of Hillsborough, being part of Lot No. 129.. Also that Lot in the town of Fayetteville, joining the house and lot of the late Thomas BURNSIDE.. Also that Lot in said town..joining a lot of the late Isaiah PARVISOL.. Also, that lot in..Fayetteville, joining the lands of the late Richard GROVES.. And also all that Tract..of Land containing 320 acres..in Duplin county, on a branch of Rockfish, called JAMES' Swamp. Also..will be sold, a Negro Man named BOATSWAIN, and another named TOM. The above..(heretofore mortgaged by the late John ROBESON, dec.) will be sold to satisfy a Decree obtained in the Court of Equity for the District of Wilmington, in a certain cause, wherein the Administrator of Abraham LOTT is complainant and Jonathan ROBESON and others defendants... Sam. R. JOCELYN, C. & M. E. Wilmington, May 31.

(No. 87.) Thursday, August 30, 1798. (Vol. II.)

(97) Boston, August 4. The Fever. The selectmen having had a conversation with the physicians of the town find from their reports, that from the first appearance of the fever, viz. from the 1st of July..but 16 persons have died..and but 10 persons are now sick... By order of the Selectmen, Wm. COOPER, Town Clerk.

(98) Baltimore, August 16. This day, the federal sloop of war, Baltimore, Isaac PHILIPS, esq. commander, weighed anchor and went down river...

(99) Wilmington, August 30. The Hon. Judge STONE, is elected Representative in Congress, for the Division of Edenton; and Willis ALSTON, Esq. for the Division of Halifax.

(100) Died) At Philadelphia, on the 3d instant, Col. James INNES; American Commissioner under the British treaty, for the settlement of the claims of British subjects against the American citizens.

(101) Tuition. The subscriber respectfully informs..that he intends continuing his school during the Summer months... W. MACVURRICH. Wilmington, July 26.

(102) Advertisement. A Sober Industrious Man who can be well recommended, and is acquainted with making and burning of Bricks-may meet with great encouragement, by taking under his direction, from 12 to 20 Negroes..for one, two or three years. John BURGWIN... Hermitage near Wilmington, July 5.

(103) Sheriff's Sale. Will Be Sold On Wednesday the 19th day of September next, at the Court-House in Wilmington, The following Lands, in the County of New-Hanover, for the Taxes due thereon, viz. 2984 acres entered by James CARRAWAY..on the south side of the North-east branch of Cape-Fear River, above the mouth of Holley-Shelter, beginning at a Pine in the county line, 24 poles south of Curling SMITH's second corner of land, formerly patented by Job HARRINGTON, and about 180 poles east of the mouth of Rockfish Creek; conveyed by said CARRAWAY to David ALLISON, and by him conveyed to J. B. BOND of Philadelphia. 14,080 acres entered by Starling WHEATON, on the east side of the Northeast branch of Cape-Fear River, including the lower and the great Holley-Shelter Pecoson, on the head of LILLINGTON and MERRICK's Creek, beginning at a Pine on the north side of ASHE's Mill Creek, thence crossing the Creek on or near Daniel MALLETT's; conveyed by said Starling WHEATON to Daniel WHEA-

(103) (Cont.) TON, and by him..to Francis Lewis TANCY of George-Town. 44,160 acres entered by Daniel WHEATON, on the east side of the North-east branch of Cape-Fear River..on the edge of Holley-Shelter Creek, on the south side thereof, about one quarter of a mile above James HOWARD's line. 2,280 acres, the estate of Richard QUINCE, jun. dec'd. on Doctor's Creek, near South-Washington. Thomas WRIGHT, Sheriff.

(104) Public Auction. On the First Monday in October next, Will commence the Sale of the remaining part of the Cargo of the Ship Betty Cath-Cart, Prize to the Schooner Bellona, a French privateer.-. G. J. M'REE, Collector, Wilmington District. Wilmington, N. C. August 9, 1798.

(105) For Cash Will Be Sold, 800 Bushels Corn, and 100 Tierces Rice. Apply to George DUNCAN. Wilmington, July 16.

(106) Wanted an Overseer, Who understands making Bricks &c.. Apply to Anthony B. TOOMER. Wilmington, June 28, 1798.

(107) LANGDON & GILES Have Imported From Europe..a General Assortment of Hard Ware.. Also..Pewter Goods..Rum..Sugar..Earthen Ware... Wilmington, July 19.

(108) Lumberton Academy Will be opened for the reception of Students, on the first of August next, under the immediate superintendance of David KER, Esq. This academy is intended as a school for the education of young Ladies and Gentlemen. In it will be taught the English, Latin and Greek languages, Arithmetic, Book-keeping, Geography, the use of the Globes, Geometry, Trigonometry, with the practical branches of Navigation and Surveying, the elements of History, Natural and Moral Philosophy, Young Ladies will be instructed in Needle work by Mrs. KER.. By order of the Board of Trustees, John WILLIS, John C. NOYES, J. P. MARTIN, Committee. N. B. Since the publication of the above..Miss TAYLOR, from New-York, last from Dublin, has been engaged as an assistant... Lumberton, July 26.

(109) To Be Sold, That valuable Plantation in Sampson County, whereon the subscriber now lives, containing about 800 acres of Land..Two Story Dwelling House with a brick Cellar... George MORISEY. Sampson County, July 16.

(110) Ran away from the subscriber a Mulatto Fellow named ISAAC, about five and a half feet high, well set.. He was lately the property of Mr. John BECK, of Sampson .. Ten Dollars Reward... George HOOPER, Wilmington, August 21, 1798.

(111) Ran away from Mrs. Susannah QUINCE, in Charleston, South Carolina, on the 17th July, 1798, a Negro fellow named DAVID, by trade a Carpenter. He is slim made, about 5 feet 8 inches high, light complexioned, 28 years of age..he originally lived in Wilmington, and was some time with Mr. ALLEN of said Town.. A reward of 30 Dollars.. Richard QUINCE, Near Wilmington. Or, Abraham MOTTE, No. 118 Bay Charleston, August 16, 1798.

(112) Ran away from the subscribers..two negro men; they both speak French & broken English-one is called GRUDGE..is about 50 years of age; the other is called PRINCE, about 25 or 30 years of age.. It is expected they will endeavour to return to the West-Indies.. A reward of 20 Dollars, if taken in Jones county,..in any other county, 30 Dollars for the two... Joseph HATCH, Edmund HATCH. Jones County, August 4, 1798.

(113) A Caution. My Wife Levisa STACKS, having left my bed and board without cause, I do hereby forwarn all persons..I will not henceforth pay any debts of her contracting. William STACKS. New-Hanover, August 16.

(114) Wanted An Apprentice to the Clock and Watch Making business... H. MEL-VILLE. Wilmington, July 29.

(115) At a respectable meeting of inhabitants of (Rockingham) county, the foregoing address was unanimously adopted and ordered to be signed, by the Chairman, Major SCALES, and transmitted to the President by the first opportunity. Nathaniel SCALES, Chairman.

(No. 93.) Thursday, October 11, 1798. (Vol. II.)

(116) Wilmington, Oct. 11. On Monday the 16th Inst. Will Be Sold To the highest bidder, That House and Lot in Market-street in the possession of Mr. John CALHORDA, for the benefit of John CALHORDA and Co... Thomas FITZGERALD, V. M. Wilmington, October 9.

(117) Just Landed From the Brig Industry, Captain WEBB, from Tortola, and for sale by the subscriber, 22 Puncheons of 3d and 4th proof Rum, and a few Barrels Sugar. George GIBBS... October 11.

(118) The subscriber respectfully informs..that he intends opening on the 15th inst. in the Town of Wilmington, a School, where Reading, Writing and Arithmetic will be taught... Robert HARLEY. Wilmington, October 8.

(119) C. F. HUGUNIN, Clock and Watch-Maker, From Switzerland, Informs the Public, that he has arrived in this place with a variety of Ladies and Gentlemen's Gold Watches And French and English Silver Watches.. He will mend and repair Clocks and Watches..while he remains in Wilmington. Apply at Mr. Jonathan JENNINGS's. Wilmington, October 11.

(120) List of Letters in the Post-Office. Samuel ASHE, 2; Mrs. Peggy ALLEN, Captain Titus ALSTON, Benjamin AYDELOT, 2. Citizen BOSCH, French Consul, 3; Canady BREER, William BROWNE, Offin BOARDMAN, Captain William BARTLETT, John BROWN, junr, Captain Stephen B___ARD, William BLOODWORTH, 2; Samuel BLOODWORTH, Benjamin BOLITHA?, Amherst? BARTLET. Captain Weare COFFIN, John CURRIE, John COLVIN?, Captain James COFFIN, Li__ CASON, Peter CARPENTER, George CAMERON, John CREWS, John CLIFTON, Captain Thomas C___, 2. Christopher DUDLEY, Onslow; James DAWNEN, Edmund DUNKIN, the Matter of the Duplin Lodge. Captain John FELT. Joshua GEE; Clarke GILBERT, James GUNNING, 2; James GORHAM, 2; Mr. GEBAROCHE, 2; William GEWELL, Onslow; Mary GRANGE, Stephen GODKIN, Mons. GAMACHE. Jacob HARTMAN, Daniel HEARTWELL, Wm. HANNAY, Geroham HOMER, M__n HARDY, Henry HULL, Cornelius HOLT, Joseph HODGES, Joshua HARRISON, Gabriel HOLMES, Mr. HULETT, Benjamin HUTCHINS, Jeremiah HAND, William HOOPER, David HOOPER, care of Joseph DEANE. Joseph LUCAS, Captain William LIGHTBOURN; Mr. LOMES, Bernard LASPYRE, 2; Nathaniel LOOMIS, Onslow. Henry MOORE, James MOORE, Samuel MORGAN, John MC FARLANE, Moody MOORE, William G. MARSHALL, Alfred MOORE-William BURN, Thomas MURPHY, James MURRAY, John MURPHY, Mr. MITCHEL. Oza__ NETTLETON. George ORCHARD, John O'NEIL, the Sheriff of Onslow, Monsieur OUSSE. Mr. John PEABODY, 2; John POURCENT, Richard PARISH, James PARISH, John PLAIN, Mrs. POWERS. Moses RETTER, George REED, George ROUSE, Thomas ROBESON, Joseph ROBINSON, Edward ROBESON, William RUSEL, Mrs. S. ROBESON, Patrick RILEY, Edward RUSSEL, 2; Gen. Joseph RHODES. John STORIE, Peter STAUNTON, William STEWART, 2; Jennet SPENDLOVE, Elizabeth SIMPSON, James SHETO, Stephen SMYTH, Duplin; Simon SELLERS, William STUDWICK, Duncan SMITH, Mrs. SELLERS, Mrs. M. SWANN, George STEELE, Selah SULLIVAN, Edward SULLIVAN, John SWANN, John STANTON. Charles THOMPSON, Onslow, 2; John THOMPSON, James TOWNING, Robert TRASH, 2; Anthony B. TOOMER, Wm. TURNER, 2. Mrs. WILLIAMS, Michael WALSH, 2; Gilbert WILSON, Mr. WISS, 2; Captain Samuel WILLIAMS, 2;

(120) (Cont.) Captain William WILLIAMS, Serjeant WILLIAMS, Col. John Pugh WILLIAMS, 2; Howel E. WRIGHT, John Storie WRIGHT, Isaac WRIGHT, Duplin. R. BRADLEY, A. P. M. Wilmington, N. C. October 10.

(121) Notice, The subscriber has it in contemplation to leave South Washington, therefore requests his friends and customers to make payment of the respective balances due him, immediately, as he has already waited a considerable time beyond any degree of reason. Pay to William TAYLOR, in Duplin, and in South-Washington, to Geo. M'DONALD. Sept. 28.

(122) Just Received and for Sale, by Daniel WHEATON, Ladies Sandals, Humhums, Ginghams, Writing Paper..Rum, Madeira, Sherry and Claret Wines.. Who will also sell for cash, or exchange for likely Negroes from 16 to 24 years of age, several very valuable Tracts of Land in Tennessee, not far distant from Nashville. Wilmington, Sept.6.

(123) Just Arrived In the Sloop Jamaica Packet, Captain LIGHTBOURN, from Bermuda, and for sale..Old Windward Island Rum..Muscovado Sugar... George HOOPER. September 27.

(124) State of North Carolina, Wilmington District. Superior Court of Law and Equity, November Term, 1798. Rule of Court. New-Hanover and Brunswick, the 1st, 2d, 3d, and 4th days. Bladen, Duplin and Onslow, and causes out of the District, 5th and 6th days. Criminal and Argument Causes, 7th and 8th days. Equity Causes, 9th, 10th, 11th, 12th, and 13th days. By order of Court, James W. WALKER, D. Clk.

(125) Notice. The Copartnership of POTTS and GIBBS expires by mutual consent, on the 30th of this instant (September)... Joshua POTTS, George GIBBS. Wilmington, Sept. 25, 1795.

(126) George GIBBS Intends continuing in the Commission Business..particularly to those who have hitherto been pleased to favor POTTS and GIBBS with Orders. Wilmington, Sept. 26.

(127) Ran away from the subscriber, on Sunday night, the 30th ultimo, a Negro fellow named CATO..has long hair..a high nose for one of his colour, a remarkable good foot, and plays on the violin. He is well known in Wilmington, by Dr. HILL and Mr. David JONES.. Ten Dollars reward..deliver him to me at MOSELEY Hall, on Rockey Point... Tobias COBB. October 1.

(128) To be Let or Hired Out for 2, 3 or 5 years..That healthy pleasant Plantation in New-Hanover county, Called Castle Haynes, Including Legers and the Rice Field, adjoining, Together with between 20 and 30 Working Negroes, with their families. There is about 1500 acres including Legers and the Swamp belonging to said Plantation, all enclosed between Prince George's Creek and the North east River..within eight or nine miles of Wilmington.. The owner being far advanced in years and very infirm... John BURGWIN. Hermitage, Sept. 10.

(129) Advertisement. The subscriber will give great encouragement to an industrious honest, sober Man who understands the making and burning of Bricks... John BURGWIN. Hermitage. Sept. 10.

(130) Grand Lodge. The Officers and Members of the Grand Lodges, and the Representatives of Lodges, are hereby requested to attend the annual communication in the city of Raleigh, on the evening of the day the 22d of November next, at 6 o'clock. By order of the most worshipful Grand Master, W. R. DAVIE. Robert WILLIAMS, Jun. Grand Sec'ry.

(131) New-York, August 28. Interesting Law Case. Ann BURNS, vs. John BAKER. Action of damages for a breach of promise of marriage, before the honorable Judge KENT, at the sittings held after July term, Friday, the 17th August 1798. Counsel for the Plaintiff, Mr. HARRISON-Mr. MONROE. For the Defendant, Mr. EVERTON-Mr. LEE. Mr. MONROE, on behalf of the plaintiff, opened the cause. He stated..that his client was a young woman of respectable family and connections; that she had been addressed by the defendant, in the character of a lover, who sought a connection with her on honorable terms; that he continued his attention to her till he had effected her seduction, and when he had discovered she was pregnant, had abandoned her; that the defendant was a man who belonged to the society of the Methodists, and had introduced himself to his client as a preacher of the gospel, and under the cloak of religion effected her ruin.. Thomas IVERS was the first witness called for the plaintiff. He swore that he knew the parties; that the defendant was a preacher in the Methodist church, and as such became acquainted with the plaintiff, who was his grand-daughter.. Roderick M'CLOUD, the next witness, was called to prove the defendant's hand writing... the following letter was produced and read in evidence.. addressed to Mrs. Nancy B_RN, Woodbridge.. I am your affectionate Friend, John BAKER. New-York, July the 28, 1797.

Ebenezer DOUGHTY was next called.. William VALLEAD swore that he saw the defendant frequently visiting the plaintiff.. Margaret MORGAN was then called as the last witness-She said she was present when the defendant was sent for and told of the plaintiff's situation, and charged with his baseness to her, and reproached by her that he had seduced her under a promise of marriage. He admitted that he was the father of the child..that if he had promised her marriage, she could not prove it, nor could she recover any damages if she did, for he was not worth anything. The counsel for the preacher opened the defence by stating..they should shew, in mitigation of damages, some very improper conduct on the part of the plaintiff..and next shew that the defendant was worth nothing. Roderick M'CLOUD was then called again, as a witness for the defendant. He was asked by Mr. LEE if he was not knowing to the plaintiff having at some time granted improper liberties to a certain person? He answered..that he was..asked who..confessed he..was the person. He was then asked to tell the jury exactly what these freedoms were..she had permitted him to wait upon her home, four or five times, and-to kiss her, and he had once laid his hand on her neck; but it appeared from further examination, that she had resisted him even when he attempted to kiss her, and absolutely refused him when he attempted to take any further liberties. He acknowledged this was after she was in a state of pregnancy; but denied that it was produced by any preconceived plan between the defendant and himself.. James GOURLAY was called to prove the defendant's circumstances..

The evidence being closed, Mr. EVERTSON, for the defendant..addressed the jury ..as to this person; it having been proved by their own evidence, that she had had a child by means of illicit commerce, they could not think her a very virtuous woman, but that her behaviour to the witness, the Rev. Mr. M'CLOUD was in his mind a forfeiture of all character-for a woman who was courted by one man, to suffer another to wait upon her home, to kiss her, and fondle with her so much as even to lay his hand on her neck, evinced he would say, "a violent propensity to concubinage", and no virtuous woman would do it, especially at the age of five and twenty, when the passions may be supposed in some measure to have cooled.. The Jury brought in their verdict next morning for the plaintiff-damages 750 dollars.

(132) Ran Away from the subscriber..a Negro fellow named TONEY, about 19 years of age, formerly the property of Col. Sampson MOSELEY. He is well known on Rockey-Point, and is probably about Mrs. MOSELEY's plantation. I will give Five Dollars

(132) (Cont.) to any one that will deliver him to me, at the Sound... William MOSELEY, Guardian to Maria A. S. MOSELEY. October 4.

(No. 97.) Thursday, November 15, 1798. (Vol. II.)

(133) The Wilmington Gazette Will be enlarged and printed on a new and elegant Type, twice a week, after the First Day of January, 1799.. Price of Subscription Five Dollars per Annum.. It is requisite that those who subscribed after the fifth day of January, 1797, when the Gazette was commenced, should settle up to the first day of January, 1799. Wilmington, N. C. October 24th, 1798.

(134) Notice. The Copartnership of John CALHORDA and Co. was dissolved on the 11th of September last by mutual consent... John CALHORDA. Wilmington, Nov. 8.

(135) The subscribers since the fire, have removed their Goods to the back part of the store occupied by Mr. NUTT, facing Mr. GEER's where they have A General Assortment, Suitable for the season. WILLKINGS & SCOTT. Nov. 8.

(136) Robert ADAM & Co. Have received by the Ship Hazard from Liverpool, & are now opening for sale at their Store in Wilmington, an assortment of Goods Suitable to the season... November 6, 1798.

(137) Knoxville, Oct. 16. ___ of Kentucky, Sept. 17th '98. Major KINGSBURY, Commandant of Massac, Sir, For the purpose of exploring the country to the southward of this, my friends with me are desirous to descending the river Ohio, by your garrison-not being acquainted with the rules of the place, has induced me to write you, for information how to act, whether we are to descend the river or not.. The migration to Smithland has far surpassed the calculation of many.. Your humble servant, Zach. COX. Fort Massac, July 17, 1798. Sir, I received your letter of this date by Mr. GIST, and must inform you, that no armed party is permitted to pass this place, and should you presume to attempt forcing by the galley or garrison you must expect to pass under a heavy fire from every piece of ordnance, which can be brought to bear on you from the fort and galley. Your humble servant, Jacob KINGSBURY, 2d U. S. Regiment commanding Fort Massac and its dependencies. Mr. Z. COX.

Kentucky, 3 miles above Fort Massac. July 18, 1798. Col. Moses SHELBY. Dear Sir, On my rout down the river Ohio, in pursuit of the journey contemplated, and fully communicated to you when at Smithland; there appears some difficulty with the officers of the garrison of Massac, in permitting our descending the river, as you will see by the inclosed documents.. Zach. COX. One Mile above Massac, July 21, 1798. Major KINGSBURY, Sir,.. I now beg you, if consistent with your power and order, to admit the barge of Col. COX, and one flat bottom boat, with five perogues to pass, with five men on board, of each, or I suppose five less might do by getting hirelings to work up. I have thought from the date of your order..they must have originated with and came from Col. HAMTRAMMOCK... Moses SHELBY. .. Col. Zachariah COX has permission to pass the garrison of Massac, with his company..of himself and 32 others... Thomas ELMORE, officer of the day, 3 miles above Fort Massac, 22d July, 1798.

(138) Philadelphia, Oct. 23. Communication. (Concerning the Fever.) Beware citizens, of a premature return to town..we have sorrowfully to mention that Mr. John MAN, tailor, in Water street, was buried this morning, having returned only 4 days ago.

(139) Norfolk, November 1. John SEVIER, Gov. of the state of Tennessee, and Briga-

(139) (Cont.) dier general of the provisional army, has addressed the regiment of Cavalry of the district of Washington in that state...

(140) Baltimore, October 25. A Cherokee chief, of the name of BOWLES, picked up at sea, by the Isis man of war, is arrived in England.. He had been a prisoner with the Spaniards six years, from whom he had just made his escape.

(141) Alexandria, October 20. From the Columbian Mirror.. Need it asserted be by what authority has Thomas JEFFERSON presumed to intercourse with foreign nations. He is yet but vice president; and in usurping the function of the chief majestrate, he has given a proof of ambition, the ruling passions of his heart, that cannot soon be forgotten...

(142) Letter from Captain M'DOUGAL of the ship Two Friends to his owner in Philadelphia. Ship Two Friends, Margate Road, Sept. 13, 1798. Dear Sir, I have the pleasure to inform you of the safe arrival of our ships Two Friends, after being taken by the French privateer Good Fortune..who took out my two mates and nine of my hands, and sent me for Spain, with a prize master and 17 men..with three men and myself, I retook the ship with very little trouble.. I am dear sir,.. John M'DOUGAL.

(143) Wilmington, Nov. 15. The subscriber informs..that he continues to do business in the Vendue & Commission Line... Thomas FITZGERALD. Wilmington, Nov. 13.

(144) The Trustees of the University of North-Carolina, are earnestly requested to attend the annual meeting of the Board, at the City of Raleigh, on the first Monday of December next. W. R. DAVIE, Trustee. Oct. 20, '98

(145) For Sale, A Few Tierces of good Coffee-Also-Muscovado Sugar..Bottled London Porter..Liverpool Ware..Salt, and Four double fortified Six Pound new Cannon and a quantity of Cannon powder... George HOOPER. Wilmington, Nov. 15.

(146) Notice. The subscribers understand that several persons have of late undertaken to inspect Lumber &c, contrary to an Act of the General Assembly, and to the great injury of the Lawful Inspectors. Notice is hereby given..if any..persons are found attempting to do so in future, they shall be prosecuted..without discrimination. Henry HOSKINGS, Isaac BERNARD, Archibald CUTLAR. Inspectors for the Town of Wilmington. Wilmington N. Carolina, Nov. 10, 1798.

(147) Smithville. The Commissioners for Smithville having resolved that a framed House 24 feet long, and 16 feet broad, shall be erected without delay in the said town, as a temporary School-House; any persons willing to contract for the same are desired to send their proposals to the subscriber on or before the 10th day of November next... Benjamin SMITH, Chairman. Wilmington, Oct. 24, '98.

(148) John PEABODY Clock and Watch-Maker, Returns thanks to his customers for past favors-informs..that he continues his business... Wilmington, Oct. 25.

(149) The Races At Charleston, South-Carolina, will commence on Wednesday the 13th day of February, 1799.. First Day's Purse of at least 1,000 Dollars-Four Mile Heats ... Obrien SMITH, James BURN, Alexander NISBETT, St'wds. October 20.

(150) Just Imported, And for Sale At the Store in Wilmington, Market-Street, formerly THACKER's, by Robert MITCHELL..A general assortment of Dry and West-India Goods... Nov. 8.

(151) From (J. RUSSEL's) Boston Gazette. Elegiac. To the Memory of Mr. John FENNO, of Philadelphia. Late Printer of the Gazette of the United States.. Mr. John Ward FENNO-a young gentleman of talents and merit.

(152) New-York, Oct. 16. Extract of a letter from the agent of the U. S. resident in the Chickasaw nation, dated August 25, 1798. "Lieutenant Samuel R. DAVIDSON, died some weeks ago, at the Walnut Hills, many other officers have died, and the troops are sickly in every post on the Mississippi."

At an election held at Knoxville, on the 21st and 22d inst. for a Senator to represent the county of Knox..the famous William BLOUNT was duly elected, with only one dis‌centing vote!!!

(153) The subscriber informs..that he has taken that large and commodious house in TOOMER's ally, where he has opened a house of accomodation for people at the ensuing Superior Court... John NICHOLS.

(154) Notice. All persons who have any demands against the Estate of James COCHRAN, of Brunswick County, North-Carolina, deceased, are requested to have them properly attested and given to Mr. William WHITE, at Mulberry, Brunswick County, State aforesaid... Thomas COCHRAN. Charleston, 27th Sept. '98

(155) Will be Sold for Cash, On the fourth day of the Wilmington Superior Court, in November next..Six or Seven likely Negroes, and three well blooded Mares... Richard QUINCE. Moorfields, Oct. 16.

(156) Notice. The subscriber informs..that in a few days he will again open his School on the same terms as formerly... Robert HARLEY. Wilmington, Nov. 3, '98.

(No. 99.) Thursday, November 29, 1798. (Vol. II.)

NOTE: Illegibly dark film.

1799 - All issues missing except for the following from Harvard University Library- March 7; April 4, 19; June 13; August 8; September 5; October 3, 10, 17, 31; December 12.

THE WILMINGTON GAZETTE
Three Dollars per Annum.) Thursday, March 7, 1799. (Vol. III.-No. 113.

(157) Published Weekly By Allmand HALL, Printer To The State of North-Carolina.

(158) New-York, Feb. 27. We understand..that two other gentlemen will be added to Mr. MURRAY, in the proposed mission to the French Republic, that the President of the United States on Monday nominated for that purpose, Patrick HENRY, Esq. of Virginia, and Oliver ELLSWORTH, Esq. of Connecticut, the present Chief Justice of the United States. -Am. D. Adv.

(159) A gentleman of the first respectability..arrived from Philadelphia..informs us, that..a report was circulated..that the Senate had confirmed the nomination of Ms. Vans MURRAY as Minister Plenipotentiary from the United States to treat with the Directory of France...

(160) Congress. House of Representatives. February 20. Mr. LYON, from Vermont, took his seat in the House this day. Mr. BAYARD proposed the following resolution to

(160) (Cont.) the house: "Resolved, That Matthew LYON, a member of this house, having been convicted of being a notorious and seditious person, and of a depraved mind, and wicked and diabolical disposition, and of wickedly, deceitfully and maliciously contriving to defame the government of the United States, and John ADAMS, the President of the United States..be therefore expelled this house". ..not carried.

(161) The subscribers give notice that the sum of 234 Dollars and 62 Cents, being a collection made by the Ancient York Masons, in the state of South-Carolina, for the poor and distressed sufferers by the late Fires in this town, has been remitted to them for the purpose of being distributed amongst those who are in the greatest distress... Benjamin SMITH, Griffith J. M'REE, George HOOPER. Wilmington, March 5.

(162) For New-York, The Schooner Juno, Jonathan THOMPSON, Master, Intended as a regular Packet, will sail by the 12th inst..apply..THURSTON, SMITH & PELHAM. Wilmington, March 7.

(163) Sheriff's Sales. On the tenth day of April next, Will Be Sold At the Court-House in Wilmington, One moiety of a parcel of Land on Island creek, containing about 1500 acres, with a good saw-mill..500 acres of Land adjoining. Also..Negroes .. The above property is levied upon, and..will be sold to satisfy sundry writs of fieri facias to me directed, against John B. MOORE, Esq. William NUTT, Sheriff. Wilmington, March 1.

(164) Taken up and committed to Wilmington Goal, a Negro Woman named BET and her daughter, belonging to the estate of Thomas LUCAS of Bladen... Miles KNIGHT, goaler. March 7.

(165) Will Be Sold On Thursday the 4th day of April next, at the Court House in Wilmington, A Plantation on the Sound, called Myrtle-Grove, alias The Vineyard, containing about 500 acres of Land.. Also, A vacant Lot of Ground in Wilmington, on the south side of Dock-street, to satisfy an execution in my hands, John BURGWIN against William MOSELEY, deceased. John ALLAN, coroner. February 19.

(166) For Sale, The Schooner Polly, As she now lies at Mr. William CAMPBELL's wharf, with all her Tackle and Furniture... John LORD. Wilmington, Feb. 11.

(167) For Sale, The American Sch'r Two Friends, James GILDEA?, master... Apply to George GIBBS. January 31.

(168) The subscriber will sell upon a short credit, the Lot whereon his late dwelling-house was situated; the Lot formerly possessed by Mr. Robert WILLKINGS; and the House and Lot now occupied by Mr. RUSS, with a vacant Lot fronting it on Prince's-street. Jos. G. WRIGHT. February 21.

(169) For Sale. 1013 acres of Land in Bladen county, on the west side of Waccamaw river, being one-third part of a Tract of Land entered by John SLOAN, and known by the name of SLOAN's Tract. Also, Between one & two hundred acres of Land in New-Hanover county, on the west side of MOORE's-creek, patented by Joseph WOODCOCK... Michael SAMPSON. February 18.

(170) District Court-House. Any person willing to contract with the Commissioners appointed by an act of the last Assembly..to slate or otherwise secure the Court-House in Wilmington from fire, are desired to send their proposals..to the subscriber ... Benjamin SMITH, Chairman of the Board. February 27.

(171) Notice. The subscriber having qualified as Administrator to the estate of Maurice CUNNIAM, dec'd, requests all persons indebted to said estate..to make payment... Richard KELLY, Adm'r. February 27.

(172) Martin ETTINGER, Blacksmith, Whitesmith, Gunsmith, and Nail Manufacturer, Informs..that he carried on the several branches of business at his Manufactory on Mr. William CAMPBELL's wharf... Wilmington, Feb. 21.

(173) United States of America, North-Carolina District. Whereas Benjamin WOODS, Esq. attorney for the North-Carolina District, hath exhibited his Libel..against Four Cases of Gin... Francis HAWKS, Clerk of said court. February 18, 1798.

(174) Smithville Academy. The Trustees of the abovementioned Seminary are requested to meet at Smithville on Friday the eighth day of March next, at the house of Mr. GAMACHE..to fix a plan of one or more Lotteries for raising the sum granted by the Legislature for erecting an Academy in the town of Smithville, at the mouth of Cape-Fear River. Benjamin SMITH, President. By order, John CONYERS, Sec'y. February 27.

(175) For Sale by LANGDON & GILES West-India Rum..New-England Rum..Muscovado Sugar ..Coffee... February 7.

(176) Just Imported And for Sale by the subscribers, at their Store in Second street ..A General Assortment of European, East and West-India Goods. A. I. BROWN & Co. Wilmington, February 1, 1799.

(177) To Be Leased, And possession given immediately..The Plantation lately the residence of Col. Thomas WRIGHT.. Also, about 40 acres of tide swamp... Jos. G. WRIGHT. M. R. WILLKINGS. Feb. 11.

(178) The Commissioners Appointed by an act of the last General Assembly, for the purpose of selling the Palace lots in the town of Newbern, Give Notice, That the sale of said lots will commence on the 22d day of March next, at noon... J. C. BRYAN, Lewis BRYAN, Wm. JOHNSTON, Jas. CARNEY, Com'rs. Newbern, January 12.

(179) Twenty Dollars Reward. Ran away from the subscriber in the month of September 1797, a Negro Fellow named QUACO, (formerly the property of John HALL, Esquire) a Blacksmith by trade. He is about five feet 10 inches high.. He is supposed to be harboured about the plantations of Jennet SPENDLOVE and of William JONES, in Bladen county. Any person delivering said fellow to the subscriber on the North-east.. shall receive the above reward... William HOOPER. Wilmington, February 7.

Thursday, April 4, 1799. (Vol. III.-No. 117.)

(180) Congress of the United States. House of Representatives. Saturday March 2. The House agreed to the resolution in favor of Joseph WHEATON.. Sunday Morning.. "Resolved, That the thanks of this House be presented to Jonathan DAYTON, in testimony of their approbation of his conduct in discharging the arduous and important duties assigned him, while in the chair."

(181) Public Auction. On Tuesday the 9th instant, Will Be Sold, The Hull, Masts and Spars of the Brigantine Enterprize, Edward ATKINSON, master, of New York. Thomas FITZGERALD, V. M. Apprril 3.

(182) Sheriff's Sale. On the first day of the ensuing Superior Court, Will Be Sold At the Court-House, A Tract of Land on Black? river, about 1000 acres, with a good

(182) (Cont.) saw mill..commonly called SAMPSON's Mills-levied upon to satisfy an execution in my hands, Henry TOOMER vs. the Executors of John GILIARD, dec'd. And on the same day will be Sold 100 acres of Land adjoining Joseph CHADWICK's line, by virtue of a vend. expo. Peter CARPENTER vs. James EARL. And on the third day..will be Sold, Three Negroes, viz. JOB, DICK and PEG, to satisfy an execution Thomas COHHAM? vs. Administratrix of Sampson MOSELEY. And on the same day The following Negroes, viz. BACCHUS and SARAH his wife, GEORGE, FLORA, JIM, JENNY, old ABRAHAM, old NAN, ISAAC and MARY a child, to satisfy an execution Charles JEWKES vs. Administratrix of Alexander LILLINGTON. Wm. NUTT, Sheriff. Wilmington, April 2.

(183) Public Auction. Monday the 23d of the present month, Will Be Sold, Part of the perishable property of the late Mr. Henry TOOMER.. By order of Anthony B. TOOMER, Executor. A. JOCELYN, Auct'r. Wilmington, April 2.

(184) To be Rented at Public Auction, On Monday the 8th instant, The Barn Plantation near the bridge on SMITH's creek, belonging to the estate of the late Mr. Henry TOOMER. At the same time will be Sold, The plantation tools, &c. and between 40 and 50 Negroes... A. B. TOOMER, Ex'r. Wilmington, April 2.

(185) List of Letters remaining in the Post-Office at Wilmington, N. C. A. John ALLAN, 1; Benjamin AYDELOTT, 1; Capt. Edward ATKINSON, 1; Hon. Samuel ASHE, 1. B. Timothy BLOODWORTH, jun'r. 3; Mrs. R. BLOODWORTH, Washington, 1; Capt. Richard BULLOCH, 2; Capt. George BOOCOCK, 1; Captain John BULKLEY, 1; Messrs. William BLANCHARD and Son, 1; Capt. William BASDEN, 1; Mr. John BURKE, 1; Thomas BRICKLE, 1; Madame BOISSON, 1. C. Commissioners of Taxes for the District of Wilmington, 1; Clerk of the Superior Court, 1; William CEVIL, 2; Capt. Ebenezer CHINEY, 1; John CALLON, 1; Thomas COLE, 1; Stephen CASS, 1, Joseph CASSE, 1; John CRESTON, 1. D. Ezekiel DAY, care of POTTS and GIBBS, 2; Christopher DUDLEY, 1; Christopher D DLEY of Onslow, 2; Samuel DENHURST, 1; William DAVIS, 1; Madame DOMNIGO, 1; Capt. Nathaniel DONNEL, care of POTTS and GIBBS, 1; Thomas F. DAVIS, 1; Edward DOLITSON?, 1; A. DULUC, 1; James DEVAUNE 1; James DICKSON, Duplin, 1; Doctor James DUBOIS, 1. E. Mary EDWARDS, 1; Rufus ELLIOT, 1. G. Mons. GAMATH, 1; William GUEL, M. GALBARUSH, 1; James GREEN, 1. H. Capt. Benjamin HUTCHENS, 1; Cornelius HOLT, 1; Daniel HEARTWELL, 1; Gabriel HOLMES, 1; Henry HOSKINS, 1; Isaac HENDRICKSON, 1; John HALL, North-west, 1; Wm. HENDRY, care of Mr. URE, 2; Walter HUSSEY, 1; Mrs. Catharine HUNTER, 1; Henry HULL, Rockey Point, 1; Doctor N. HILL, 1; Mr. HULET, 1; George HOOPER, 1. J. Edward JONES, Solicitor-General, 7; Mrs. JONES, 1; S. H. JOCELYN, 1. K. John KAYS, 1; John KENNEDY, care of H. URQUHART, 1; William KEDDIE, 1; Captain Conkling KETCHOM, 1; Ephraim KEMPTON, 2. L. Mr. LASPEYSE, 1; Stephen LELLY, 1; James LARKINS, Longcreek, 1; Capt. Andrew LAURENCE, 1; Lew LATOUR, 1. M. Amasa MASON, 4; Roger MOORE, 1; Henry MOORE, 1; D. MALLET, 1; Benjamin MOSLES, 1; Wm. M'KERRAL, 1; Wm. G. MARSHALL, 1; Ronland? M'DUGAL, 1; Donald M'INTIRE, 1. N. Richard NIXON, Topsail, 1; William NUTT, 2; Henry NORMAN, 1; Jarrot NOBLE, 1; John NUYS, 1; Peter NICHOLSON, 1. P. William PULLY, 1; Arthur PAREMAN, Onslow, 1; John PLAIR, 1; Miss El za PRATT, 1; Capt. William PARKER, 1; David PERRY, 1. R. Capt. Joseph ROBBINS, 1; Edward RUGGLES, 1; Wm. RUSSELL, 1; Gen. ROUSE, 1; Edward ROBESON on the sound, 1. S. Capt. Gamalu SMALL, 2; Captain Robert SAGE, 2; William SNELL, 1; Daniel SHOALER, 1; James SHAW, 1; James STEWART, Esq. 1; Mrs. Sulan SELLERS, 1; Capt. John STANTON, 1; Jacob SAARS, 1; Geo. STEMUR, care of Cornelius HURST, 1; Simon SELLERS, 1. T. Capt. John THOMPSON, 2; Charles THOMPSON, Onslow, 1; Wm. TURNER, 2; Mrs. Amey TURNER, 1; Captain William TOLMAN, 1. U. Henry URQUHART, 1. W. Richard WATTS, 1; Henry WATTERS, 1; James WEAR, 1; Mrs. Rebecca WILKINSON, 1; John WARKINS, 1; Capt. James WALKER, 1; James WALKER, Esq. 1; Capt. John WOOD, 2; Gilbert WILSON, 1. Should the above letters not be taken out of the Post-office before the first day of July next, they will then be forwarded to the General Post-office as dead letters. John LORD, A.P.M. April 1, 1799.

(186) Ran Away from the Subscriber on Thursday night last, two Negroes, one a mulatto fellow named WILL, about 30 years old, 5 feet 9 or 10 inches high..the other a wench about 18 years old..(reward) of Ten Dollars. J. LANE. Rockey-Point, March 25.

(187) Proposals For publishing by subscription, Notes on Agriculture Adapted to the soil, climate and markets of South-Carolina..by Lewis DU PRE. Subscriptions will be taken in by Maurice SIMONS, Esq. near Georgetown; Mr. Samuel DU PRE, St. James' Santee; Mr. Andrew BURNET, Combahee; Mr. David CRUGER, Messrs. GAILLARD & MAZYCK, and Messrs. FRENEAU & PAINE, in Charleston; ELLIOTT & BURD, in Georgetown, March 20. Samuel I. THURSTON engages to furnish the book subscribed for at Wilmington, (N. C.)

(188) United States of America; North Carolina District. Whereas Benjamin WOODS Esq. District Attorney for the North-Carolina District, has exhibited..a libel setting forth that Griffith J. M___, Esq. Collector of Wilmington,..on the 10th day of March instant..seized as forfeited..a certain schooner called the Ranger..cargo..of coffee, sugar and molasses..for this cause..departed from the port of Boston..Massachusetts..on a foreign voyage, commencing after the..1st day of July, and..(did) proceed to a port..under the acknowledged government of France... Francis HAWKS, Clk. March 15.

(189) Will Be Sold, On Wednesday the 17th of April next, at the Plantation of the late Charles SIMPSON, All the perishable and personal part of his estate... Elizabeth SIMPSON, Adm'x. New Hanover, March 27.

(190) List of Laws, passed at the third session, of the fifth Congress of the United States, begun..at the city of Philadelphia..Pennsylvania, on Monday the third of December, 1798, and ending the third of March, 1799.. 5. An act for the relief of Jonathan HASKILL.. 7. An act for the relief of GAZZAM, TAYLOR and JONES; and of Samuel WATT, of the city of Philadelphia.. 16. An act for the relief of Thomas LEWIS.. 19. An act allowing James MATTHERS, compensation for services done for the United States, and expences incurred in rendering said services, as searjeant at arms to the senate.. 45. An act for the relief of Comfort SANDS and others.

(191) Five Dollars Reward. Will be given for securing goal an elderly Negro fellow named QUAMINA..the property of Mrs. Sarah J. CAMPBELL... Thomas ROBESON. March 14.

(192) Edward WOODYEAR and Samuel SMYTHE Having taken out a license to carry on business as Auctioniers..shall be always ready to attend..having taken a store suitable for their purpose, next to Messrs. BENNER and KEIGHLOR's, in Pratt-street, near BOWLY's wharf... Baltimore, January 26.

(193) Tanning & Currying. The subscribers are determined to carry on the aforesaid business... Lemuel NOYES, Zephaniah LEONARD. N. B. During our absence from Wilmington, which will be about 15 days, application must be made to Mr. John BROWN, merchant. Wilmington, March 21.

(194) Notice. The subscriber once more requests all persons indebted to the firm of Matthew JOHNSTON and Maurice CUNNIAM, to make payment. Those who neglect to do so immediately will be sued indiscriminately. Matthew JOHNSTON, Surviving Copartner. Wilmington, March 21.

(195) The subscriber forbids the sale of a vacant Lot of Ground on the south of Dock-street in Wilmington, as advertised by John ALLEN, coroner; and forwarns any person from purchasing the same, she having a deed therefor. Mary TUCKER. March 28.

(196) Boarding & Lodging. The subscriber having provided himself with a very convenient House, in Princess' street, can accomodate a few Boarders... F. BEAUFORT. Wilmington, March 14.

Thursday, April 19, 1799. (Vol. III. No. 119.

(197) Ton Timber wanted, For which a generous price will be given in cash for about 30 tons of good yellow pine timber, to square from 10 to 14 inches clear of sap, and as free from knots as possible, to be from 20 to 30 feet in length. J. BURGWIN. April 11.

(198) Died, At his seat in Frederick county, Virginia, immediately after his return from Congress, Major-General Daniel MORGAN.

(199) Wax-Work. MOULTHROP & STREET, Respectfully inform..that they will open this day, April 18, at Mr. NICHOL's Billiard room, a most elegant collection of Wax-Work .. A striking likeness of Mr. HUTTON, late of Philadelphia, aged 110 years. The American Dwarf, taken from the life. This miniature of Man, whose name is Calvin PHILIPS, was born in Bridge-Water, Massachusetts, he is seven years old, 26 inches high, and weighs only 12 pounds...

(200) State of North-Carolina, Wilmington District, Superior Court of Law & Equity, ss. Notice is hereby given that the rule for the trial of causes at the next Court is as follows... James W. WALKER, D. C. S. C. L. April 18.

(201) The Laws & Journals of the last session of the General Assembly of North-Carolina will be completed and ready for delivery the latter end of this week.. The deprivation of a house and the destruction of a part of my printing apparatus, by the late fire, have in a great measure retarded their publication.. In consequence of a promise to the members of the General Assembly, to establish a Printing-office at the seat of government, previous to the ensuing session, and in obedience to an act entitled "An act more fully to ascertain the duties of the Public Printer" I.. am in daily expectation of receiving from New-York, a complete set of printing apparatus..which..will be immediately forwarded to Raleigh, where I shall hold myself in readiness to perform the requisites of the above mentioned act-and where I intend publishing..a Newspaper, to be entitled The Courier, or North-Carolina State Gazette; (notwithstanding the opposition lately manifested by the removal of the Fayetteville Minerva office to that place.)... A. HALL. Wilmington, April 18.

(202) Just Received and for sale by A. T. BROWNE, & Co..Gin..Brandy..Wine..Rum.. Sugar..Tea..Coffee..Bar Iron & Sheer moulds, Nails, Iron Potts, Kettles... And a general assortment of Dry Goods... April 18.

(203) Marshal's sales. Will Be Sold..Sundry Negroes and parcels of land (unidentified)... John S. WEST, Marshal. April 11.

(204) For Sale, The Sloop Sally,.. John SHUTER. Wilmington, April 11.

(205) Notice. The subscribers having qualified to execute the last will and testament of John JAMES, Esq. deceased, request all who are indebted to the estate..to make immediate payment... Benj. LIDDON, John HOLDON, Ex'rs. Or to Alice JAMES, Ex'r. South Washington, April 8, 1799.

(206) Sheriff's Sale. Will Be Sold On the 19th inst. at the Brick House opposite Wilmington, 32 Negroes..sold to satisfy sundry writs of fieri facias to me directed,

(206) (Cont.) at the suits of the Administrators of Richard QUINCE against James CARSON. Thomas LEONARD, Sh'ff. April 6.

(207) Ran Away from the subscriber a negro fellow named MICHAEL, stout and well made of a yellow complexion.. It is supposed he will make for Brunswick Old-Town, at which place he has a wife, formerly belonging to the estate of Hezekiah DAVIS, named NANNY, a yellow wench.. This fellow is outlawed agreeably to law and the subscriber will give 50 dollars reward for his head, if dead, or 10 dollars to any person who will secure him so that his master can get him again. J. W. BRADLEY. April 4.

(208) March 23. Pennsylvania Legislature... War Department. (To) His Excellency Gov. Thomas MIFFLIN. Sir, To suppress the insurrection now existing in the counties of Northampton, Bucks and Montgomery, in..Pennsylvania..the President has thought it necessary to employ a Military Force, to be composed in part of such of the Militia of Pennsylvania, whose situation and state of preparation will enable them to March with promptitude. The corps of Military first desired..are the..cavalry belonging to this city, and one troop of each of the counties of Philadelphia, Bucks, Chester, Montgomery and Lancaster..to march on or before the 28th instant under the command of Brigadier General MACPHERSON. Your..humble servant, James M'HENRY.

(209) Ran Away from the subscriber on Monday the 8th inst. a negro fellow named ASTON, a country born slave, about 24 years of age, 5 feet 8 or 9 inches high, of a yellowish complexion..he was born in the county of Wake.. Any person who will..secure the said slave shall have a reward of 30 dollars & all reasonable charges, by delivering him to me at Rockfish, Duplin county.. Shadrick STALLINGS. .. April 12.

Thursday, June 13, 1799. (Vol. III.-No. 127.

(210) As little or no attention has been paid to a former advertisement of mine, this is..to give notice..that unless they who are indebted to me will come forward and pay up their accounts, I shall be under the disagreeable necessity of enforcing payment agreeably to law. Payments will be expected to be made at South-Washington. George M'DONALD. May 23.

(211) Wilmington, June 13. Yesterday arrived from Jamaica, the armed brig Thomas, capt. John MARTIN.-Consigned to John MACLELLAN-cargo Rum and Sugar. Same day, from Nassau (N. P.) in 14 days, the armed brig Mary-ann, capt. G. CUNNINGHAM-cargo Sugar and Fruit...

(212) Married) On Thursday evening last, Mr. John A. ABRAMS to Miss Polly RUNDEL. In Fayetteville, Robinson MUMFORD, Esq. of Rowan county, to Miss Polly HAND.

(213) Notice. The subscribers having declined business here, in favor of Malcolm MACKENZIE, requests all those who owe them to come forward and make payments to him ... Robert ADAM, & Co. Wilmington, N. C. May 10, 1799.

(214) University. The annual examination in the University of this state, will commence on the 4th of July. The committee of visitation..to pronounce judgment on the examination so far as relates to the conduct and proficiency of the students, will consist of the following Trustees: Mr. Walter ALVES, Hillsborough, Mr. Wallace ALEXANDER, Morgan, Mr. Thomas BLOUNT, Halifax, Mr. James GLASGOW, Newbern; Mr. William B. GROVE, Fayetteville, Mr. John HAMILTON, Salisbury, Mr. Samuel JOHNSTON, Edenton, Mr. Duncan MOORE, Wilmington... By order of the President, William E. WEBB, Sec. April 26.

(215) The subscriber having obtained letters of administration on the estate of the late John GIBBS, dec. requests all persons who have any demands against said estate, to render them in properly attested... Robert GIBBS, Adm'r. May 23.

(216) Fifty Dollars Reward. Ran-Away from the subscriber about the 10th of May last, a negro fellow, named LARRY, yellow complexion, between 5 feet 10 and 6 feet high..about 25 years of age..formerly hired to Virgil DRY..delivery at Belvedere... Benjamin SMITH. June 6.

(217) To Be Rented And entered the first of July next, that convenient and well situated House in Market street, at present occupied by Mrs. MEEK. For terms, apply to Thomas HILL. June 6.

(218) Public Notice. Proposals in writing will be received at this office until the 15th day of June, from any..persons who will contract with the United States, to furnish any quantity of provisions, fuel and straw, that may be required for the troops thereof, that are or may be at Occacock, Fayetteville, Salisbury and Charlotte..the residue of the current year, 1799, Wilmington & Fort Johnston excepted... G. J. M'REE, Agent War department. Custom-House, Wilmington, May 2, 1799.

(219) The subscriber having qualified as Executor to the last will and testament of Henry TOOMER, dec. requests all persons indebted to the estate..to make payment ... Anthony B. TOOMER. May 30.

(220) A Lottery. The subscriber intends to dispose of, by way of Lottery, at one dollar per ticket, several Gold and Silver Watches, some patterns for gentlemen's apparel, &c... Duncan LIVINGSTON. May 30.

(221) For Sale By Robert MITCHELL, Muscovado Sugar..Rum..Brandy..Barrel'd Pork and Beef. Tobacco. Fresh Souchong Tea... June 13.

(222) Any person who will undertake to supply the subscriber with 100,000 Red Oak hhd. Staves dressed, in the month of August next, will please to inform him as speedily as possible. Geo. HOOPER. June 13.

(223) Wanted Three or four active Negroes, either on purchase, mortgage or hire... J. BURGWIN. Hermitage, June 12.

(224) Ran-Away On Friday the 17th of May last, a negro fellow named JIMMY, he is a stout black fellow, of a yellowish cast, he is about 5 feet 10 or 11 inches high, rather slim made..about 26 years of age.. Whoever will apprehend said fellow and commit him to jail..or deliver him to Mrs. John MAGILL, Old-Town, Brunswick county, or to myself, shall receive a reward of 20 Dollars... William MAGILL. Brunswick county, June 1.

(225) Notice. The subscriber for the last time, earnestly requests all persons who have lodged any species of goods with him, in the line of his business, to apply immediately, as he intends leaving the state... D. LAMBERTOZ. June 13.

(226) A Reward of 10 Dollars will be paid to any person who will deliver into the goal of Wilmington, a certain negro man named JOHNY, a fellow I purchased from Mr. John WADDELL.-He is of a yellow complexion, about 5 feet 10 inches high, strait and well made:..about 35 or 40 years of age. It is probable he may be about Mr. WADDELL's plantation, having a mother and uncle there... George GIBBS. June 13.

(227) Sheriff's Sales. Will Be Sold On Monday the 17th day of June, at the Courthouse in Wilmington, the following Lands, situated in the county of New-Hanover, for the taxes for the years 1796 and 1797. 29,084 acres entered by James CARRAWAY, situate on the north side of the north-east branch of Cape-Fear river, above the mouth of Holley-Shelter, beginning at a Pine in the county line, 24 poles south of Curling SMITH's second corner of land, formerly patented by Job HARRINGTON, and about 180 poles east of the mouth of Rockfish Creek; conveyed by said CARRAWAY to David ALLISON, and by him conveyed to J. B. BOND, of Philadelphia. 14,080 acres entered by Starling WHEATON, on the east side of the north-east branch of Cape-Fear river, including the lower and the great Holley-Shelter pecoson, on the head of LILLINGTON and MERRICK's Creek, beginning..on the north side of ASHE's Mill Creek, thence crossing the Creek on or near Daniel MALLETT's line; conveyed by said Starling WHEATON to Daniel WHEATON, and by him conveyed to Francis Lewis TANCY, of George-Town. 44,160 acres entered by Daniel WHEATON, on the east side of the north-east branch of Cape-Fear..about one quarter of a mile above James HOWARD's line. The above lands are liable to a double tax for the year 1796, and will be also liable for a double tax for the year 1797, unless the amount of a single tax is paid before the sale. William NUTT, Sheriff. May 9.

(228) From The Monthly Magazine, Printed at New-York By T. & J. SWORDS...

(229) From the Eastern Telegraph. At the close of the last session of Congress, the honorable Matthew LYON, Esq. member from the State of Vermont, applied to the Serjeant at arms to settle his bill for mileage and attendance during the session. Mr. LYON had come to Congress only a very short time before the session ended, having in the fall of last year been imprisoned in the goal of Vergennes, in..Vermont..for Sedition.. But it may be proper to observe, that two other bills for Sedition were cut and dry for Mr. LYON, on his return to Vermont; and that he chose to retire for shelter with his friend MASON of Virginia; and has lately announced his intention of going to Kentucky.

(230) Virginia. May 6. The following Ten characters will truly represent this State in the Sixth Congress..viz. Henry LEE, John MARSHALL, Leven POWELL, Samuel GOODE, Edwin GRAY, James HAYMOND, George HANCOCK, Josiah PARKER, Thomas EVANS, and Robert PAGE.-The three last gentlemen are re-elected-The Democratic Members will be, if they repent not, of which there are some hopes-Matthew CLAY, John DAWSON, Anthony NEW, Joseph EGGLESTON, John NICHOLAS, John RANDOLPH, David HOLMES, Samuel Jordan CABAL, and one other cabaler, whose name we have not asertained. The members who have leave to stay at home, are the Ex-Hon. Messrs. CLAIBORNE, HARRISON, MACHIR, TRIGG, JONES, CLOPTON, BRENT and VENABLE.

(231) Philadelphia, May 18. Yesterday morning, Mr. LEWIS concluded the pleadings in support of his motion for granting a new trial to John FRIES, when after taking some time for consideration, Judge IREDELL delivered his opinion on the several reasons which had been assigned by the counsel of the prisoner, as a ground for their motion.. The new trial cannot..take place till the next Circuit Court..held in October next.

Thursday, August 8, 1799. (Vol. III-No. 135.

(232) A Saw-Mill To Be Hired Out. As I wish to embark for the Northward this Summer, for the benefit of my health, I will hire out the Saw-Mill on Island-creek, with upwards of 3,000 acres of Land..with 8 or 10 able Negroes. Payment will be received in Lumber, at Eight Dollars per thousand, at the Mill Landing. John BURGWIN. Hermitage, July 4, 1799.

(233) Martin ETTINGER, Blacksmith, Whitesmith, Gunsmith, & Nail Manufacturer, Informs..that he has removed his shop to Mr. TELFAIR's ship-yard, near Sam. R. JOCELYN, Esq's... May 9.

(234) Taxes for the year 1798. The subscriber will receive taxes for the year 1798, on the days of the Election, and at any time in Wilmington, preceeding those days. Wm. NUTT, Shff. Note.-The following persons, viz. Peter MAXWELL, James LARKINS, John BLOODWOTH, William JONES, Sam. BLOODWORTH, William GREEN, Robert NIXSON, and John P. WILLIAMS, Esq. were appointed at the last Court to receive lists of taxable property, for the year 1799. July 18.

(235) For Freight or Charter, To any port of the United States, The schooner Sally, John MACFARLANE, master.. For terms apply to John TELFAIR or John BROWN. July 25.

(236) Secretary's Office, Raleigh, June 17, '99. This is to notify all whom it may concern, That Grants have been lately executed for all the lands returned to this office,..for most of the counties in the state of North-Carolina, to the number of about 2500, which are ready to be delivered:-the claimants are requested to come forward and take them away... Wm. WHITE, Sec. of State.

(237) Notice. Deserted from the 2d Regiment of Artillerists Engineers, at Fort-Johnston, North-Carolina, on the 2d July, 1799, a Soldier by the name James MARLER, 5 feet 7 inches in height, dark eyes, short black hair, 38 years of age, born in Camden County, S. C..reward of 10 Dollars. The said deserter is supposed to have made his way to St. Mary's, in Georgia. J. FERGUS, lieut. 2d Regiment of A. and E. Fort-Johnston, August 1.

(238) For Philadelphia or New-York, As freight may offer, the Stout, strong and fast sailing Schooner Two Friends, James GILDEN, master..apply to Geo. GIBBS. August 1.

(239) Michael MOLTON begs leave to inform..that he has opened a public house in Fayetteville, at the house of the late Col. ROWAN, on Bow-street, lately occupied by Mr. James KERR... June 27.

(240) Lottery. All persons who purchased Tickets in T. FITZGERALD's Lottery, are requested to call upon Hugh STALLINGS and get them, as the drawing will commence on the day of the Election, in Wilmington. Tim. BLUDWORTH, jun. August 1. N. B. Tickets may be had at Mr. H. KELLY's store.

(241) New-York, July 9. Extract of a letter from one of the owners of the schr. Nancy, capt. JACKSON of Providence, dated Baltimore June 24. "By Capt. Wm. HURST, of the brig William, who arrived here last evening from London, I have received a truly melancholy account of our schr. Nancy, capt. JACKSON, which is related to me as follows, by Capt. HURST: That on the 13th inst. in the Gulph Stream, saw a sail in distress..and..saw a man on deck, who gave him to understand that he must keep to windward, which he did..he went on board the schooner, and found that Capt. JACKSON was the only living person on board, and he in a very feeble state: That capt. JACKSON informed him he buried his mate (Mr. Welcome ALLEN of Cumberland, son of the late capt. Nehemiah ALLEN) a few days after leaving St. Thomas's; and that the remaining 3 hands (James SCOTT, Henry ARNOLD, and Samuel DAILY) had then lain below, dead three days, he being unable to bury them: That he took capt. JACKSON on board his own vessel and gave him all the assistance in his power..and restored him to a good state of health. That capt. SIMPSON, who was a passenger on board the William, & two sailors went on board the schooner, buried the dead, made some sail, and kept in company with the brig until Thursday the 20th June..."

(242) Norfolk, July 27. The Retaliation captured again! Last evening arrived in town captain Joseph CANBY, 14? days from St. Bartholomew's; by him we are informed that 18 days ago..the U. States sloop of war Merrimack fell in with and captured the Retaliation French privateer, just out of Guadaloupe, with 150 men on board.

(243) Sheriff's Sales. Notice Is hereby given that the following Lands, situated in the county of Jones were not given in by any list or lists exhibited in said county, for the year 1798, agreeably to law; and that so much of the same as will satisfy the taxes due thereon..Will Be Sold At the Court House of said county, in Trenton, on Thursday, the 29th of August next. 1280 acres on the head of Gum Swamp, beginning..near John ISLER's line. 8320 acres on the north side of White-oak river, and West side of HUNTER's creek, beginning at..the mouth of Pometer branch and.. HUNTER's creek-James WICK's corner. 640 acres joining the Onslow county line, beginning at..J. SAUL's corner, on the road. 5120 acres on the north side of Trent river, beginning at..Samuel DELIHUNTER's beginning of his 100 acre patent. 13,705 acres on the north side of Trent river & head of BACHELOR's creek, beginning at Hezekiah MERRITT's beginning pine of his 100 acre patent. 35,200 acres on the south side of Trent river beginning at a tree..known by the name of the Royal Oak the beginning of two patents in the name of Daniel SHINE. 1408 acres on the south side of the Trent river, including the head waters of Rattlesnake Branch, beginning at..the beginning of Jacob JOHNSTON's 200 acre survey, on the head of Tuckahoe branch. 1280 acres on the north side of Whiteoak river..beginning at..JOSEPH & RICHARD's corner. 640 acres beginning at..Jonathan KEY's corner of his 250 acres survey. The foregoing lands appear on record as the property of David ALLISON, Esq. late of Philadelphia. 1920 acres on the north side of Trent river..beginning at..the last corner of Willie GURGANUS' 100 acres survey. 640 acres on the north side of Trent river, including Black swamp pecoson, beginning at ..James WESTBROOK's corner, near Wm. MORGAN's house. 1300 acres on the south side of Tuckohoe creek, beginning at..Hall JARMAN's corner. 1280 acres on the south side of Trent river, beginning at..David ALLISON's second corner of his Royal Oak survey. 640 acres on the north side of Trent river, including HERRITAGE's percoson, beginning at..Benjamin DAVIS's beginning in Lenoir county line. 640 acres on the south side of Trent river, beginning at..his and T. THORNTON's corner. 2560 acres.. 640 acres in Dover pecoson, beginning..in Gum Swamp, on the east of KENT's old field, the beginning of his grant in Craven county, for 19,200 acres. 15360 acres including the BACHELOR's creek and Dover pecoson, beginning at a ..corner of his own, surveyed by James FOY. The foregoing lands were granted to David ALLISON, but are reported to be the property of Solomon MARKS and Henry BECK. 1600 acres, the property of Eli WEST, on White oak. 6400 acres, the property of David WITHERSPOON and ___, on Island-Creek, in Jones County. 500 acres, belonging to the heirs of Samuel HILL. 500 acres, the property of J. SHINE, on the waters of Trent. 14800 acres, the property of Gideon DUNISON. Ben. BROCKETT, Shff. Jones County, July 1.

(244) Wilmington, August 8. Sheriff's Sales. Notice is hereby given That the following Lands, situate in the county of Jones, were not given in by any list..for the year 1798..so that so much of the same as will satisfy the tax due thereon for said year..will be sold at the Court-House in Trenton, on Monday the 30th day of September next. 670 acres, the property of the late George MITCHELL, Esq. in the Whiteoak pecoson. 620 acres, the property of Waightstill AVERY and Wife on Trent river called the White Rock. 640 acres, patented by James TAYLOR, lying on Whiteoak, near John JONES' land. 100 acres whereon James HARRIS now lives. 80 acres on Deep Gulley, entered by Edward WHITTY, Esq'r. now said to be Eusibeus CRUTCHFIELD's. 320 acres, said to be the property of the heirs of Martin WARSTER?, whereon James WILLS now lives. 150 acres patented by Thomas WILLIAMS, on or near Island creek, said to be the property of Hardy BRYAN. Benjamin BROCKETT, Shff. of Jones county. August 2, 1799.

(245) The subscriber takes this opportunity of informing his former liberal customers..that he is just arrived, and intends as usual, to follow his business as a Taylor, at the store lately occupied by Mr. A. T. BROWNE... He has on hand a general assortment of Dry Goods... Peter WI__. August 1.

Thursday, September 5, 1799. (Vol. III.-No. 139.

(246) Philadelphia, August 15. Extract of a letter from John GAVINO, Esq. American consul at Gibraltar, dated 19th June, '99...

(247) Address. From the officers of the Gun Room on board the U. S. ship Constellation, To Commodore TRUXTON. Ship Constellation, August 8, '99. Sir, It is with a degree of regret, scarcely to be conveyed in words we have understood you mean to decline the command of the United States ship Constellation.. We are, sir, Your most grateful, Obliged and obedient Humble Servants, Andrew STERRET, Ambrose SHIRLEY, John ARCHER, S. B. BROOK, John B. DENT, T. ROBINSON, R. HARRISON. S. M. I. HENRY, Surgeon, M. GARETSON, Pursur. Answer To the Address. 9th of August, '99.. Thomas TRUXTON. To Lieut. STERRET, &c.

(248) Mr. Jacob PERKINS, of Newburyport, has obtained a patent of an invention to detect counterfeit bank paper...

(249) Indian Affairs. Augusta, August 3. A Talk from the Chusseittaw King, to Col. Joseph PHILIPS of Green county, dated 24th June, '99. Friend & Brother,... CUSSEITAW MICO. King of Cusseittaw.

(250) Louisville, July 30. Extract of a letter from col. HAWKINS, to his excellency Governor JACKSON, dated Creek Nation, 17th July, 1799. "The CHEEHAW MICO has visited me and shewed me your address to him,.. I sent a demand down in the neighbourhood of Kinnard, for some negroes in that quarter..and lately an Indian informs me, that two belonging to the late Joel WALKER, one to Mrs. BAILY, one to Mr. WALDREN, are taken down by Kennard, and that one other has been apprehended on his way to the nation, and delivered to lieut. THOMPSON at Fort James.. I believe the murderer of MORELAND is discovered-he is said to be a Cussital man.. A young half breed, who under some pretence of claim to them plundered Mrs. M'INTOSH, of Malo, in M'Intosh county, prime hands-leaving the unfortunate widowed lady with six small children, with scarcely the means of subsistence."

(251) New-York, August 15. (Communicated by capt. STANWOOD for publication.) In the ship Montezuma from Kingston, in the island of Jamaica, arrived at the port of Philadelphia, on the 30th ult. came passenger capt. Lemuel STANWOOD, late master of the from (sic) Chatham, of this port, which vessel was owned by Mr. Thomas BUCHANAN, merchant, of this city. Capt. STANWOOD sailed from Montego Bay, in the said island, on the 15th of may last..on the north side of the island of Cuba, was brought to by the British frigate Maidstone, Ross DONNELLY, commander, who sent some of his officers on board to examine..her papers.. Some time after he returned to his vessel, himself and a Mr. Peter BROWN, a passenger, were ordered on board the frigate... A true statement of facts, Lemuel STANWOOD.

(252) Philadelphia, Aug. 15. Piracy! I am informed by Joseph YZNARDI, Esq. acting as American Consul at Cadiz, that the mate and four of the seamen of the American brigantine Nancy, whereof Stephen MUNIONS was master, piratically cut her cables in the Bay of Cadiz..the 7th of June last and carried her out to sea without her papers. The said brigantine is a square sterned vessel, 86 feet in length, 26 in breadth, 10 in depth, of the burthen of 191 63-95 tons.. All custom-house officers

(252) (Cont.) and others are therefore requested to seize and detain the brigantine and the said mate and seamen... Timothy PICKERING, Secretary of State. Department of State, 12 Aug. '99.

(253) Charleston, August 14. A Gallant Exploit. Yesterday arrived the letter of marque brig Maria, capt. John MORRISON, mounting 11 guns, and carrying 30 men, last from the bar of Nassau (N. P.) in 5 days. The Maria is owned by capt. MORRISON,..of this city, and was bound from New York to la Vera Cruz, with a cargo of 50,000 dollars...

(254) Wilmington, Sept. 5. From the Virginia Federalist. August 28. By Col. William MAYO who arrived here yesterday evening from New-York and Philadelphia, we are informed that the fever prevailed in those cities to an alarming degree.

(255) Returns of the Election for Members of the next General Assembly. Mecklenburg-Robert IRWIN, Senate. James CONNER and Sherid GRAY, Commons. Chowan-Frederick LUTON, Senate. John B. BENNET and Shadrach FELTON, Commons. Edenton-John BLOUNT, jun. Tyrrel-Charles SPRUILL, Senate. Jordan ARMISTEAD and Samuel SPRUILL, Commons. Perquimans-Joseph HARVEY, Senate. Charles BLOUNT and Charles HARVEY, Commons. Wayne- R. M'KINNIE, Senate. Needham WHITFIELD and R. CROOM, Commons. Lenoir-Simon BRUTON, Senate. Hardy CROOM and J. FATTE, Commons. Glasgow- ___ mere HOOKER, Senate. Grove BRIGHT? and William TAYLOR, Commons. Pitt-Mr. BRYAN, Senate. Hollon JOHNSTON and Wm. MAY, Commons. Hyde-Henry SILBY, Senate. William CLARK and John JORDAN, Commons. Carteret- ___ BISHOP, Senate. William FISHER & Nathaniel PINCKAM, Commons. Bertie-George OUTLAW, Senate. Joseph JORDAN and James TUNSTALL, Commons. Northampton-John M. BINFORD, Senate. James LONG and ___ COTTON, Commons. Martin-Samuel JOHNSTON, Senate. Thomas WIGGINS and Jesse CHERRY, Commons. Edgecombe-Thomas BLOUNT, Senate. Laurence O'BILAN? and Jeremiah HILLSARD, Commons. Nash-J ARRINGTON, Senate. Redmund BUNN and Archibald HUNTER, Commons. Franklin-Jordan HILL, Senate. Archibald DAVIS and Britain HARRIS, Commons. Warren-James CALLIER, Senate. James TURNER and Oliver FITT, Commons. Orange-David RAY, Senate. Samuel BENTON and Wm. F. STRUDWICK, Commons. Hillsborough-Absalom TATOM.

(256) Taken up and committed to goal, in Fayetteville..a mulatto fellow; he says that he belongs to Abram BURNAP, near Swansborough... Jesse LEE, Goaler. Fayetteville, Sept. 5.

(257) Stolen From the subscriber about three weeks ago, out of my room, at Mr. JONES' boarding-house, a handsome Gilt Watch..20 Dollars, to any person who will give such information, as may convict the thief, or 10 Dollars for the Watch. A. CUTLAR. Sept. 5.

(258) Mr. HALL, The situation I have been in for some time past being intimately connected with the commercial interest of this place, as well as that of my owners, I shall without apology state to the public a recent occurrence, which has been very injurious to myself, owners, and all who had property on board of my vessel.. On the 8th of August last..fell in with an armed ship, who after passing athwart my bow within less than half a gun shot, hoisted French National colours. The vessel I commanded being unarmed..I was obliged to run off into the gulph.. On my arrival here I was much surprised to find the ship alluded to, the Nancy of Wilmington, Capt. CUNNINGHAM, mounting 16 guns. I understand Capt. CUNNINGHAM endeavours to excuse his conduct, by saying there was an armed brig in sight, of which he was fearful... Jon. THOMPSON, Schooner Juno. Wilmington, Sept. 3, 1799.

(259) Sheriff's Sales. Will Be Sold, On the 1st day of October next, at the Court-

(259) (Cont.) House in Brunswick county, the following Lands, for the payment of the Taxes due thereon, viz. 100,480 acres consisting of three tracts, one situated on the west side of Waccamaw river between the state and Bladen lines, the other two tracts situated on the eastern side of Waccamaw and upon Shallott, the waters of LOCKWOOD's Folly and Elizabeth rivers, also on or near the waters of Governour's, Orton?, Lilliput and Town-creek, and running northwestwardly to the road leading from Town-creek to LOCKWOOD's Folly, or near the same; sold for the taxes of the years 1797 & 1798. 8000 acres..on the eastern side of Waccamaw river, joining William GRISLET?'s and Thomas HICHMAN's lands, and touching on the waters of Shallott river, said now to be or late was the property of the late Patrick HENRY, Esq. of Virginia; sold for the taxes of the years 1795, 1796, 1797 & '98. 80 acres being part of 100 acres..on the south side of LIVINGSTON's-creek, said to have been granted to Joel ALLEN; sold for the taxes of 1798. 100 acres on the west side of Waccamaw river, near..the Green swamp and Snake island, called HARPER's land, to whom it was granted; sold for the taxes of the years 1795, 1796, 1797 & 1798. 50,000 acres situate in..Green swamp; the same appears to have been entered for taxation in the names of Benjamin STODDART and John MASON, trustees of Francis Lewis TANCY, by George G. M'DANIEL, their agent for the year 1798. Thos. LEONARD, Shff. Brunswick county, Aug. 28.

(260) All persons are hereby forwarned from buying or dealing with the subscriber's or Mr. Francis B. BEAUFORT's negroes on Greenfields, any corn or other articles whatever, without a permit from one or the other of the owners... Wm. GREEN. Any person apprehending the subscriber's negro fellow APOLLO..shall be generously rewarded. Aug. 30.

(261) For Freight or Charter, To any Port in the United States, The Sloop Sally, In good order for sea. John TELFAIR. Sept. 5.

(262) For Sale A House 25 by 18 feet..on Market-street, between Fourth and Back-streets, on the lot No 5; at present occupied by the subscriber Wm. SMEETON. Wilmington, Sept. 5.

(263) Wanted Immediately. Two or three boys of about 14 years of age, and of good parentage, as apprentices to the Black, White and Gunsmith business, and Nail Manufactory... M. ETTINGER. Sept. 5.

(264) Notice. The proprietors of Carriages in the county of New-Hanover, are informed, that the month of September next, is the time appointed by law, for the entry of their Carriages for the year to end on the 30th September, 1800.. Retailers of foreign distilled spirits and wines are also informed, that the first day of October next, is the time appointed by law to renew their licenses for the year to end on the 30th day of September, 1800... Robert MUTER, Collector of Revenue in the 6th division of the 1st Survey, North-Carolina. Wilmington, August 27, 1799.

(265) Twenty Dollars Reward. Ran away from the subscriber, a large black Negro Man, named JACK, about six feet one or two inches high... Hardy ROYAL. Sampson county, August 18.

(266) For Sale My Mills on the raft swamp, about four miles above Lumberton.. This seat is on 12,000 acres of land, on which are six plantations, a saw-mill with two saws, a grist-mill with two pair of stones..a rice machine..that will beat 120 bushels per day; a large and well finished two story house, kitchen, meat house, stables.. I have also a plantation (1,000 acres in the tract) joining the town.. also two town houses..and about 5000 acres of other land..near and joining the town

(266) (Cont.) I would take one-half or two-thirds of the value of the above premises in western lands in the state of Tennessee, in Mero district... J.? WILLIS. Lumberton, Aug. 4.

(267) Mr. Printer, (letter)... John PEABODY. August 27.

(268) Wanted Immediately. Three or four Apprentices to the House Carpenter's business. Boys from 14 to 16 years of age... Alex. ROUSE. Wilmington, August 15.

(269) Sheriff's Sales. Will Be Sold On Saturday, the 2_th of September next, at Sampson Court-House, the following Lands, in Sampson county, to satisfy the Taxes due for the year 1798: 11,950 Acres between Little Coherry and Bearskin swamp above Lazarus HALL's land. 445 acres between Doctor's-creek and Quewhistle, including HARVEL's pecoson. 6207 acres on Bearskin swamp, beginning at..PAGE's and HONEYCUT's corner. 2266 acres between Little Cohery and Bearskin, joining Perigreen JOHNSON's land. 20,000 acres between Little Cohery and South-river, on both sides of the main road, joining Peter MALLET's land. 30,000 acres between Little-Cohery and South-river, joining Ozius BEAMAN, on Starling swamp. 4896 acres between Great Cohery and Little Cohery, on both sides of the old road, joining Lazarus HALL's land. 1110 acres on the east-side of Black river, joining the county line, at William JOHNSON's land. 2366 acres on the east-side of South-river..joining John HARVEY's corner. 657 acres between Little Cohery and South river, including part of James HERRINGTON's pecoson. 4502 acres.. All the above mentioned land returned by John DICKSON, agent for Robert C. JOHNSON. 4480 acres on the east side of South-river, returned by Peter MALLET, Esq. 355 acres on the east side of Great Cohery, returned by Stephen BECK. 150 acres on Roan swamp, returned by Miles CARSON. 300? acres on the west side of Great Cohery, returned by Hallasha ODOM. 190 acres near or joining do. returned by Silas ODOM. 50 acres near or joining do. returned by Dempsy ODOM. 400 acres near the head of Great Cohery, returned by Joel LEE. 750 acres on Black river, returned by Jane FRYER. 90 acres on the west side of the Six Runs, returned by Moses CUMMINS. 232 acres between the Six Runs and Goshon, returned by John ROSE. 440 acres near Goshon swamp, returned by Lewis BARFIELD. 10 acres near the head of Great Cohery, returned by Joel TAYLOR. 100 acres on the Beaver dam, returned by Mary SESSUMS. 200 acres on the east side of Great Cohery, joining Daniel KINZEY's lines, and no return made. 350 acres on Blackmingo supposed to be the property of B. ROBERSON of Bladen county, and no return made. 1000 acres on Little Cohery, joining Mary WILLIAMS, the property of William KEDDY, and no return made. 100 acres on the east side of South river, joining John FOWLLER, the property of said KEDDY, and no return made. Two 640 acre Tracts on South river, one below and the other above Macom PETERSON, supposed to be the property of Wm. KEDDY, of Wilmington. Owen GREGORY, Shff. August 23.

(270) Whereas Daniel MALLET mortgaged to me as security for the repayment of a certain sum of money lent..to him, a certain Negro Fellow named ELIJAH, on the 19th inst. and delivered..into my possession on the 20th-That on the 22d the said fellow..eloped from my service..reward of 10 Dollars... John BURGWIN.

(271) Albany, July 19. (The following is extracted from an address delivered at Cooperstown, on the late national fast-by John M'DONALD, A. M.-After detailing the measures adopted by this country, to preserve a good understanding with the French, previous to the system of arming for the defence of our property, and the security of our rights, the orator proceeds as follows:)...

Thursday, October 3, 1799. (Vol. III.-No. 143.

(272) Raleigh, September 17, 1799. On Wednesday last, the Governor of the state left this place on his way to Philadelphia, in order to take on him the important duties of his mission to France. Previous to his departure, the inhabitants of Raleigh and its neighbourhood, met and caused him to be presented with an address, of which the following is a copy. To His Excellency Wm. R. DAVIE... Signed by appointment and under the direction of the inhabitants present. John HAYWOOD, Wm. POLK, Wm. WHITE, J. CRAVEN, S. HAYWOOD.

(273) We learn that the Yellow Fever is in Newbern-a person direct from that place informs us that on Tuesday and Wednesday last, inclusive, 16 persons died-Mrs. CRADDICK has lost during the last week, the whole of her children 5 in number-The inhabitants are flying in every direction.

(274) Wilmington, October 3. We are authorised to state, that Benjamin SMITH, Esq. Speaker of the Senate, was to assume the duties of the Executive of this state, on the 12th inst. and that he had been requested by Gov. DAVIE to repair to the City of Raleigh for that purpose.

(275) Mr. HALL, I See in your last papper a very scandalous advertisement put in against me by David MIMS jun. concerning losing sadel bags, I deny Leeon stealing Mr. MIMS bags, or any of my family, as much as Mr. MIMS wod, and if I am a mid to gambel I can gambel on my one money, Mr. MIMS bags was not in my hose nor in my cear, I wod thank Mr. MIMS for the future to keep himself sober when he cols at my hose and tak cear of bags and himself; no man can ever say, that ever cold at my hose and put anything in my cear or in any of my family, that ever lost 6 pence; no, nor never shall. Benjamin ROWELL. October 3.

(276) Public Auction. Will Be Sold, On the 15th inst. at Mr. CAMPBELL's ware-house in Princess-street for the benefit of the underwriters, sundry packages of Dry Goods, damaged on board the ship Hazard, John JACKSON, master, from Liverpool. Joshua WINSLOW agent for R. & J. DONALDSON, & Co. October 3.

(277) A List of Letters remaining in the Post-Office at Wilmington, October 3, '99. A. Colonel Samuel ASHE, _ ; Peter AUBINAUD 1; Cain ALLEN, Brunswick county, 1. B. Mrs. Mary BARTLETT, 1; Timothy BLOODWORTH Esq. 1; Timothy BLOODWORTH Jun. 1, Joseph BLAND, 1; Mrs. Mary BALLANTINE, 1; John BROWN, Blk. 1; Doctor BURTEN?, Duplin, 1 C. Mr. CLIFTS (carpenter,) 1; Miss Rhoda CHURCH, 2; Peter CARPENTER, 1; Jesa. CARMAN, 1; James CR___FORD, 1; R. Wm. CUTLAR, 1; Wm. CUTLAR, 1; Wm. COIT, 1; Gorton CHASE, 1; John CURRIE, 1; Arch. CUNNINGHAM, 2; Thomas COOKE, (Sampson,) 1; Mrs. CLINTON, (Sampson,) 1; Thomas Hereson COLEMAN, (Duplin,) 2. D. Elihu DOTY, Captain, 2; John DRYSDALE, Captain, 1; Nimrod DYE, 1; James DENNY, 1; James DOWLING, 2; Christopher DUDLEY, (Onslow,) 1. F. John FENBRACE, care of George GIBBS, 1; Lieut. John FERGUS, 1; Mrs. Christian FLEEMING, 1; Margaret FERGUSON, 1; Elizabeth FULLER, 1; Thomas FOHEY, 1; James FARSON, (Sampson,) 1. G. James GUFFORD, Long creek, 1; Captain Jereamiah GROSS, 1; Elias GOODWIN, Brunswick county, 2. H. Hardy HOLMES, Sampson, 1; Owen HOLMES, do. 1; James HAIL, Duplin county, 2; Gabriel HOLMES, Sampson, 1; Capt. Wm. HALL, Brunswick, 1; John HARGRAVE, 1; John HUSKE, 1; John HARFORD, 1; Wm. HUDSON, 1; James HUTCHINS, 2; Thomas HUDSON, 1; Isaac HOUSEMAN, 1; Jane HARTLEY, 1; Capt. Benjamin HUTCHINS, 1; Mr. S. George HENSEN, 1; Jonathan HUNTINGTON, 1; Jacob HARTMAN, 1; Zekiel HILL, Brunswick 1. J. Edward JONES, 6; Jesse JENNETT, 2; John JACKSON, 1; John JOHNSTON, jun. 1. K. John KENNEDY, 1; David KETCHUM, 1; Master Wm. KING, 1; Henry KER, 1; James KENAN, Duplin, 1; Thomas KENAN, Duplin, 2. L. Joseph LONGFORD, 1; Kenan LOVE, Sampson, 1. M. Major M'CREE, 1; George MERRICK, 1; Elizabeth MORGAN, 1; James MOORE Esq. 1; Henry MOORE, 1; Peter M'KELLER 1; James MANSFIELD, 1; Hugh M'KAY, 1; Benjamin MOSES, 1; Benjamin MORGAN, 1; Mrs. Ann MILLER,

(277) (Cont.) 1; George M'KENSIE, 2; Alexander Duncan MOORE, 1; Wm. M'GILL, 1; John M'GILL, 1; D. P. MORSE, 1; Alexander MORGAN, 1; Wm. M'KERRELL, 2. N. Samuel NOBLE, 1; Thomas NORMAND, Duplin county, 1. P. William PUNCHARD, 1. R. Thomas RUFFES (or RUSSES), 1; John ROBERSON, 1; James RICHARD, 1; Joseph ROBERSON, 1; Adjutant General, James Thomas RHODES, Duplin county, 2. S. Thomas SLADE, 1; Catharine STANLY, 1; Jannet SPENDLOVE, Bladen, 1; Elizabeth SIMPSON, 1; Michael SAMPSON, 1; Jacob SNARES, Thomas SWANN Esq. attorney at law, 1. Thomas SEWELL, Sampson county, 1. T. Barker W. THACKER, care of Geo. HOOPER, 1; Wm. TULON, Sampson county 1; Geo. TAYLOR, Sampson, 1. U. Henry URQUHART, 1; W. Burgwin L WHITE, 2; John P. WILLIAMS, 1; Sylvester WILLESTON, 1; Wm. WELSBY, Sampson, 1; William WALDERMAN, Duplin county, 2; Elisha WIGGENNS, 1. John LORD. October 3.

(278) District of North-Carolina, Supervisor's Office, Raleigh, Sept. 16. The citizens of the District of North-Carolina are hereby informed that the Press and Dies for stamping vellum, parchment and paper, are now at this place; and that Merchants, traders, & others, may be supplied with such stamps as they may require... Wm. POLK, Supervisor N. C. D.

(279) Will Be Sold On Tuesday the eighth day of October next, at the Dwelling-House of the late John GAILLARD deceased, in Market-street, the personal estate of the said deceased consisting of a few Dry Goods and household Furniture... Eliza. SIMPSON, Adm'x. Wilmington, Sept. 26.

(280) Notice is hereby given, That the lists and valuations made by the United States assessors for the District of Wilmington, will be kept open at the store of the subscriber, from the 27th September to the 12th of October..for the purpose of hearing and deciding on any appeals... R. BRADLEY, Principal assessor. Wilmington, Sept. 26.

(281) Sheriff's Sales, On the 29th day of October next, the following Lands in Duplin County, Will Be Sold For the taxes due thereon for the year 1798. 9530 Acres granted to Roger ALDEN, including the upper part of Holley Shelter pecoson, beginning at three pines the last station of James CARRAWAY's survey of 2,184 acres. 12,800 Acres granted to Roger ALDEN lying on the east side of the North-East River, and both sides of Cypress creek and Back swamp, beginning at a pine the corner tree of Duplin County and New Hanover. 5120 Acres granted to Roger ALDEN, on the head of Panther Swamp, and Beaver dam of Limestone, joining the boundaries of Jones and Lenoir counties, beginning at..Jacob MACNON's corner tree, on the north side of a small drain of Cherrytree branch. 3200 Acres granted to Roger ALDEN, on both sides of the said branch, including the Goard pecoson, beginning at a pine, William HALL's line, on the boundary of Onslow county. 640 Acres granted to Roger ALDEN, on the drains of BURNCOAT & MATTHEW's branch, beginning at..the fourth corner of a survey of 500 acres patented by George SMITH. 1280 Acres granted to Roger ALDEN, on the drains of Rockfish creek, beginning at..Aaron WILLIAMS's corner, in the edge of the northeast corner of ALDERMAN's Great Bay or pecoson. 3200 Acres granted to Roger ALDEN, on the west side of the North East River, and in LOVEL's pecoson, beginning on the river bank, the lower corner of James PICKET's 50 acres. 640 Acres granted to Samuel JOHNSTON, on the east side of the North-East River, including the Indian Grave Bluff. 640 Acres granted to Samuel JOHNSTON, on the west side of the North-East River, opposite the Indian graves. 640 Acres granted to James PHOEBUS, joining the land of Jacob TEACHY. 2 0 Acres granted to John THALLY, on both sides of MAXWELL swamp, joining Nathaniel M'CANNE and Richard CHASTEN's lines. 640 Acres granted to Roger ALDEN, on the drains of the Little Rockfish creek, in the pecoson, beginning.. west of the main road George DOHORTY and William JONES' corner. 640 Acres granted to Roger ALDEN, on the head of FUSSEL's creek, a branch of Rockfish creek, beginning at

(281) (Cont.) the second corner of Jacob WELL's survey of 640 acres. 640 acres supposed to be granted to John JOHNS, joining Jacob BROWN's line, and Broad Branch. Hugh M'CANNE, Shff. September 15.

(282) Sheriff's Sales. On the 21st of October next, Will Be Sold, At the Court-House, A Parcel of Land, situate on the north side of the North-west river, immediately opposite ROWAN's Plantation, being the field on the low land, and that part of said Tract which lies in New-Hanover county-levied upon by virtue of a writ of fieri facias, at the suit of the Executors of Thomas LUCAS, vs. the Heirs of John ROWAN. Wm. NUTT, Shff. Sept. 19.

(283) By virtue of a writ of fieri facias, to me directed, at the suit of John BURGWIN vs. the Heir of Robert SCHAW, On the first day of November next, at 12 o'clock Will Be Sold, At the Court-House, in Wilmington, That valuable Lot with improvements thereon, situated on Front-street, containing 66 feet on Front-street, and running down to the river. Wm. NUTT, Shff. September 19.

(284) United States of America, N. Carolina District. Court of Admiralty. Whereas Richard NIXON, of New-Hanover County..N. Carolina, hath exhibited his libel before the Honorable the Judge of the Court of Admiralty..setting forth that on the 7th day of July last past, on the high seas, near New-Topsail Inlet,..the libellant discovered and took possession of the hull of a schooner named the Patty of Yarmouth, wrecked and abandoned..and praying that the same as derelict, or otherwise a reasonable salvage therein may be deemed to the said libellant... Attest, Francis HAWKS, Register of said Court. Newbern, September 17, 1799.

(285) North-Carolina, Treasury-Office, Sept. 1, '99. The Sheriffs and other Revenue Officers of the state aforesaid, are reminded of..the act of Assembly, which requires that their accounts shall be settled and..collections paid into the Public Treasury, on or before the first day of October annually... John HAYWOOD, P. Treasurer...

(286) Grand Lodge, The officers and members of the Grand Lodge and the Representatives of Lodges, are hereby requested to attend the annual communication in the city of Raleigh, on the evening of Thursday the 28th of November next, at 6 o'clock. By order of the most worshipful His Excellency Wm. R. GAVIE (DAVIE), Grand Master. Robert WILLIAMS, Grand Secretary. Wilmington, Sept. 15.

(287) To Be Let, And entered upon on the first day of October, That store & warehouse at present occupied by Mr. CABRAL, adjoining to Messrs. Robert ADAM & Co. in Market street. J. BURGWIN, Wilmington, September 15.

(288) Sheriff's Sales. On the first day of November next, Will Be Sold, at the Court-House, the following Lots in the town of Wilmington, to pay the Taxes due thereon: No. 155, situated on Back-street, said to belong to Samuel MORGAN.. No. 10, 15, 20, 25, situated on Back-street, said to belong to the heirs of Richard PLAYER, dec. No. 185, on Back-street, said to belong to Joseph RICHARDSON. No. 190, on Back-street, said to belong to the estate of Myer DYE. No. 200, on Back-street, said to belong to Thomas A KINS. No. 205, on said street, said to belong to the heirs of James CAMPBELL.. No. 96, 95, situated between (Third and Fourth) streets, said to belong to EAGLES' estate. No. 24, situated between said streets, said to belong to the heirs of Thomas JAMES. No. 29,34,44,49,54, situated between said streets, said to belong to the heirs of Peter LORD. No. 7 , situated between Second and Third-streets, said to belong to the heirs of E. HARRISON.. No. 75, situated between said streets, said to belong to the heirs of WAYNE. No. 70, 69,

(288) (Cont.) between said streets, said to belong to EAGLES' estate. No. 66, do. Jos. JOHNSTON's estate. No. 65, do. Rob. HOGG's estate. No. 43, 53, do. do. Joshua GRAINGE's do. Two thirds of a lot undivided, No. 79, opposite the Church, situated between Sam. BENTON's and James WALKER's, said to belong to the heirs of J. LONG and J. CAMPBELL. A vacant piece of ground on Dock street, being part of lot No. 28, between Isaac BERNARD's lot and Geo. HOOPER's, owner not known, supposed to belong to the estate of Joshua GRAINGER. No. 139, situated between Front and Second-streets, said to belong to Geo. LUCAS. No. 52, between Front and Second Streets, said to belong to E. HARRISON. No. 50, between do. heirs of CARVER. No. 49, do. do. heirs of WAYNE. No. 46, do. do. W. NORTON.. (No.) 39, do. do. estate of Rob. HOGG. (No.) 37 do. do. Hugh WADDEL. (No.) 36, do. do. Gen. CLARKE.. Part of lot No. 52, situate on Orange-street, between P. HARRIS & S. SPRING's, about 102 feet by 33, said to belong to GRAINGER's estate. Part of lot No. 62, at the corner of Orange and Front-streets, lately purchased by Butler ASHFORD.. No. 137, belonging to H. DHERBE.. (No.) 24, a water lot at the upper end of the town, owner not known. No. 22 do. do. said to belong to GRAINGER. No. 196, at the lower end of the town, said to belong to the estate of Gen. CLARKE. A small part of a lot on Front-Street, immediately before the lot belonging to George DUNCAN, about 30 by 20 feet-said to belong to Mr. CAIN, in Bladen. There are a number of lots belonging to the heirs of WIMBLE, not on the tax list, which will be to be sold, unless some person comes forward to pay the taxes. The numbers as herein mentioned are from the old plan. Wm. NUTT, Shff. Sept. 5.

(289) For Sale, That valuable Plantation, containing 300 acres of Land, lying on the east side of Cape-Fear river, opposite Brunswick, and adjoining the Plantation of Peter MAXWELL, Esq...apply to Ronald M'DUGALL. Wilmington, Sept. 19.

(290) Deserted From the 2d Regiment of Artillerists and Engineers stationed at Fort-Johnston, N. Carolina, Joshua WILSON, born in Cumberland County, England, 38 years of age, 5 feet 8 inches high, sandy complexion, blue eyes and sandy hair..a reward of 10 Dollars. Pat. C. HARRIS, Lieut. 2d Regt. A. & E. Fort-Johnston, Sept. 26.

(291) 1500 Dollars Was delivered to the Post-Master here, in the Post-Office, on the evening of Tuesday the 27th ult. in a Letter directed to Mr. John MILLS, Merchant, Baltimore, containing two Alexandria Bank Notes, No. 4320, in favor of Wm. TAYLOR, dated 30th April, '98, for 1000 Dollars, and No. 4522, in favor of John P. PLEASANTS, and dated the 10th of December, 1798, for 500 Dollars; which letter has been Suppressed in a Post-Office, and the Bank Notes taken out-as the Public Mail was not Stopped, Molested, or Robbed. Bankers and merchants are particularly requested to watch the circulation of said notes and stop them; and any person giving such information as will lead us to our money, shall have 500 Dollars reward. WILSON & SWANN. Fredericksburg, (Virg.)

(292) For Sale or Exchange, The Plantation adjoining Old-Town on Cape Fear River.. The situation for a house is beautiful having..a pleasing view of every vessel that passes to or from Wilmington, from which it is distant about four miles..apply to James CARSON. Wilmington, Sept. 12.

(293) Being determined to remove to the back country, I wish to dispose of the Plantation whereon I now live-it contains 320 acres.. There is now a good crop of Rice growing on it-the situation is pleasant, and there is a tolerable dwelling-house and good out-houses..a quantity of good fruit trees..and good stream for a Mill and Rice Machine... M. SAMPSON, Wilmington, Sept. 19.

Thursday, October 10, 1799. (Vol. III.-No. 144.

(294) Wilmington, October 10. At Baltimore. Interesting! By the arrival of the schooner Moncrief, captain E. PEARCE, in 21 days from Surinam, we are favoured with the following...

(295) Died-On Thursday last, at Fort Johnston, Mr. Philip SPAULDING, of this place.

(296) Notice is hereby given, That in Smithville on Saturday the 26th of October, the skirts of land on the water around the borders of the town, not heretofore granted or appropriated, will be leased in convenient Lots or Parcels..(at) 12 o'clock at the corner of Potts and Bay-street... By order, Joshua POTTS. October 10

(297) Deserted From the 2d Regiment of Artillerists and Engineers Stationed at Fort-Johnston N. Carolina, John BROWN, 5 feet 6 inches high, light hair, blue eyes, dark complexion, plays the fife..at this Fort..a reward of 15 dollars, and 10 if delivered to any Officer in the service of the United States. Pat. C. HARRISS, Lieut. 2d Regt. A. & E. Fort-Johnston, Oct. 10.

Thursday, October 17, 1799. (Vol. III.-No. 145.

(298) Halifax, Oct. 7. University of N. Carolina. In consequence of information received from the faculty of the University of North-Carolina, on Thursday the 19th of September, 1799, by the Trustees residing at Raleigh and Hillsborough, Mr. JONES, Mr. HOGG, Mr. POLK, Mr. HILL, Mr. HINTON and Mr. HAYWOOD immediately repaired to the seat of the University. They met on the 20th and..after..deliberating on the measures..to be adopted they returned to their respective homes, having first requested of their chairman, that publication of the issue of the business of this meeting be made in the Raleigh and Halifax Gazettes.

In compliance..the public are hereby informed, that the anarchy and confusion which lately prevailed among the students at the University, have fortunately subsided.. We are sorry to add, that the riotous and disorderly behaviour of Mr. William BAKER, Mr. Samuel M'CULLOCH, and Mr. Robert ALSTON had been such, as to lay the Trustees under the disagreeable necessity of ordering them to be expelled. The Trustees unanimously approved of the expulsion of Mr. William MARTIN which had taken place previous to their arrival, for and on account of his disorderly conduct, and disrespectful and indecent behaviour to the faculty. During the above disorder, several of the students professed their ____ amidst the tempest and conformed to order; in Honour to them and to give satisfaction to their parents and guardians, we do, with pleasure, publish their names, as follows, John HENDERSON, Thomas HUNT, William CHERRY, George THORNTON, Frank DANCY, Solomon WILLIAMS, Joseph GILLESPIE, George PHIFER?, Moses LOCKE, Jeremiah BAULE?, Johnston BLAKELY, John TOOMER, Richard CASWELL, Alexander MARTIN, John HUSKE, James HENDERSON, Henry MARTIN, Richard HILL, Henry HILL, Thomas NEAVES, James BATTLE and Edmund HARVEY... Willie JONES. John HAYWOOD. Raleigh, September 2.

(299) Wilmington, October 17. State of N. Carolina, Wilmington District, ss. Order for the Trial of Causes at November term 1799... (Witness) James MOORE, Clk. October 17.

(300) Sales At Auction, Will Be Sold On Friday the 25th inst. for the benefit of the concerned-at TOOMER's wharf at 10 o'clock in the forenoon-36 Tierces of Rice, and 6 Hhds. Tobacco-damaged on board the Schooner Polly, Jonas WARREN, master, bound from Charleston South Carolina to the Island of Babadoes-put in here in distress. ISAACS & LEVY. October 17.

(301) Depatment of State, Philadelphia, 27th July 1799. Sir, I beg leave to refer you to the enclosed duplicate of my letter of the 13th of this month, for my opinion concerning your answer to the speech of the Creek Chief, METHLOGY.. I am, sir,.. (Signed) Timothy PICKERING. P. S. By letters lately received from Mr. ELLICOTT, I find that col. HAWKINS stands high in the confidence of the Creek Nation. To James SEAGROVE, Esq. St. Mary's.

(302) Extract of a letter from John KINNARD, King of the Hitchicaw Tribe of Creek Indians, to James SEAGROVE, esq. dated in the Creek Nation, 26th August, 1799...

Thursday, October 31, 1799. (Vol. III.-No. 147.

(303) Ten Dollars Reward. Ran away on the 7th instant a stout Negro Man named JACK, formerly the property of Wm. JACKSON, Goaler of Wilmington..about 5 feet 8 inches high... Holden M'GEE. Little-Bridge, Oct. 24.

(304) Will Be Sold On Thursday the 14th of November next..at the Store of the late Philip SPAULDING, deceased, in Market-street, The Personal Estate of said deceased... Marg't SPAULDING, Ex'x. John FURGUS, Ex'r. Wilmington, Oct. 24.

(305) At Public Vendue On the 15th of November, will be sold, the Wearing Apparel &c. of the late Thomas HERRINGDINE, deceased. October 22.

(306) Notice. The subscriber having obtained letters of administration on the estate of Thomas HERRINGDINE, dec'd, requests all persons who have any claim thereon to bring it forward for settlement... Gorton CHASE. Cash-Alley, October 23.

(307) Wilmington, October 31. The Printer of this Gazette is under the unpleasant necessity of informing his subscribers..-That in consequence of a positive avowal of the Post-Master at this town, to stop the circulation of this Gazette, by preventing the post riders from carrying it to its subscribers in the country, after this day, although the Printer has made contracts with the carriers of the mails, to that effect, with whom he presumes that right exclusively exists-he is apprehensive that the existence thereof will soon be extinct, which must eventually cause the removal of his Printing-Office...

(308) To Be Sold At public vendue, on the third day of the Superior Court..a likely Negro Fellow. A. B. TOOMER. Wilmington, Oct. 31.

(309) Notice. All persons indebted to the firm of WHITFIELD and BROWN formerly of this town, are requested to come forward and settle their accounts, otherwise suits will be commenced without further notice. Richard BURDEN. Wilmington, October 31.

(310) Notice. The subscriber informs..that the drawing of his Lottery, will commence on the first day of the ensuing Superior Court. Timothy BLUDWORTH. Wilmington, Oct. 31.

(311) Ten Dollars Reward. Ran away from the subscriber, a Negro Fellow named QUA, Known by the name HOOPER's QUA. A. B. TOOMER. Wilmington, October 31.

(312) Sheriff's Sales. Notice is hereby given, that the following Lands in the county of Bladen, were not given in by any list..exhibited in said county for..1798 ..and the sale of the same will commence at the court-house..on the 14th day of December 1799..to satisfy the taxes due thereon for said year.. 640 Acres on the North-east side of the North-west River, joining Gen. BROWN and Governor ASH's lands,

(312) (Cont.) the property of John JOHNSTON, decd. 140 Acres.. 500 Acres in the fork of little & big Colley swamp, patented by Walter GIBSON, adjoining his old survey. 300 Acres on Wam Squam 400 do between little and big Colley swamp. 400 Acres lying on the East side of the North-west River, and on the South side of Gum swamp patented by David LLOYD. 200 Acres on the South-west side of Colley swamp, patented by John JORDAN, supposed to be the property of C. A. BELOAT, dec'd. 320 Acres on the South-west side of the North-west River, the property of William SANDERSON. 250 Acres on both sides of WHITE's creek, patented by Duncan M'COULSKY, joining Duncan RAY's land, supposed to be the property of John BURGWIN. 80 Acres lying between Benjamin FITZRANDOLPH and James MOORHEAD's land, supposed to be the property of ____ HOWARD. 1013 Acres lying on the East side of the Waccamaw, patented by John SLOAN, and granted by SLOAN to Jacob RHODES, supposed now to be the property of Michael SAMPSON. 100 Acres joining Archibald CAMPBELL, supposed to be the property of Lawyer DUFFEE, Senior. 200 Acres on both sides of WHITE's creek, supposed to be the property of Charles JEWKS, dec'd. 70 Acres on CARVER's creek, known by the name of PIKE's land. 320 Acres on same creek, known by the name of Girsham BEMBOE's land. 500 acres in the fork of Colley swamp, supposed to be the property of Thomas GRAYHAM. 500 acres on the upper part of the same swamp, supposed to be the property of Henry GRAYHAM. 640 acres on the South-west side of Colley swamp, joining the Tar-Kiln, supposed to be the property of Faithful GRAHAM. 126 acres sold by Amos JOHNSTON to William PARKER. 50 acres sold by do. do. to Eli SMITH. 50 do. sold by do. do. to William REGISTER. 100 do. sold by do. do. to John DANIEL. 225 do. sold by do. do. to Shadrack DANIEL. 245 do. sold by do. do. to Charles EDWARDS. 100 do. sold by do. do. to William WILKINSON. 200 do. sold by do. do. to Britton HARGROVE. 290 do. sold by do. do. to Iver M'MILLAN. 296 do. sold by do. do. to Drury HADDOCK. 500 do. sold by do. do. to James CROMMARTY. 640 do. sold by do. do. to Bailey SUTTON. 50 do. on PORTER's swamp supposed to be the property of Robert HODGE, dec'd. 66,130 acres sold by Jacob RHODES and William R. DUNHAM to William WHEELER of Robeson county. 960 acres on the south side of the White M_r_h, joining lands of ____ SESSIONS and ____ TOWKES, late the property of Elizabeth RICHARDS. E. MORSE, Shff. Bladen, October 29.

(313) To Be Sold As Escheated property..a Lot of Land opposite Wilmington... Jos. G. WRIGHT, attorney for the Trustees of the University. Wilmington, October 31.

(314) Notice. The subscribers having obtained Letters of Administration on the Estate of Mr. Roger HALL, deceased, request all persons who have any claim thereon, to bring it forward for settlement... John HALL, Michael MOLTON, Admr's. Fayetteville, October 28.

(315) Twenty-five Dollars Will be given to any person who will apprehend and deliver to the Goaler in Wilmington, the Negro fellow ELIJAH, formerly advertised in this paper..-he has been harboured at John TELFAIR's plantation down the river, as well as in Wilmington-..and at Mr. Daniel MALLET's plantation.. He has lately been guilty of a crime for which he deserves to suffer capital punishment... John BURGWIN. Wilmington, Oct. 21.

(316) Vermont Election. We have felt an interest in the recent elections in Vermont; and we with pleasure announce the election of His Excellency Isaac TICHENOR to the chair of that State.. The exertions of that fomenter of evil works, Matthew LYON, and his cubs, have been indefatigable and violent...

(317) Lexington, Sept. 12. By a gentleman just arrived from the Natchez, we are favored with the following proceedings: "At a court of general quarter sessions, commenced and held for the county of Pickering, Misissiippi Territory, on the 27th June, 1799. We the grand jury of the county of Pickering..present as a grievance,

(317) (Cont.) That so respectable a body of people, as inhabit the Misissippi Territory, are allowed in no manner of shape to interfere in their own government.. That the judges should assume to themselves the liberty of making laws.. That the government and judges, should ascertain the sum proposed to be levied on the county.. The impolitic appointment of officers civil and military; all confidence appears to be destroyed between them and the people.. That persons well known to be hackneyed in Spanish duplicity..should be nominated to posts of profit, honor and trust.. That the executive of this government, should deny to the citizens who were permanent residents in this Territory, previous to the running the boundary line between the United States and Spain, the privilege of removing slaves, from the Spanish dominions.. That any citizen should be confined as a criminal, without an oath being prefered against him.. That merchants should keep their shops open..on Sundays; also that tavern-keepers should be allowed to keep open houses for rioting, drinking and gaming on the above day... Col. WEST, Foreman, Maj. HINDS, James TRULY, A x. MONTGOMERY, Felix HUGHES, Robert MILLS, Gibson CLARK, William MOSS, Thomas CALVET, Parker CARODINE, George SOTLOR, Thos. M. GREEN, Jesse HARPER, Thos. WHITE, John BROOKS, Eben. SMITH.

Thursday, December 12, 1799. (Vol. III.-No. 153.

(318) Public Auction. Pursuant to the last will of Matthew JOHNSTON deceased will ____ at the Court House in ____ on Wednesday the 18th of December next..Lots & Lands, viz. One Lot on Market street containing 26 feet 10 inches front, and running back to Maiden Lane.-A water Lot with a Wharf and Warehouse thereon-Two other water Lots near or adjoining the above.-580 acres of Land in Sampson county..at or near the Six Runs-Also 100 acres of Land in said county... George JENNINGS, Ex'r.

(319) Public Vendue. On the third Monday of December next, will be peremtorily sold to the highest bidder, The Plantation adjoining Old-Town, on Cape-Fear River.. The situation for a house is beautiful, having..a pleasing view of every vessel that passes to or from Wilmington, from which it is distant about four miles... ISAACKS, LEVY & BISHOP. Wilmington, Nov. 28.

(320) Will Be Sold On the 9th day of January, at Public Sale, At the house of R. W. SNEAD, dec. part of the perishable property of said deceas'd consisting of Merchandize, Horses, Cattle, Hogs, household furniture, plantation Utensils, Naval Stores, two Turpentine Stills, and two Vessels, &c... H. M. SNEAD, Adm'x. Onslow county, Nov. 28.

(321) Wilmington, Dec. 5. The subscriber acquaints his friends and the public that he intends transacting Commission Business..at his store near the Court House, and next door to the Post-Office... C. D. HOWARD.

(322) Notice Is hereby given that Thomas NORMENT, Esq. of Duplin county is dead, and the subscribers have qualified as Executors to his last will and testament... Thomas WRIGHT, James WRIGHT, David WRIGHT, Kenan LOVE, Ex'rs. Duplin county, Nov. 21.

(323) Dissolution of Partnership. The copartnership of ISAACKS & LEVY being dissolved on the 31st ultimo, those who are indebted to them are requested to make payment.. Abraham M. ISAACKS, Jacob LEVY. Wilmington, Nov. 6, '99.

(324) Wilmington, December 12. Official. Extract of a Letter from Wm. F. HULINGS, Esq. Vice-Consul of the United States at New-Orleans, to the Secretary of State, dated October 18, 1799...

(325) Notice. I Wish to rent my Holly-Shelter Plantation to a good Tenant, for a term of seven years.. Ran away from me about the middle of June last, a Negro fellow named SAMBONY-he is supposed to be lurking about the plantations of Major A. D. MOORE and George DAVIS, Esquire... M. SAMPSON. December 12.

(326) Turk's Island & Lisbon Salt, Jamaica Spirits, St. Croix and Windward Island Rum, Brandy, Molasses and Sugar, for sale..by the subscriber... John MACLELLAN. Dec. 12.

(327) To Be Rented On the first day of January next, The house lately occupied by Benjamin ROWELL-Also, the Saw-Mill on VAUGHAN's creek... Wm. HOOPER. December 12.

(328) Notice. The purchasers at the sale of the personal property of the late Henry TOOMER, Esq. are hereby informed, that the time of payment has elapsed-they are..requested to come forward and make payment without delay. A. B. TOOMER, December 12.

(329) Notice. The subscribers having obtained letters of administration on the estate of Benjamin ROBERSON, dec'd, requests all persons who have any claim thereon to bring it forward for settlement... Alice ROBERSON, W. ROBERSON, Adm'rs. Sampson County, Nov. 21.

(330) To Be Leased, For one year or..longer. The whole or a part of my plantation on Rocky-Point..apply to Col. S. ASHE, on Rocky-point, or Dr. HILL, in Wilmington... W. H. HILL.

(331) I Have taken the house that Mr. John NICHOLS lately left, and intend taking in Boarders, by the day, week, month, or year... Thomas HOWARD. December 5.

(332) For Sale, The Ship Clermont, As she came from sea, well found with materials. Apply to M. MACKINZIE. Wilmington, Nov. 28.

(333) The subscriber has opened a store three doors above the Court-House, on the North-east side, where he has for sale..An Assortment of Groceries... James CARSON. November 28.

(334) U. States of America, N. Carolina District, Court of Admiralty. Whereas Thomas YOUNG and Elizabeth his wife, by their procurators and advocates duly admitted, have exhibited their libel before the honourable the Judge of the court of admiralty for the aforesaid District, setting forth their claim to certain negro slaves brought as a prize into the port of Wilmington in the year 1780, by a certain Martial BOITAR, commander of the armed schooner called the Fortunate; which said negro slaves, the said libellants alledge, are in the possession of John WALKER, Roger CUTLAR, the executor of Henry TOOMER, and the executors of James SPILLER... Francis HAWKS, Clk. November 28.

(335) Notice. The subscriber having obtained letters of Administration on the Estate of Robert W. SNEAD of Onslow county requests all those indebted to said estate to make payment... Harriet M. SNEAD, Adm'x. November 28.

(336) Raleigh, Nov. 26. Yesterday Col. Samuel BENTON, of Hillsborough, was chosen Brigadier General of the 6th Brigade, vice Gen. MOORE, resigned. James MILLER was chosen Brigadier General of the 10th brigade, vice Gen. DICKSON, resigned. No choice for a Brigade, vice Gen. BRICKELL, placed on the federal establishment, was made: on counting the votes, there appeared for Col. Wm. WILLIAMS, of Martin, 51 and for

(336) (Cont.) Col. INGLES 40. Yesterday a bill for establishing a court of errors and appeals, was introduced in the Senate, by Mr. S. JOHNSTON, of Martin...

(337) Legislature of N. Carolina. House of Commons. Nov. 20, '99. John R. EATON, esq. Private Secretary to his Excellency Wm. R. DAVIE, esq. laid before the house a message from his Excellency the Governor.. Thursday, Nov. 21. The following messages from..the Governor were read: To the Honourable the General Assembly of N. Carolina. Gentlemen-Being appointed a Minister Plenipotentiary to the French republic, in conjunction with Oliver ELLSWORTH, Chief-Justice of the United States; and Mr. Vans MURRAY, Minister at the Hague, for the purpose of discussing and settling by treaty all controversies between the U. States and France, I thought it my duty to accept the appointment... No. 2. Gentlemen, Basil GAITHER and Samuel B. PURVIANCE, Esquires, two of the Commissioners appointed for the purpose of completing the investigation of the frauds suggested to have been committed in the Secretary's office, and that of the late John ARMSTRONG, met on the 3d of March... No. 3. Gentlemen, In pursuance of the resolution of the late General Assembly, I appointed General John WILLIS and Francis LOCKE, Esquires, Agents, for the purpose of procuring from the Governor of the state of Tennessee, the books of Martin ARMSTRONG's office, lately kept at Nashville, and which had unfortunately been put into his possession in the month of January, '99... No. 4. Gentlemen.. A letter from Blake BAKER, Esquire, under date of the 28th of August, on the subject of the employing an agent on behalf the state, for the purpose of collecting & arranging the evidence against the offenders, is also submitted with these documents... Wm. R. DAVIE.

Raleigh, Sept. 10. Ordered, That the foregoing message be referred to a joint committee; and that Messrs. PORTER, John MOORE, Robert SMITH, LACY, SEAWELL, YANCEY, R. LONG, PLAYWELL?, MONTGOMERY, HINTON of Pasquotank, STANLEY, GRIST, ASHE, Thos. HILL, HAY and PURVIANCE, compose the same on the part of this house.

(338) Notice. The subscribers having qualified as Executors to the last will and testament of the late James BLOODWORTH, sen. dec'd, request all those indebted to said estate to make immediate payment... Ann BLOODWORTH, Ex'x'. James BLOODWORTH, Ex'r. December 1.

(339) The subscribers having entered into copartnership under the firm of ISAACKS, LEVY & BISHOP, solicit the favours of their friends and the public, in the Vendue & Commission business. Abraham M. ISAACKS, Jacob LEVY, Isaac BISHOP, jun. Wilmington, Nov. 6, '99.

(340) For Sale, An Elegant Eight Day Clock, With a Mahogany Case, almost new-Enquire of John PEABODY. Wilmington, Nov. 7.

1800 - All issues missing except for the following from Harvard University Library-January 2, 9, 16, 23, 30; February 13; March 6, 13, 20, 27; April 3, 10, 17, 24; May 1, 29; June 5, 26; July 3, 10, 31; August 14, 21; October 23, 30; November 6; December 4.

Thursday, January 2, 1800. (Vol. IV.-No. 156?

(341) Published Weekly By Allmand HALL.

(342) A List of the Laws Passed By The General Assembly of North-Carolina, at their Session commencing the 18th of November, and ending the 23d of December, '99.. 4. An act to amend an act, entitled, "An act for establishing a town on the lands of Wm. GRAY, on Cashy river." .. 9. An act to alter the name of Lawrence TOOLE, to

(342) (Cont.) that of Henry Irwin TOOLE. .. 14. An act to establish an Academy at or near the dwelling of the Rev. Wm. PEASLY, in the county of Moore. 15. An act for the relief of Archibald CAMPBELL. .. 17. An act to secure to Nancy POWELL of Johnson county, wife of Nathan POWELL, such estate as she may hereafter acquire. 18. An act to restore to credit J. HOKARD?, of the county of Lincoln. .. 20. An act to secure to Frances SMELLEY, wife of John SMELLEY, such estate as she may hereafter acquire. 21. An act to secure to Sarah DAVIS, wife of Richard Child DAVIS, such estate as she may hereafter acquire.. .. 26. An act to secure to Priscilla HALL, of Randolph county, wife of Levi HALL, such property as she may hereafter acquire, by her own industry, legacy, or otherwise.. .. 51. An act to alter the names of Charles and Basil MANLSLEY?, to that of Charles and Basil MANLY, of the County of Chatham.. .. 53. An act to alter the name of John BRYAN, of Johnson County, to that of John Arthur BRYAN. .. 65. An act to empower Abner WEATHERLY, sheriff of Guilford county, to collect the arrears of taxes due him in said county, for the years 1797 and 1798. 66. An act to secure to Catharine DICK, wife of Joseph DICK, such property as she may have acquired since her husband has left her, and such as she may hereafter acquire.. .. 68. An act to empower William SASSER, Isaac WILLIAMS, and John STEPHENS, late sheriffs of Johnston county; Solomon ALCOCK, late sheriff of Currituck county; Samuel SPEIGHT, late sheriff of Glasgow county; Thos. MORRIS, late sheriff of Iredell county; Edward HALL, late sheriff of Perquimans county; Thomas LEONARD, late sheriff of Brunswick; Ed. HATCH, late sheriff of Jones county; Lewis WILLS (or WELLS), late sheriff of Nash county; James BOWLES and W. CATE, sheriffs of Rutherford county; and the administrators of Annanias NELSON, late sheriff of Carteret county, to collect the arrears of taxes which may be due them for the years 1796, 1797 and 1798. 69. An act to secure to Jenny Jarrett THOMAS, wife of Charles THOMAS, such property and estate as she may hereafter acquire. 70. An act to reinstate John M'LENNON in the rights and privileges of a citizen. .. 72. An act to establish a town on the lands of John SPEED, in the County of Richmond.. .. 76. An act to enable Ephraim ELSBEE, sheriff of the County of Hyde for the year 1796, and the Administrators of Zach. SPENCER, deceased, sheriff, for the year 1797, to collect the arrears of taxes due them respectively, for said years. 77. An act to empower Richard RANKIN, late sheriff of Mecklenburg county, to collect the arrears of taxes due him for the years 1796, 1797 and 1798. 78. An act to authorize Freeman KILLINGSWORTH to erect a milldam across Neuse River, at his mill in the county of Johnston.. .. 80. An act to secure to Rachel HARE, wife of Marmaduke HARE, such estate as she may hereafter acquire. .. 91. An act to suspend the operation of an act, entitled, "an act more liberally to endow the University of N. Carolina, and to secure the titles of certain inhabitants of Mecklenburg ..to certain lands heretofore purchased from Henry Eustace M'CULLOH, so far as it respects the sales of confiscated lands.." 104. An act to _____ the title of Officers _____ tinental line of th___ State, and of Claimants _____ Entries made in the office of John ARMSTRONG. 105. An act to restore Zebedee HASELL to the rights and privileges of a free citizen.. .. 110. An act to secure to Mary BOWERS wife of Barnabas BOWERS, such estate as she may hereafter acquire. 111. An act to pardon and restore to credit Elijah BELCH. .. 113. An act to alter the name of Green CARR to that of Green SIMMONS, and to entitle him to inherit in the same manner as if born in wedlock. 114. An act to authorize Marmaduke KINBROUGH, of Surry County to collect the arrears of taxes due in said County, for the year 1798. 115. An act to empower Thos. JOHNSTON, of the County of Onslow, to collect the arrears of taxes due in said County, for the year 1798?.

(343) Notice. The subscriber hereby forbideth all and every person..from hunting or trav_ling over any part of his lands with dog or gun, or on lands in his possession, lying at and near the head of the Sound, in New-Hanover-County... Peter MAXWILL. December 26.

(344) Boston, December 6. Mr. GRIFFITH, a passenger with captain DRINKWATER, from Portland, has favored us with Mr. JENK's Gazette of Monday last, which contains the following Postscript. Gazette-Office, 3 o'clock, Dec. 2. I delay the press to mention the arrival, this moment, of the ship Cornelia, captain B. PRINCE, 49 days from Liverpool...

(345) New-York, Dec. 11. From a Jamaica paper of the 2d ult. received yesterday by the Venus. Interesting to Merchants.. Arrete, declaring that all American and other neutral vessels, coming from English ports in Europe or America, shall not be admitted into the ports of St. Domingo.. 1. The American schooner the Nantucket, commanded by captain Winslow LEWIS, dispatched from Boston to Martinique, in virtue of a sea letter granted by the President of the United States, under date of the 3d June last, and which came from Martinique to Cape Francois..shall be obliged to depart in 12 days, without any excuse...

(346) Congress. Monday, Dec. 9. .. The credentials of William Henry HARRISON, Esquire, who has appeared as a Delegate of the Territory of the United States N. W. of the Ohio, were referred to a committee of Election, to report their opinion thereon to the House.

(347) Wilmington, January 2. The subscribers to this Gazette are informed that this day commences its fourth year-They are earnestly requested to pay up their arrearages.

(348) Monday morning last, on the receipt of the following melancholy and distressing account, the citizens of this town..went into mourning-all the vessels in the harbor wore their colors half mast-the stores and shops were immediately shut up.. Baltimore, Dec. 17. Of all the disagreeable engagements which have devolved on the Editor of the American, none have ever occurred equal to the announciation of the Death of the most virtuous statesman, the most able General and the most inflexible patriot, that ever dignified a human nature; Geo. WASHINGTON, the hero, patriot sage, is no more. This amiable character, this virtuous statesman, this inflexible patriot yielded up his pure and uncontaminated soul, at about eleven o'clock on Saturday night last-about 24 hours preceeding which he was seized with a violent inflammation in the throat, and expired, "without a sigh, without a groan," on the following evening...

(349) Fayetteville & Wilmington Stage. The Stage will, for the present, ply once a week between Fayetteville and Wilmington-leave Michael MOLTON's, at Fayetteville, on Wednesday morning at 7 o'clock, & arrive the next day at Wilmington-leave DORSEY's Hotel, at Wilmington, Sunday morning, 7 o'clock, and arrive at Fayetteville Monday afternoon, by way of Point Peter and Black river.. Seats may be engaged at Fayetteville of M. MOLTON, and at Wilmington of C. D. HOWARD...

(350) Notice. The subscriber having obtained letters of administration on the estate of John NICHOLS, deceased, requests all persons indebted thereto, to make payment... Jere. NICHOLS, Adm'r. January 2.

(351) Will Be Sold, At public auction, on Friday the 10th day of January inst. on the premises, six miles from town, The personal Estate of the late John NICHOLS, consisting of Negroes, a Horse, Cattle, Hogs, plantation Utensils, and Household Furniture... Jere. NICHOLS, Adm'r. January 2.

(352) Taken up and committed to Jail, on Wednesday the 25th ult. a Mulatto Fellow named DICK, formerly belonging to F. SHACKELFORD, of Fayetteville-he has been sold

(352) (Cont.) to persons from Georgia, once or twice. The owner is requested to come and take the said fellow away. John GALE. January 2.

(353) Notice is hereby given, That the Land purchased by the Deep and Haw-River Navigation Company, in the fork of said Rivers, for the purpose of erecting the Town of Hawwood, has been laid off.. The sale of the Lots will commence on the second Thuesday of February next, on the premises.. John HENDERSON, President. N. B. Notice is also given to the company, that the general annual meeting will be held at Chatham Court-House on the second Monday in February next... J. H. Dec. 19th.

(354) Notice. The subscriber having obtained letters of administration on the estate of Robert HENDERSON, dec'd, requests all persons indebted thereto to make payment without delay... John HENDERSON, Adm'r. Wilmington, Dec. 23, 1799.

(355) New-York, December 11. We mentioned in yesterday's Mercantile Advertiser, the arrival of a cutter in this port, prize to the United States brig Norfolk. Lieutenant Henry KENYON (who commands the cutter) has since favored us with the following extracts from his log book...

(356) For Sale That valuable corner lot, and Brick Building thereon, between Market Street and TOOMER's alley on Second-Street-the dwelling house and kitchen may be easily repaired, as the walls are but little hurt by the fire... John BURGWIN. December 26.

Thursday, January 9, 1800. (Vol. IV.-No. 157.

(357) To the Honourable the General Assembly of the state of North-Carolina, Gentlemen, Basil GAITHER and Samuel D. PURVIANCE, Esquires, two of the Commissioners appointed for the purpose of completing the investigation of the frauds suggested to have been committed in the Secretary's office and that of the late John ARMSTRONG, met on the 3d of March.. Wm. R. DAVIE. Raleigh, Sept. 10. (Report) (A.) To His Excellency William R. DAVIE, Raleigh, June 6. Sir,.. Basil GAITHER, Samuel D. PURVIANCE.. Copy from the original, William WHITE, Secretary. (B.) .. Sir, The board of Commissioners for the further investigation of frauds committed in the office of the late Secretary, after sitting 63 days..have now the honour to present.. a general report, of their proceedings.. Among these your Excellency will perceive, that James GLASGOW, Esq. the late Secretary, holds a conspicuous place;.. 1st. He has issued duplicate warrants (without proof of loss).. 2d. He has issued two warrants to the same soldier, without expressing either to be a duplicate, and executed grants for both. 3d. He has issued warrants for the full bounty of land, to persons..mustered only for nine months. 4th. He has issued warrants to soldiers, who..have deserted and executed grants to others as the asignees of such soldier.. 10th..grants to himself on unsigned warrants, as the asignee.

No evidence is perhaps necessary to support these charges, but what the records on which they are founded, will supply, unless it is the charge contained in no. 10; to establish which it may be necessary to procure the testimony of Samuel HOLLADAY, of the county of Glasgow. In this case, the Secretary issued a warrant in favour of James HARRISON, a soldier who mustered; on the back of the warrant, there is an assignment from HARRISON to James GLASGOW, attested by Samuel HOLLADAY; the body of the assignment is written by GLASGOW, the name of Samuel HOLLADAY, as a witness to it, is forged, and the warrant has no signature.-On this warrant and assignment the Secretary issues a grant to himself.. As it was the opinion of the Board that frauds of this kind would be the subjects of criminal prosecution, they have endeavoured to discover the persons concerned in them. They..are of opinion that John

(357) (Cont.) M'NEES, Nathan LASSITER, Moses SHELBY, Wynn DIXON, Mann PHILLIPS, Benjamin SHEPPARD, Samuel SAMFORD, Thomas BUTCHER, John PRICE, John SHEPPARD, Joshua DAVIS, William FAIRCLOTH, Joseph FERREBEE, John BONDS, Arthur PEARCE, Willoughby WILLIAMS, Joshua HADLEY, Stockly DONELSON and William TYRRELL, are the persons who have been principally concerned in making and forging the false assignments...

(358) Congress. House of Representatives. Thursday, December 19. A message was received from the President of the United States, by Mr. SHAW, his Secretary, and read.. Gentlemen of the Senate, and Gentlemen of the House of Representatives, The letter herewith transmitted will inform you, that it has pleased Divine Providence to remove from this life, our excellent fellow citizen, George WASHINGTON.. John ADAMS. Mount Vernon. Dec. 15, 1799. Sir, It is with inexpressible grief, that I have to announce to you the death of the great and good General WASHINGTON. He died last evening between 10 and 11 o'clock, after a short illness of about 24 hours. His disorder was an inflammatory sore throat, which proceeded from a cold, of which he made but little complaint on Friday. On Saturday morning about 3 o'clock he became ill. Dr. CRAIK attended him in the morning, and Dr. DICK of Alexandria, and Dr. BROWN of Port Tobacco, were soon after called in... Tobias LEAR.

(359) The President, with deep regret, announces to the Army, the death of its beloved Chief, General George WASHINGTON.. Given at the War Office of the United States in Philadelphia, this 19th day of December, A. D. 1799, By command of the President, James M'HENRY. Secretary of War.

(360) Wilmington, January 9. Extract of a letter from John MORTON, Esq. American Consul at Havanna, dated Nov. 14, 1799. "The Governor has just issued a proclamation requiring all strangers to depart hence in two months."

(361) The President of the United States has nominated to the Senate, Alfred MOORE, Esq. to supply the place of James IREDELL, Esq. as an Associate Judge of the Supreme Court of the United States. The Legislature of Virginia has elected Mr. MONROE the Governor of that state.

(362) The Mechanical Society will meet this Evening at 6 o'clock, at the house of Mr. Thos. HOWARD... John MARTIN, Treas'r. January 9.

(363) State of North-Carolina, Wilmington District. Pursuant to a decree of the Court of Equity for the district aforesaid, in a certain cause wherein SMITH, DESAUSERE and DARREL were complainants, & Nathaniel CROCKER defendant, will be sold in Wilmington, at public auction, to satisfy said decree, on the first of February next, a certain House and Lot in said Town, on the east side of Front street..now in the possession of Benjamin BLANEY, merchant... Sam. R. JOCELYN, c. & m. e. Equity-Office, 6th January, 1800.

(364) The subscriber having qualified as Executor to the last will and testament of William MEREDITH, deceased, requests all persons indebted to the estate..to make payment... Jesse JENNET. January 3.

(365) The subscribers having qualified as Administrators on the estate of John HARRISON, deceased, request all persons indebted thereto, to make payment... William KEDDIE, James COXETTER, Adm'rs. January 9.

(366) Five Dollars Reward. Eloped from my service a Negro Fellow named MANUEL, belonging to David JONES, Esq. but mortgaged to me.. He has been heretofore harboured by a Negro Woman belonging to Mrs. HERON, who he has for a wife, and was there last Sunday night... John BURGWIN. January 8.

(367) Federal Legislature. House of Representatives. Thursday, Dec. 5. A message was received from the President of the United States..to wit: Gentlemen, ..I herewith transmit to Congress, certain documents, which relate to the late insurrection in Pennsylvania... John ADAMS.. Dec. 5, 1799. .. 1st Insurrection in Northampton, &c. A letter from the hon. Richard PETERS, to the Secretary of State, inclosing a declaration of William NICHOLS, Esq. Marshall of the District of Pennsylvania; a deposition of VALENTINE --; and the deposition of John FYETLY, Esq.. A letter from Patrick HENRY, Esq. to the Secretary of State, declining the appointment of Envoy, owing to his indisposition.. A message was received from the Senate informing the House, that the Right Rev. Bishop WHITE had been chosen on their part, as chaplain to Congress.

(368) Papers referred to in the President's message, Department of State. Philadelphia, March 6th, '99. Sir, ..your obedient servant, Timothy PICKERING, (to) Wm. Vans MURRAY, Esq. minister of the U. States, at the Hague. (Copy.) The Hague, 5th May, 1799. Citizen Ministers, It is with greatest pleasure that I hasten to fulfil the instructions..from the government of the United States of America, by informing you that the President has appointed Oliver ELLSWORTH, Chief Justice of the United States, Patrick HENRY, late governor of Virginia, Vans MURRAY, Minister Resident.. at the Hague, to be Envoys Extraordinary and Ministers Plenipotentiary of the United States to the French Republic... Wm. MURRAY.

(369) An Act Granting longer time to survey certain Lands in this state, and prescribing the manner in which entries of claims to the vacant Lands in this state shall in future be made.. Read three times, and ratified in General Assembly the 21st day of December, 1799. Benj. SMITH, S. S. M. MATTHEWS, S. H. C.

Thursday, January 16, 1800. (Vol. IV.-No. 158.

(370) New-York, Dec. 20. Extract of a letter from an officer on board the United States ship, Adams, R. V. MORRIS, Esq. Commander, dated on board the Adams, off Guadaloupe, 30th November...

(371) Philadelphia, Dec. 18. Fire! Last evening, about 9 o'clock, the city was alarmed by the cry of Fire. It proceeded from RICKETT's Circus, which, in a few minutes after the discovery, was enveloped in Flames. These communicating to a range of new three story brick buildings in Sixth street, the wooden part of five of them was nearly all destroyed. The flames also communicated to O'ELLER's Hotel and left nothing but the bare walls unconsumed..

(372) Almanacks for the year 1800 for sale at A. HALL's Book Store.

(373) Notice. The New-Hanover Troop of Light Horse, are requested to attend at Captain HILL's, at 9 o'clock on Sunday morning, properly equipped, to attend the procession in memory of General George WASHINGTON, By order of the Captain, A. CUTLAR, Cornet. January 1_.

(374) For Sale, That valuable Lot in the Town of Wilmington, running 99 feet on Front-Street, and 99 on the River, with..a well finished two story Dwelling-House, with an excellent Store-Cellar, Kitchen and Out Houses; at present occupied by Mr. George GIBBS-and a Wharf with a new Ware-House thereon, 50 by 60 feet. For terms apply to George DUNCAN. January 16.

(375) To Be Rented, Two convenient stores 22 by 16, the corner of Front and Dock-Streets. Apply to Thos. ROBESON. January 16.

(376) Advertisement. A Large Box supposed to contain Books, was shipped on board the Schooner Juno from New York-The Consignee may receive the Box by calling on A. T. BROWNE, and paying freight and charges. Jonathan THOMPSON. Wilmington, January 13.

(377) Ten Dollars Reward. Ran away from the subscriber, a Negro Man named WILL, formerly the property of Thomas LOPER, on the Sound... Proudfoot JOHNSTON. Wilmington, January 13, 1800.

(378) Dancing School. Monsieur LOYZELL acknowledges with gratitude the support and encouragement with which the ladies and gentlemen of Wilming have hitherto favoured him... Nov. 6.

(379) Legislature of North-Carolina. Papers referred to in the Governor's Message. (Concluded from our last.) (C) His Excellency Wm. R. DAVIE, Esq. Sir, It was the care of the last Board of Commissioners for the investigation of frauds committed in the office of the late Secretary, not to interfere generally with such of that business as had been thoroughly examined and reported by the former Board. But as the duplicate warrants issued from the office of John ARMSTRONG, and in which John Gray BLOUNT and Thomas BLOUNT, had a concern, although selected and reported on by the former Board, were perhaps not so arranged and methodized in the books accompanying their report, as might be necessary to a full and complete knowledge..The Commissioners have made them an exception to this rule.. In these lists..we have referred to distinct classes. Those duplicate warrants drawn by the BLOUNTS, where they had made no assignment either of the original or duplicate, but where they had obtained grants on the one, and DONELSON and TYRRELL on the other. Those cases where they assigned the original to James KING, and obtained grants for themselves on the duplicate.. Those cases in which they have obtained grants on the duplicate and assigned the original to Stockly DONELSON, who thereupon obtained grants for himself.. There have been no assignments from the enterers to the BLOUNTS, that we have been able to discover; the assignments from the BLOUNTS to others we take to be genuine, and not forged, as the former Board appear to have imagined... Basil GAITHER, Samuel D. PURVIANCE, Copy from the original, Wm. WHITE, Secretary.

(380) House of Commons, Dec. 13, 1799. .. The committee who were appointed to examine whether the names of these persons reported on by the Commissioners, as being concerned in the frauds committed in the Secretary's office, have at any time been made known to the proper authority previous to the meeting of the present General Assembly, and if so, why they were not apprehended and bound over, Report.. But among a numerous croud of offenders none have been arrested except James GLASGOW ... Thos. WYNNS, Chairman. In Senate, Dec. 21, '99. Read and resolved, That this house do concur therewith. Benj. SMITH, Speaker. By order, M. STOKES, Clerk. In the House of Commons, Dec. 23, '99. Read and concurred with. M. MATTHEWS, Speaker. By order, J. HUNT.

(381) The following is the Order of the Funeral Procession, in honor of the Memory of the late General WASHINGTON, as agreed upon by the Committee of Arrangement,..Jas. M. HUGHES, Chairman, Ebenezer STEVENS, Jacob MORTON, James FARLIE, John STAGG, jun. New-York, Dec. 29, 1799.

(382) From the Philadelphia D. Advertiser. Funeral Procession In Honour of the late Commander in Chief of the armies of the United States, Lieut. Gen. Geo. WASHINGTON.. Having arrived at the Zion church, the Bier was conveyed to the centre of the middle aisle-Here the ceremonies commenced with soft and solemn music-the Rt. Rev. Bishop WHITE made suitable prayers; and..an eloquent Oration..was delivered..by Major Gen. Henry LEE, a member of the House of Representatives from the state of Virginia.

Thursday, January 23, 1800. (Vol. IV.-No. 159.

(383) Wilmington, January 23. On Sunday last the funeral obsequies in honor of General Geo. WASHINGTON, deceased,..were solemnized in this town.. (Procession) Mechanical Society, preceeded by Mr. John ALLAN, president. Masonic Societies in the mourning of the Fraternity, preceeded by the worshipful Samuel MASON..William CAMPBELL, Esq. in full mourning.

(384) Notice. All persons having demands against the estate of Matthew JOHNSTON, Sen. dec'd, are requested to exhibit the same to the subscriber... George JENNINGS, Ex'r. Wilmington, Jan. 23.

(385) Mr. John Charles CRAFTS, As every one may not be acquainted with your celebrity for lying..I am under the necessity of declaring you to the public as a base unprincipled scoundrel and liar... Henry WILLIAMS, Wilmington, Jan. 15, 1800.

(386) Congress. House of Representatives, December 23. .. Mr. SEWALL presented a letter of Winthrop SERGEANT, Esq. governor of the Missisippi territory.. Mr. RUTLEDGE presented a petition of Nicholas I. ROOSAVELT, on behalf of himself and associates, praying for an act of incorporation, for the purpose of continuing and facilitating the works of SCHUYLER's Copper Mine in New-Jersey...

Thursday, January 30, 1800. (Vol. IV.-No. 160.

(387) Pennsylvania Legislature. House of Representatives, January 3. To Thomas M'KEAN, Governor of the commonwealth of Pennsylvania. Sir,...

(388) From the Newburyport Herald. Remarkable Phenomenon. Mr. MARCH, Being requested to communicate the following remarks, to the public,-I send them to you.. On my late passage home, from the island of St. Domingo, being in lat. 29, long. 71, on the 12th Nov. 99 half past one o'clock in the morning, the weather being very clear and pleasant, the wind to the eastward, the moon near the full, and shining very bright, observed the stars to shoot in great numbers, from every point in the compass and at twelve o'clock, the whole atmosphere appeared to be full of stars. I may say thousands of thousands, shooting and blazing in every direction..and so continued till day light, the day following the wind came round with the sun, till it got to the north, and the whole atmosphere was filled with smoke, attended with a strong smell, like the burning of woods, and so continued for several days till I got into lat. 35 N. and further... Joseph H. WOODMAN. Newburyport, Dec. 20, '99.

(389) Wilmington, January 30. Died at Fayetteville, on Wednesday last, in the bloom of life, Mrs. WINSLOW, consort of Mr. John WINSLOW. All who had the happiness of being acquainted with this admired and accomplished lady, are touched with an unfeigned sympathy at her premature separation from her respected partner and relations.

(390) In behalf of the Grand Lodge of North Carolina. To all and every our right worshipful and loving Brethren, Greeting: It is recommended to the officers and members of the Grand Lodge of North-Carolina,..that they wear a black crape for 60 days commencing on the 22d of February next, in memory of their regret of the death of their illustrious friend and brother Geo. WASHINGTON. By the most worshipful the Hon. William POLK, Grand Master: Robert WILLIAMS, Grand Secretary. Raleigh, Jan. 23. A. L. 5890, A. D. 1800.

(391) Notice. The subscriber has obtained letters of Administration on the estate

(391) (Cont.) of Joze Roiz SILVA, late of New-York, merchant, deceased-Those indebted to the said estate are requested to make payment... Antonio C. SILVA, Adm'r. Wilmington, Jan. 24, 1800.

(392) Sales at Auction, On Thursday the 4th of February next, Will be Sold At the Store occupied by Mr. A. C. SILVA, A large and valuable Assortment of Dry Goods, Groceries & Cordage.. By order of the Administrator upon the estate of Mr. Joze Roiz SILVA, late of New-York, deceased. ISAACKS, LEVY & BISHOP. Wilmington, 29th January.

(393) Advertisement, To Be Sold At Public Auction, on Friday the 14th of February next, A Bay Horse... L. A. DORSEY, jun. January 30.

(394) Congress. House of Representatives. January 4. Another member, viz. Richard D. SPAIGHT, esq. from N. Carolina, appeared this day, was qualified and took his seat. A message was received from the President of the U. States, by Thomas B. ADAMS, esq. in the absence of his secretary, Mr. SHAW, informing the house, that the President had approved and signed the following acts, viz. An act for extending the privilege of franking to Wm. H. HARRISON, a delegate, from the territory N. W. of the river Ohio.. Mr. WALN presented a petition of Absolesm JONES and others, freemen of colour, of the city and county of Philadelphia, praying for a revision of the laws of the U. States, relative to the slave trade...

Thursday, February 13, 800. (Vol. IV.-No. 162.

(395) Treaty of Peace and Friendship between the United States of America, and the Kingdom of Tunis. John ADAMS, President of the United States of America. To all whom these presents shall come, Greeting: Whereas a Treaty of Peace and Friendship was definitely arranged and concluded, between the United States of America, represented by William EATON and James Leander CATHCART, Esquires commissioners for that purpose especially appointed, & the most illustrious and most magnificent Bey and government of Tunis, which treaty is in the following words..

Whereas the President of the United States..dated the 18th day of December, 1798, vested Richard O'BRIEN, William EATON and James Leander CATHCART, or any two of them..with full powers to confer, negotiate and conclude with the Bey and Regency of Tunis on certain alterations in the Treaty..concluded by the intervention of Joseph Etienne FAMIN on behalf of the United States, in the month of August 1797.. and entered in the foregoing treaty, certain alterations in the 11th, 12th and 14th articles... In testimony Whereof, I the said John ADAMS..signed the same..at the City of Philadelphia this 10th day of January..1800. John ADAMS. By the President, Timothy PICKERING, Secretary of State.

(396) Wilmington, February 13. Smithville, February 3, 1800. Funeral obsequies in memory of General George WASHINGTON, were observed this day at the Military Station of Fort-Johnston, on the river Cape-Fear; attended by the inhabitants of this town and its vicinity.. Order of procession. The Federal Troops commanded by Lieut. FERGUS.. Pall Bearers. Lieut BURCH, Lieut. SNELL, Lieut. HARRIS, Capt. BROWN. Mourners. Joshua POTTS, Abram BAKER, Henry LONG, Joseph HUMPHRIES, Luke SWAIN, Isaac DAVIS. Physician, Doctor EVERET. Mrs. LONG and Mrs. GALLOWAY.. Dr. EVERET..read the Funeral Service.. On the evening of the same day, a discourse was delivered by Abram BAKER, Esquire...

(397) For London, The Ship Perseverance,   COTTLE, Master, will sail in all this month. For Freight or Passage apply to LANGDON & GILES. February 13.

(398) Ran away from the Brig Hannah, John DAGGET, Master, now lying in this Port, two seamen, one named Richard ____ED, the other William GIPSOM... Thomas BURTON. Wilmington, February 13.

(399) A Caution. The crew of the English Letter of Marque Venus, commanded by John WELLS, now lying in this Port, having absented themselves from duty on board said vessel, all persons are hereby forwarned from harbouring them at their peril, or from giving them credit on any account, as I will not pay any debt they may contract ... John WELLS. Wilmington, February 12.

(400) Hector PAYNE, Hair-Dresser, From Fayetteville, Offers his services to the Ladies and Gentlemen of Wilmington..at their own houses. Wilmington, February 13.

(401) Ten Dollars Reward. Ran away from the subscriber..a Negro Woman,..by the name of BLANEY's NAN.. I have empowered Mr. Ezekiel LANE to dispose of said Negro wench, should she be taken up and lodged in Goal, or as she runs. Edward WILLIAMS. February 13, 1800.

(402) Charleston, January 7. On Saturday last, the inhabitants of this city, paid the last honors..to the remains of their late most worthy and beloved Chief Magistrate, Governor RUTLEDGE.. Major RUTLEDGE attended as chief mourner.. His body was deposited with military honors, in the family burying ground in St. Philip's church yard...

(403) An Act for the better regulation of the Inspection of Lumber in the Sea-Port Towns in this State... Benjamin SMITH, S. S. Mussendine MATTHEWS, Speaker of Commons. Read three times and ratified in General Assembly the 23d of December, 1799. A true Copy, William WHITE, Secretary.

(404) Sheriff's Sales. The following is a list of lands in New-Hanover county, the taxes of which remain unpaid-The same will be sold on the 13th of May next..or as much thereof, as will pay the taxes, and expence. 100 acres given in by Francis HENRY, and due for the year 1797. 130 do. do. John MARSHALL, do. 250 do. do. Benj. ALEXANDER, do. 100 do. do. J. CULLEN, sen. do. 190 do. do. John MORRISS, do. 612 do. do. John SIMPSON, do. 360 do. do. John WALLIS, do. 200 do. do. John BURNS, do. 300 do. do. John CORBET, do. 770 do. do. James CORBET, do. 250 do. do. Edgerton MOTTE, do. 165 do. do. Archibald MACARIBE?, do. 200 do. do. Jacob POWELL, do. 244 do. do. James THOMAS, do. 317 do. do. Daniel MORGAN, do. 1334 do. do. John MILLER, do. 325 do. do. John PRESCOTT, do. 600 do. do. W. TAYLOR, do. 1076 do. do. Ex'rs. of D. JAMES, do. 300 do. do. Edmond MOORE, do. 150 do. do. Henry HOLLY, do. 160 do. do. John WALKER, (MOORE's Creek,) do. 410 do. do. Joseph BRINSON, due for 1797 & 1798. 125 do. do. Hardy PARKER, do. 200 do. do. Frederick ROWE, do. 108 do. do. White BURWICK?, do. 400 do. do. Peter GATSON?, do. 50 do. do. Jacob EASON, do. 960 do. do. James PRICE, do. 283 do. do. James TOWNING, do. 320 do. do. Wm. DWAUN, do. 375 do. do. George DWAUN, do. 160 do. do. Benj. GIDEON, do. 200 do. do. Thomas GIDEON, sen. do. 158? do. do. Michael LOPER, do. 100 do. do. John MALPUS?, do. 650 do. do. James ROGERS, do. 400 do. do. John SWINSON, sen. do. 200 do. do. Frederick BUFORD, do. 360 do. do. John ERWIN, do. 250 do. do. Arthur STUCKEY, do. 150 do. do. John STOKELY, do. 122 do. do. Jonathan WILLIAMS, do. 175 do. do. Fen? FULLER, do. 730 do. do. Arther SAVAGE, do. 400 do. do. Henry BLAKE, do. 100 do. do. Thos. SCARBOROUGH, do. 800 do. do. James KINNEA_, do. 1175 do. do. Mores WRITTER, do. 141 do. do. Absalom TAYLOR, do. 2607 do. do. Wm. WALKER, do. 200 do. do. Wm. ANDERSON, for the year 1798 only. 762 do. do. Thomas BEESELY, do. 795 do. do. Daniel BOURDEAUX, do. 400 do. do. Thomas BARLOW, do. 120 do. do. Wm. BUXTON, do. 410 do. do. Joseph BRINSON, do. 2_0 do. do. Nathan COOK, do. 50

(404) (Cont.) do. do. Jacob COSTON, do. 50 do. do. Peter CAESAR, do. 100 do. do. Isaac COTTEN, do. 150 do. do. John CURRIE?, do. 1720 do. do. James DWAUN, do. 570 do. do. John EDENS, do. 50 do. do. Jacob EDENS, do. 50 do. do Jacob EASON, do. 1100 do. do. John FELLOWS, do. 500 do. do. Nicholas FENNEL, do. 150 do. do. Samuel GURGANUS, do. 400 do. do. David HALL, do. 100 do. do. John HUNT, do. 340 do. do. James HOWARD, sen. do. 351 do. do. Wm. HENNESSEY, do. 260 do. do. William HUFFHAM, do. 100 do. do. Allan HENNESSEY, do. 500 do. do. Thomas JAMES, do. 100 do. do. Joshua KNOWLTON, do. 310 do. do. Daniel KERR, do. 466 do. do. James LEE, do. 40 do. do. Thomas LEDDON, do. 195 do. do. Isaac LAMB, do. 400 do. do. Woney M'LAMMY, do. 100 do. do. Henry MILLER, do. 200 do. do. Peter MACBRIDE, do. 2360 do. do. Mark M'LAMMY, do. 100 do. do. Mary M'LAMMY, do. 135 do. do. Joshua M'LAMMY, do. 50 do. do. John MALPUS, sen. do. 300 do. do. Benj. ATOTT?, jun. do. 450 do. do. Simon MALPUS, do. 200 do. do. Henry MALPUS, do. 500 do. do. George NEWTON, do. 150 do. do. Joseph NEWTON, do. 400 do. do. George NIXON, do. 620 do. do. Hardy POWEL, do. 100 do. do. John PACE, do. 50 do. do. Francis PRIDGGN, do. 365 do. do. Wm. H. RAMSAY, do. 75 do. do. Charney RUSSEL, do. 325 do. do. James STANDLEY, do. 860 do. do. Edward SPEARMAN, do. 61 do. do. Thomas SIMMONS, do. 700 do. do. James SMITH, do. 455 do. do. Jonathan STANDLEY, do. 111 do. do. Thomas WOODSIDES, do. 350 do. do. James WILSON, do. 200 do. do. George WHITE, do. 2 0 do. do. Luke WHITE, do. 310 do. do. John WHITE, do. The foregoing is the names of the persons who gave in the lands for taxation. Since then it is probable some of the said land may have been conveyed, and now in possession of others. .. Any person who may come forward to pay the taxes before the day of the sale, will apply in case of my being out of town, to Marshall R. WILKINGS... Wm. NUTT, Shff.

(405) State of North-Carolina, Onslow County. Notice is hereby given, That there has been apprehended and is now in my care, a Ranaway Negro Man by the name of TOM; he is about 5 feet 5 or 6 inches high.. Said Negro was formerly the property of Edward DUDLEY, Esquire, of Onslow, and said DUDLEY carried him to the State of South-Carolina, & as he told me, sold him to a Mr. Andrew BURNETT, and the Negro says he now belongs to said BURNETT..(apply) to the subscriber about three miles from Onslow Court-House. Lemuel DOTY. January 19, 1800.

(406) The subscriber wishes to Sell or to Lease for a term of years, the place in Fayetteville where he now lives... John SIBLEY, Fayetteville, Jan. 28, 1800.

(407) The subscriber begs leave to inform..that he has taken the house at present occupied by Mr. Thomas MURPHY, where he intends carrying on the business of Saddle and Harness making... David DUDLEY. Wilmington. February 6.

(408) Removal. A. HALL has removed his Books and Stationary to the new store in Front-street, nearly opposite to Messrs. MILNE and BLANEY's.. He has for sale a few copies of the system of Bookkeeping and Dr. PERKINS Metallic Points... February 6.

(409) The Trustees of the Fayetteville Academy are happy..to announce..that the difficulty..in suitable boarding for young ladies..is now removed. Mrs. EMMET has concluded to open a Boarding House for that purpose...

(410) Dissolution of Copartnership. The Copartnership of M'FEDRAN and ALLEN, will dissolve by mutual consent, on the first day of April next, owing to the former's intention of leaving the state shortly after that period... John M'FEDRAN, James ALLEN. Feb. 6.

Thursday, March 6, 1800. (Vol. IV.-No. 165.

(411) Congress. House of Representatives, February 4. Mr. KITTERA, from the committee to whom was referred the petition of Lardner CLARK, made a report.. Resolved, That inasmuch as the governor of the North-West territory has full powers under existing laws, to settle and adjust the claims of Lardner CLARK..the interference of Congress..is therefore unnecessary. .. On Motion of Mr. SMITH, the house went into a committee of the whole on the bill for the relief of James YARD.. February 5. Mr. LIVINGSTON, from the committee appointed to wait on the President of the United States with the resolution requesting information relative to the requisition for, and delivery of Jonathan ROBBINS, under the 27th article of the British treaty.. February 7. .. Mr. HARRISON presented a memorial of sundry inhabitants of the Little Miami, purchasers of lands from John Cleves SYM NS, praying a confirmation thereof.. Gentlemen of the House of Representatives. In consequence of your request..I directed the Secretary of State to lay before me, copies of the papers intended. These copies together with his report, I now transmit to the House.. John ADAMS... Feb. 7, 1800.. No. 1 Copy of a note from Robert LISTON, Esq. Minister Plenipotentiary, &c of the king of Great Britain, to the Secretary of State, requesting that application might be made to the President..to issue his order for the delivery of Thomas NASH.. No. 2 A letter from the Secretary of State to the Honorable Thomas BEE, Judge of the District Court of the United States for South Carolina, stating it to be the opinion of the President, that Thomas NASH ought to be given up under the 27th article of the British treaty, if upon due investigation it should be found, that he had committed the crime of piracy and murder in the manner imputed ..

No. 5 Extract of a letter from Admiral Sir Hyde PARKER, dated Port Royal, to Mr. LISTON, stating that NASH had been tried, convicted & hung in chains-and that he confessed himself to be an Irishman.. No. 4 Danbury, September 16th, 1799. We, the subscribers, Select Men of the town of Danbury in the state of Connecticut, certify,-that we have always been inhabitants of said town, and are from 45 to 57 years of age, and have never known an inhabitant of this town by the name of Jonathan or Nathan ROBBINS, and that there has not been nor now is any family known by the name of ROBBINS within the limits of said town. Certified per-Eli MYGOT, Ebenezer BENEDICT, Justus BARNUM, Benjamin HICHCOK. Danbury, September 16, '99. The subscriber late town clerk for the town of Danbury..Connecticut, certifies that he kept the town records 25 years, viz. from the year 1717 until the year 1769, that he is now 56 years of age, and that he never knew any person by the name of ROBBINS, born or residing in the said town of Danbury during that term of 25 years, before or since. Major TAYLOR.

(412) To John ADAMS, President of the United States. Sir, The general assembly of the territory north west of the river Ohio..are anxious to embrace the earliest opportunity of declaring their confidence in your virtue and talents.. Edward TIFFIN, Speaker of the House of Representatives. H. VANDERBURGH, President of the Council.

(413) Notice, The Copartnership of DEAN and LOWDER, being by mutual consent this day dissolved.. Business will be carried on in the place they occupied by Joseph DEAN in the same manner as formerly. Joseph DEAN, Samuel LOWDER. N. B. As Samuel LOWDER will leave this state in a short time, he requests those indebted to him to make payment... Samuel LOWDER. February __.

(414) Wilmington, March 6. Fire! Fire! Fire! On Tuesday morning about nine o'clock, the inhabitants of this Town were again alarmed by this most distressing cry. The workmen of a large new house in Second Street, the property of Mrs. TOOMER, having left fire in the chimney place, while gone to breakfast, it communicated to some shavings, and in a few moments the whole building was wrapt in flames..the great

(414) (Cont.) and timely exertions of the citizens aided by the masters and crews of vessels in the harbour, prevented this destroying element from extending any further than the adjacent building owned by Dr. DE ROSSET, corner of Market & Second-street, where after consuming that building also, its progress was arrested. Some careless person having put a cannister of powder near one of the engines, it blew up, and several persons were very much burnt. Captain ABRAMS, who was employed on the top of the machine, received the most injury, but it is thought he is not dangerous...

(415) To Be Sold, As She now lies stranded on Barron? Inlet, the schooner Pluto, with all her tackle and apparel... John MACLELLAN. March 6.

(416) For Liverpool The Ship Sally, John M'CARTEY master, will sail about the 20th inst. For Freight or Passage apply to LANGDON & GILES. March 6.

(417) Notice, On Saturday the 26th day of April next will be sold at the Court House in Fayetteville-the dwelling House out Houses, and Lott, at present occupied by Doctor Alexander M'QUEEN, situated on Hay-street.. Also, the Store House and Lott.. on Bow-Street..now occupied by Duncan M'AUSLAN. The above Houses and Lotts belong to the estate of the late James SPILLER, deceased... Hardy HOLMES, David DODD, D. M'AUSLAN, Executors. March 6.

(418) The subscriber informs..that he has taken the House lately occupied by Mr. George JENNINGS-and intends taking in Boarders... Thomas SNEAD. March 6.

(419) Ran Away from the subscriber, a Mulatto Slave, named ISAAC.. Should the said runaway not return home before Monday next,-from that time I do hereby declare him outlawed, and will give five dollars to any person who will deliver him to me dead or alive... A. HALL. March 6.

(420) For Sale, A Valuable Plantation,..on the North East branch of Cape Fear river within four miles of..Wilmington, consisting of 1000 acres of land... John HILL. February 20.

(421) For Sale, That valuable Lot in the Town of Wilmington, running 99 feet in Front-Street, and 99 on the River, with..a well-finished two story Dwelling-House.. at present occupied by Mr. George GIBBS-and a Wharf with a new Ware-House thereon, 50 by 60 feet. For terms apply to Robert MUTER, or John LORD, Esquires. January 16.

(422) Advertisement. If Mr. Hero Antonio UHTHOFF, or Mr. Hero A. UHTHOFF, be living, he will hear of something to his advantage by applying to the subscriber; and his friends in Europe will be obliged to any person who will give any information respecting him, whether living or dead. He resided in Carolina, previous to the year 1777, and was a native of Bremen in Germany. Geo. GIBBS. February 20.

(423) Baltimore, February 8. The publisher of Gen. WASHINGTON's Will have favored us with the following extracts..(Fed. Gaz.) "Item, I give and bequeath in perpetuity, the 50 shares which I hold in the Potomac company..towards the endowment of a University to be established within the limits of the district of Columbia, under the auspices of the general government.. Item, The hundred shares which I hold in the James River company, I have given, now confirm in perpetuity, to and for the use and benefit of Liberty Hall Academy, in the county of Rockbridge, in the commonwealth of Virginia. Item, to my nephew, Bushrod WASHINGTON, I give and bequeath all the papers in my possession, which relate to my civil and military administration of the affairs of this country.. Item, To each of my nephews, William Augustine WASHINGTON, George LEWIS, George Steptoe WASHINGTON, I give one of the swords or cutteaux, of which I may die possessed..."

Thursday, March 13, 1800. (Vol. IV.-No. 166.

(424) The Will of Gen. Geo. WASHINGTON. Virginia, Fairfax, ass. I, George DENEALE, clerk of Fairfax County Court, do certify, that the subsequent copy of the last Will & Testament of George WASHINGTON, deceased, late President of the United States of America, with the Schedule annexed, is a true copy from the original, recorded in my office. In testimony whereof, I have hereunto set my hand, this 23d day of January, 1800. George DENEALE, C. F. C...

In the name of God, Amen. I George WASHINGTON, of Mount Vernon.. Item. To my dearly beloved wife Martha WASHINGTON, I give and bequeath the use, profit, and benefit of my whole estate, real and personal, for the term of her natural life, except such parts thereof as are specially disposed of hereafter.. And to my mulatto man WILLIAM, (calling himself William LEE) I give immediate freedom, or if he should prefer it (on account of the accidents which have befallen him and which have rendered him incapable of walking or of any active employment) to remain in the situation he now is..I allow him an annuity of 30 dollars during his natural life.. Item. I release, exonerate and discharge the estate of my deceased brother, Samuel WASHINGTON, from the payment of the money which is due to me for the land I sold to Philip PENDLETON, (lying in the county of Berkely) who assigned the same to him, the said Samuel, who, by agreement, was to pay me therefore; And whereas, by some contract,..between.Samuel and his son, Thornton WASHINGTON, the latter became possessed of the aforesaid land, without any conveyance having passed from me, either to the said PENDLETON,..Samuel or..Thornton..it rests therefore with me to declare my intentions concerning the premises and these are to .. give and bequeath the said land to whomsoever the said Thornton WASHINGTON (who is also dead) devised the same ..exonerating the estate of..Thornton, equally with that..of Samuel, from payment of the purchase money which, with interest..would amount to more than a thousand pounds: And whereas, two other sons of my said deceased brother Samuel, namely George Steptoe WASHINGTON, and Lawrence Augustine WASHINGTON, were, by the decease of those to whose care they were committed, brought under my protection, and in consequence have occasioned advances on my part for their education at college and other schools, for their board, cloathing and other incidental expenses, to the amount of near 5,000 dollars over and above the sums furnished by their estate, which sum it may be inconvenient for them or their father's estate to refund-I do.. acquit them..from the payment thereof. Item. The balance due to me from the estate of Bartholomew DANDRIDGE, dec (my wife's brother) and which amounted, on the first day of October, 1795, to 425 pounds (as will appear by the account rendered by his deceased son, John DANDRIDGE, who was the acting executor of his father's will) I release and acquit from the payment thereof; and the negroes (then 33 in number) formerly belonging to the said estate, who were taken in execution, sold and purchased in on my account, in the year ____ and ever since have remained in the possession and to the use of Mary, widow of the said Bartholomew DANDRIDGE..it is my Will and desire shall continue to be in her possession..during her natural life; at the expiration of which, I direct that all of them..40 years old and upwards, shall receive their freedom..

Item. If Charles CARTER, who intermarried with my niece Betty LEWIS, is not sufficiently secured in the title to the lots he had of me, in the town of Fredericksburg, it is my Will and Desire that my executors shall make such conveyances of them..to render it perfect. Item. To my nephew William Augustine WASHINGTON,..a lot in the town of Manchester..No. 265, drawn on my sole account, and also the tenth of one or two hundred acre lots, and two or three half acre lots, in..Richmond, drawn in partnership with nine others, all in the lottery of the deceased William BYRD, are given, as is also a lot which I purchased of John HOOD conveyed by William

(424) (Cont.) WILLIE and Samuel GORDON, trustees of..John HOOD, numbered 139, in the town of Edinburgh, in the county of Prince George state of Virginia.

Item. Having sold lands..in the state of Pennsylvania, and part of a tract held in equal right with George CLINTON, late governor of New-York, in the state of New-York; my share of land and interest, in the Great Dismal Swamp, and a tract of land in the county of Gloucester-withholding the legal titles thereto, until the consideration money should be paid-and having..leased and conditionally sold..all my lands upon the Great Kenhawa, and a tract upon Difficult run, in the county of Loudoun, it is my Will..that whensoever the contracts are fully..complied with..conveyances are to be made. Item. To my brother Charles WASHINGTON, I give and bequeath the gold headed cane left me by Dr. FRANKLIN, in his will. .. To the acquaintances and friends of my juvenile years, Lawrence WASHINGTON and Robert WASHINGTON, of Chotauck, I give my other two gold headed canes..and to each..I leave one of my spy glasses, which constituted part of my equipage, during the late war. To my compatriot in arms and old and intimate friend, Dr. CRAIK, I give my bureau..and the circular chair, an appendage of my Study. To Dr. David STUART I give my large shaving and dressing table and my telescope. To the reverend, now Bryan Lord FAIRFAX, I give a Bible..presented to me by the right reverend Thomas WILSON, bishop of Soder and Man. To general DE LA FAYETTE I give a pair of finely wrought steel pistols, taken from the enemy in the revolutionary war. To my sisters-in-law, Hannah WASHINGTON and Mildred WASHINGTON-to my friends Eleanor STUART, Hannah WASHINGTON of Fairfield, and Elizabeth WASHINGTON of Hayfield, I give each a mourning ring, of the value of 100 dollars.. To Tobias LEAR I give the use of the farm which he now holds, in virtue of a lease from me to him and his deceased wife..free from rent during his life.. To Sally B. HAYNIE, (a distant relation of mine) I give & bequeath 300 dollars. To Sarah GREEN, daughter of the deceased Thomas BISHOP, and to Ann WALKER, daughter of John ALTON, also deceased, I give each 100 dollars, in consideration of the attachment of their fathers to me; each of whom having lived nearly 40 years in my family..

I proceed to the distribution of the more important parts of my estate in manner following: First. To my nephew Bushrod WASHINGTON..partly in consideration of an intimation to his deceased father, while we were bachelors, and he had kindly undertaken to superintend my estate during my military services, in the former war between Great-Britain and France; that if I should fall therein, Mount Vernon (then less extensive in domain than at present) should become his property; I give and bequeath all that part thereof, which is comprehended within the following limits, viz: Beginning at the Ford of Dogue Run, near my mill, and extending along the road, and bounded thereby, as it now goes and ever has gone..to the ford of Little Hunting Creek at the Gum Spring, until it comes to a knowl, opposite to an old road which formerly passed through the lower field of Muddy hole farm; at which on the north side of the said road, are three red..oaks..a corner, and a stone placed thence..to the back line..of the tract between Thomson MASON and myself..that line easterly..to the run of Little Hunting Creek-thence with that run, which is the boundary between the lands of the late Humphrey BRAKE? and me, the tide waters of the said creek-..to Potomac river..to the mouth of Dogue creek..to the..beginning..containing upwards of 4,000 acres. Second.-In consideration of the consanguinity between them and my wife, being as nearly related to her as to myself; as, on account of the affection I had for, and the obligation I was under to, their father when living, who, from his youth had attached himself to my person, and followed my fortunes through the vicissitudes of the late revolution, afterward devoting his time to the superintendance of my private concerns for many years..I give and bequeath to George Fayette WASHINGTON, and Lawrence Augustine WASHINGTON..my estate east of Little Hunting creek, lying on the river Potomac, including the farm of 360 acres, leased to Tobias LEAR, as noticed before, and containing..by deed, 2,027 acres..divided between them..when the youngest

(424) (Cont.) shall have arrived at the age of 21 years.. Third. And whereas it has always been my intention, since my expectation of having issue has ceased, to consider the grand children of my wife, in the same light as..my own relations.. especially by the two whom we have raised from their earliest infancy-namely, Eleanor Park CUSTIS and George Washington Park CUSTIS-and whereas the former..hath lately intermarried with Lawrence LEWIS, a son of my deceased sister, Betty LEWIS..wherefore I give & bequeath to the said Lawrence LEWIS and Eleanor Park LEWIS, his wife, ..the residue of my Mount-Vernon estate, not already devised to my nephew.. All the land north of the road leading from the ford of Dogue run to the Gum Spring..to which I add all the land I possess west of..Dogue run and Dogue creek, bounded easterly and southerly thereby-together with the mill, distillery..about 2,000 acres.. Fourth-..I give and bequeath to George Washington P. CUSTIS..the tract I hold on Four Mile run in the vicinity of Alexandria, containing 1200 acres..and my entire square No. 21, in the city of Washington. Fifth-All the rest and residue of my estate..I desire may be sold..and the monies arising therefrom to be divided into 23 equal parts and applied as follows; vix. To Wm. Augustine WASHINGTON, Elizabeth SPOTSWOOD, Jane THORNTON, and the heirs of Ann ASHTON, son & daughter of my deceased brother Augustine WASHINGTON, I give & bequeath four parts, that is, one part to each of them: To Fielding LEWIS, George LEWIS, Robert LEWIS, Howel LEWIS and Betty CARTER, sons and daughters of my deceased sister Betty LEWIS, I give and bequeath five other parts, one to each of them: To George Steptoe WASHINGTON, Laurence Augustine WASHINGTON, Harriot PARKS and the heirs of Thornton WASHINGTON, sons and daughter of my dec'd brother Samuel WASHINGTON, I give and bequeath the other four parts.. To Corbin WASHINGTON, and the heirs of Jane WASHINGTON, son and daughter of my deceased brother John Augustine WASHINGTON, I give and bequeath two parts.. To Sam. WASHINGTON, Frances BALL, and Mildred HAMMOND, son and daughters of my brother Charles WASHINGTON, I give..three parts..and to George Fayette WASHINGTON, Charles Augustine WASHINGTON and Maria WASHINGTON, sons and daughter of my deceased nephew George Augustine WASHINGTON, I Give one..part..to each a third: To Elizabeth Park LAW, Martha Park PETER, and Eleanor Park LEWIS, I give..three other parts; and to my nephew Bushrod WASHINGTON and Lawrence LEWIS, & to my ward, the grandson of my wife..one other part..

Lastly, I constitute and appoint my dearly beloved wife Martha WASHINGTON, my nephews William Augustine WASHINGTON, Bushrod WASHINGTON, George Steptoe WASHINGTON, and Lawrence LEWIS, and my ward George Washington Parke CUSTIS, (when he shall have arrived at the age of 20 years) executrix and executors of this Will & Testament... 9th of July 179 *..and of the independence of the United States the 24th. George WASHINGTON. *It appears the testator omitted the word "Nine".

(425) (Official.) Extract of a letter from Richard V. MORRIS, Esq. commander of the frigate Adams, dated Basseterre roads, St. Kitts, January 20, 1800...

(426) Extract of a letter from Wm. COWPER, Esq. commander of the United States ship Baltimore, to the Secretary of the Navy, dated Brsseterre Roads, Jan. 22...

(427) List of vessels taken by the United States brig Pickering, Benjamin HILLAR, Esq. commander, from the 2d August to the 31st Dec. '99. Schr. Cynthia, Asa FORRETT (or FORSETT), from New-York to Martinique-re-taken.. Brig Helen, Peter SAIEL, from Altona, bound to St. Domingo, a Danish vessel-recaptured from the French. Brig Brothers, Geo. PRINCE, from Savannah, to Martinique-recaptured.. Schr. Harriet, SEARS, from New-bern, N. C. to Antigua-recaptured.

(428) Wilmington District, In Equity. Charles JOHNSTON, vs. James FLEMING. Ordered that in this cause, That unless the Defendant file an answer to the Complain-

(428) (Cont.) ant's bill, at or before the next May term, the bill will be taken pro confesso, and a decree made thereon accordingly. Sam R. JOCELYN, C. & M. E. Equity-Office, March 13, 1800.

(429) Sale of Land. To be peremptorily sold to the highest bidder on Monday the 19th day of May next, under the Court-House in Wilmington, That valuable Tract..of Land in Bladen county, containing 640 acres..known by the name of PORTER's Neck, formerly the property of Gen. WADDELL... John BURGWIN. Wilmington, March 12.

(430) M. Papen LABAZDIER respectfully informs the ladies and gentlemen of Wilmington ..that he purposes opening a Dancing School... Wilmington, March 11.

(431) Horrid Murder! New York, Jan. 6. As the public mind has been much agitated to ascertain the cause of the unhappy catastrophe of Miss Juliana-Elmore SANDS, (neice of Mr. David SANDS, an eminent preacher in the Society Friends) found last Thursday barbarously murdered in one of the Manhattan wells, the following is a true account of this melancholy affair: The deceased, who, at the time of her death, was aged about 22 years-had, for some time, resided in the house of Mr. RING, Millwright, the husband of her aunt.. For some months previous..Mr. Levi WEEKS, house-carpenter, had..paid his addresses to her. On the day of her disappearance, she had told her aunt, that she was that evening to be privately married to Mr. WEEKS.. That she was murdered, is the verdict of the Coroner's Inquest.. Mr. WEEKS..is now in custody and will no doubt speedily meet the reward of his demerits.

Thursday, March 20, 1800. (Vol. IV.-No. 167.

(432) New-York, Feb. 26. The Gallant TRUXTON. Philadelphia, Jan. 25. (Official.) Yesterday morning, Lieut. SHAW, of the armed schooner Experiment, arrived at Marcus-Hook..with letters for the Secretary of the Navy from which the following are extracts -United States ship Constellation, at sea, Feb. 3, 1800. Sir,.. I have the honor to be, &c. Thos. TRUXTON. Sen. STODDART, Esq. Sec. of the Navy. (Extracts from his journal.) ..the mainmast went over the side..and carried with it the top men, among whom was an amiable young man who commanded the main top, Mr. James JARVIS, son of James JARVIS Esq. of New-York. .. I regret much his loss, as a promising officer and amiable young man... Thomas TRUXTON.

(433) United States ship Constellation, February 2, 1800. List of Officers and men wounded and missing, by the action of the 1st of February, 1800, on board the..Constellation, of 38 guns, Thomas TRUXTON, Esq. commander, with a French National ship of 58 guns. Jas. JARVIS, midshipman, missing, who was in the maintop, went overboard with the mainmast. William LIGHTFOOT, killed. Jon. ROBINSON, Seaman, do. John SMITH, do. do. Thomas STEVENSON, do. do. John WILLIAMS, do. do. John WILSON, do. do. James FOSTER, do. do. Emmanuel MANNA, do. do. Robert SMITH, do. do. Emmanuel DEIST, do. do. William POWELL, Old. do. Joseph GROWER, do. do. Christopher M'CORMICK, Mid. do. Mr. A. SHIRLEY, 2d lieut, slight wound in the leg. Mr. P. C. WEDERSTRANT, midshipman, slight wound in the head. Mr. R. WARREN, midshipman, slight wound in the head. John HIGHLAND, quarter gunner, shot through the back. John ROGERS, sergeant of marines, slight wound on the arm. Jonathan BELL, sail maker's mate, fractured leg. John HOXSE, seaman, arm shot off, and wounded in the side. William MULGROVES, seaman, fractured thigh. Jas. CARTER, seaman, wounded in the thigh and in the side. Ephraim JABINS, seaman, wounded in the arm. Benjamin BRADFORD, seaman, arm shot off-died. Antonio POYNTZ, seaman, slight wound on the head. Edward HALLMAN, seaman, slight wound in the arm and knee. George MATTHEWS, old seaman, fractured thigh. John LOGAN, old seaman, fractured leg. Thomas FITZGERALD, old seaman, gluteus maximus musle badly wounded. Charles LEWIS, old seaman, shot thro'

(433) (Cont.) the arm. John BAPTIST, boy, leg shot off. Philip SMITH, boy, wounded in the back of the neck. Cader BRANTON, marine, wound in the thigh. William SMALL, marine, shot through the thigh. William HOWEL, old seaman, slight wound in the thigh. George CARSON, marine, shot through the hand.

(434) Cash will be given for 20 or 30,000 of good well drawn Juniper Shingles, to be delivered in Wilmington between this and the first of June. John BURGWIN. March 12.

(435) Wilmington, March 20. Died in this Town on Wednesday the 19th inst. Mr. David WATTON?, sen. Prize-master of the schooner Liberty, of Norfolk, which arrived here last week, a prize to the Letter of Marque Brigantine Samuel of Baltimore, commanded by David WILSON jun.

(436) Samuel SITGREAVES has sailed for London, as a special agent to explain the causes of differences between the commissioners acting under the 6th Article of the British treaty.. Mr. SITGREAVES was some time ago appointed in conjunction with Timothy PICKERING and Oliver WOLCOTT, commissioners to adjust certain matters between the state of Georgia and the U. States,-in consequence of Mr. SITGREAVES' removal to England, Charles LEE, Attorney General of the United States, has been appointed to that duty... (Aurora.

(437) Proposals, For Printing an elegant Volume, to contain those invaluable Compositions of our late Chief and President... John RUSSELL, John WEST. .. Subscriptions for the above, received by A. HALL, in Wilmington.

(438) For Sale, By the subscribers, at the corner of Front and Dock-streets, Flour, Tobacco, Corn and Cotton... D. & T. ANDERSON.

(439) Notice. All persons indebted to Samuel LOWDER..are requested to call on Joshua G. WRIGHT, Esq. and settle the same, or they will be sued indiscr___ately by the 6th of April next. Samuel LOWDER. March 20.

(440) Notice. On Saturday the 5th day of April next, the Skirts of Land, adjoining on the ___ers about Smithville, will be leased in certain Lots..for a term of years ... By order, J. POTTS, T. C.

(441) To Be Sold, A Lot of Ground on the North-side of Market-street, whereon the late Hugh CAMPBELL, Esq. had a store-for terms apply to Joshua G. WRIGHT. March 20.

(442) Philadelphia, Feb. 21. Extract of a letter from Edward STEVENS, Esq. on board the United States schooner Experiment, of 12 guns, Lieut. MALEY, commander. Leogane, Jan. 2, 1800... Edward STEVENS. (to) Silas TALBOT, Esq., &c &c &c.

Thursday, March 27, 1800. (Vol. IV.-No. 168

(443) Philadelphia, Feb. 19. Letter from the Secretary of War, to the Chairman of the Committee, appointed on the 9th of December last, on so much of the Speech of the President, as relates to "a system of national defense commensurate with our resources, and the situation of our country."... James M'HENRY, Sec. of War. (to) Harrison G. OTIS.

(444) New-York, March 4. Extract of a letter from Capt. Moses TRYON, dated on board the United States ship Connecticut, 10 leagues E. N. E. from Descade, January 10, to a gentleman in Middletown...

(445) Wilmington, March 27. The brig Harmony Hall, captain J. SMITH, of this port, from Montego Bay, bound home, was cast away on Mattacombo Reef, off the coast of Florida, on the night of the 12th February; crew and part of the cargo saved.

(446) Brig Phenix, John Mason TUFTON, master, on Saturday March 1, sailed from Savannah bound to Jamaica and on Wednesday at 6. P. M. at 28.50 long. 74.80, was struck with a heavy squall which instantly overset him; in this condition ____ ____ until the next day when there hove in sight a brig..but she not observing us, we concluded to get into the boat which was so leaky, that the owner, Mr. MOODY would not venture; whom with 2 mates & 4 men we left on board. We missed..the brig..and then..at 5 P. M. next day was taken up by the sloop Catharine, capt. Samuel PHILLIPS, master, who offered every assistance, and tried after the wreck upwards of 12 hours but all in vain. John M. TUFTON.

(447) For apprehending and delivering to Lieutenant James MACAY, or myself..or for delivering to any Officers in the service of the United States, Arthur VENTERS, a private in my company, the reward of 10 Dollars..will be given-said VENTERS deserted on the 23d ult. from my barracks at Wilmington-he was born in Princess Anne County, Virginia but has resided for some time past in Onslow county, North-Carolina-he is 40 years of age-he has short black hair, a grey beard, fair complexion and light eyes-he is about 5 feet 6 inches and an half high... Maurice MOORE, Captain. 6th Federal Regiment. March 27.

(448) Outlawry. State of North-Carolina, New-Hanover County..march term, 1800.. Whereas the Grand Jury for the County aforesaid, pre_____ that certain Negro slaves, named JACK a cooper, and JACK commonly called Jack BACOT; and JACK, commonly called Jack ROUSE, and POMPEY, and ISAAC a Mulatto, belonging to John WALKER Esq. and a fellow called JIM belonging to Mrs. Sarah MOSEL? and SALLY, a wench belonging to Richard QUINCE, Esquire-are run away and are out lurking in swamps.. These are therefore to require and command the said negroes..forthwith to surrender themselves, and return home.. And further it shall and may be lawful for any person..to kill and destroy the said runaway slaves..by such Ways and Means, as he or they shall think fit, without accusation or impeachment of any crime, for the same... Witness, Anthny B. TOOMER, Clerk of the said Court..the third Monday of March, 1800. A. B. TOOMER, Clk. (L. S.) March 27. (April 3, 1800 issue.-"Note POMPEY and JIM have returned home.")

(449) Whereas by an act of the General Assembly..no Lumber can be exported unless it has been inspected by persons legally appointed for the inspection thereof; and whereas the subscribers were appointed by the County Court of New-Hanover, at the last Term, Inspectors of Lumber, Staves and Shingles... James MUMFORD, Thos. FITZGERALD, David JONES, Andrew URE, Junius DUNBIBBIN, Thos. BROWN. March 27, 1800.

Thursday, April 3, 1800. (Vol. IV.-No. 169.

(450) Philadelphia, March 3. (Circular.) The Philadelphia Medical Society desirous of increasing the stock of useful medical knowledge, have determined to offer a Medal of the value of 60 dollars for the best desertation in answer to the following question: "What are the effects of the following medicines upon the human body, especially upon the pulse, viz.. (Black Henbane), ..(Thorn Apple)..(Hemloc), Compher, Amber, Musk, Digitalis Purpurean (Fox Glove)..(Squill)..(mountain laurel) and the principle preparations of Lead."... By order of the Society, Benj. S. BARTON, John MOORE, George LEE.

(451) Extract of a letter from captain Charles G. RUSSEL, of the U. S. ship Herald,

(451)(Cont.) dated 25th January, 1800, of St. John's Porto-Rico...

(452) Charleston, Feb. 11. Captain D'VOL, late master of the schooner Eagle of Baltimore which upset at sea on the 30th of January last, gives the follwing information: Two days after the above misfortune, all hands on the wreck, the ship Sisters, captain STOKES, of Charleston, fell in with us. We begged his assistance; but he refused to take us up, alledging that he was short of provisions; at length after strong entreaties, he bade us swim on board. This he knew the weak state of myself and crew would not allow us to comply with; captain S. then inhumanly left us to all the calamities of starvation and lingering death. However, on the following morning..his majesty's ship Asia, admiral VANDEPUT, took us off the schooner, treated us with the utmost humanity, and landed us safe at Hampton roads...

(453) Wilmington, April 3. Caution. From an Alexandria paper-Feb. 27. The money brought from New-Orleans by John ELLIOT and others..proves to be counterfeit..the bills are well imitated..some of them are signed John KEAN, Cashier.

(454) The subscriber has just received..a neat assortment of Drugs and Medicines, which he will retail low for Cash, at his shop in Market-street... N. HILL. April 3

(455) Will Be Sold. On Saturday the 12th inst. at the plantation belonging to the late John LEVINGSTON, deceased, on the Sound near Peter MAXWELL's plantation. All the personal and perishable property belonging to said John LEVINGSTON, deceased.. Also, On Tuesday following the 15th, in the town of Wilmington, Will Be Sold The Household Furniture, and hired out until the first day of January 1801, sundry Negroes... N. HILL, J. LORD. April 3.

(456) For New-York or New-London, The Schooner William, William H. HUTCHENS master -to sail in 10 days. For passage apply to the captain, or to Thomas BURTON, at Mr. JENNINGS's. April 3.

(457) The subscribers, pilots of navigation for the Bar and River, hereby give notice, that from and after this date, they will not receive any written or verbal orders for pilotage. Corn's. GALLAWAY, Charles BETTS, Caleb DAVIS, Benjamin CRAY, William GRISSOM, Samuel LONG, Edward NEWTON, James NEWTON, Samuel POTTER, Bart. DAVIS, Elias CRAIG, Thomas CRAIG, Isaac DAVIS, Henry LONG, Henry CRAIG, Benjamin CRAIG, Wilson DAVIS, John WADE, James CLARY, Thomas WOODEN, John NEWTON, John MASH, William TODD. April 3.

(458) State of North-Carolina, New-Hanover county, March term 1800. .. Notice is hereby given..to all the creditors of the estate of Laurence A. DORSEY, that the said..DORSEY is dead, and that the subscriber qualified as Administrator, to his estate at the above term... L. A. DORSEY, jun. Adm'r. April 3.

(459) Notice Is hereby given to the subscribers of the Deep and Haw river navigation, That..every subscriber..who shall not make ___ or their payments up to 15 dollars for each of his or their respective shares, on or before the second Monday in May next,..will be dealt with according to law. The money to be paid into the hands of James NEWLAND, Treasurer; or to John HENDERSON, President. Chatham Court-House, March 10.

(460) Sixth Congress of the United States. At the first Session, begun and held at the City of Philadelphia, in the State of Pennsylvania, on Monday the second of December, 1799. An Act to suspend in part, an Act entitled "An Act to augment the Army of the United States.." Theodore SEDGWICK, Speaker of the house of Representatives. Thomas JEFFERSON, Vice-President of the United States, and President of the

(460) (Cont.) Senate. Approved, February 20, 1800. John ADAMS, President of the United States.

Thursday, April 10, 1800. (Vol. IV.-No. 170.

(461) Wilmington, April 10. The following interesting letter was received at Baltimore. United States frigate Constitution, at sea, near the island of St. Domingo, 28th Feb. Sir, I request that it may be made known thro' the United States that in consequence of the increased number of general RIGAUD's armed boats, up the Guanba (..otherwise called the Bite of Leogane) I have directed a frigate, and a small armed vessel of 14 guns, to continue cruising there, for the protection of the commerce of the United States to and from Port Republican... Silas TALBOT.

(462) List of Letters remaining in the Post-Office at Wilmington.. A. Benjamin AYDETOT 3, Major Samuel ASHE 3, Samuel ASHE senior 1, captain ABEEL 1. B. John BROWN 1, Samuel BLUDWORTH 3, captain Pearson BROWN 1, Sarah BETTS 1, Blake BAKER, Esq. 1, Mrs. BONDIES 2, captain Thomas BROWN, jun. 1, Thomas BROWN 1, Benjamin BRADSHAW, Duplin county, 1, Abraham BESSENT, Brunswick, 1, Richard BRADSHAW, Duplin, 1. C. Gordon CHACE 3, James CARD 1, Charles CLARK 1, William CARTER 1, Richard CROSBY 1, captain William COX 1, Thomas CRAIKE 1, captain Elkanah COOK 1, Mrs. C. CAMPBELL, Topsail, 1, John CAINS, Brunswick, 1, Edward CLEAMONS, LOCKWOOD's Folly, 1. D. Captain John DRYSDALE 2, Wilson DAVIS 1, Mrs. David DUDLEY 1, Monsieur DEPVERDUGON 1, Silvanus DICKINSON 1, James DICKSON, Duplin, 1. E. Captain James EDWARDS 7, Nathaniel ELLIS 1, John EGLESTON 1, Reubin EVERRETT 1, Jonathan ELLIS 1. F. Edward FULLER 1, capt. Thomas FOLLARSBEE 1, George FISHER, Fort Johnston 1, Joseph FARLEY 1. G. Captain Samuel GRAVES 2, capt. Stephen GRANT 1, John GALE 1, William GRAVES 1, capt. Joseph GAGE 2, Henry GEER 1. H. Samuel HOWARD 2, Benjamin HOWARD 2, Ann HOSKINS 1, H. HOSKINS 1, Henry HALSEY 1, capt. James HOOPER 3, capt. Edward HALEY 3, capt. James HAYES, jun. 1, Jacob HARTMAN 3, John HARFORD 1, Asa HOSMER 1, Jacob HOWLAND 1, George HAUSE, Sampson, 1. J. Edward JONES 4, capt Richard BARNEY or capt. William JORDAN 1, Dominick JORDAN 1, William W. JONES. K. Captain Charles KENNEDY 1. L. Thomas LEONARD, Brunswick, 1, William LEIGH 1, Joseph LANGFORD 2. M. Archibald M'NEIL, Esq. 1, capt. Isaac MILES 1, George M'KAY 1, John MERCER 1, Lieutenant James M'CAY 2, Daniel MALLETT 1, James MAYER 1, Fanny MYERS 1, MALLETT and MUMFORD 1, Andrew M'FARLANE 2, capt Thomas MARSHALL 1, Mrs. William MOSELY 1, James MOSELY 1, Hugh M'CANN, Duplin, 1, John MILLAR, Long creek, 1. N. Samuel NOBLE 1, Samuel NORTON 1, Mr. KNIGHT, jailer, 1, Richard NIXON, Newtopsail, 1. P. Nathan PEARCE 1, Philip PAUL 1, James PERENCHIEF 1, James PRICE 1, Mordicai PRINDLE 3, President of the Cincinati, N. C. 2. Q. Richard QUINCE 3. R. William REID, Duplin, 1, Nelly ROWLAND 1, Andrew REGUES 1. S. Captain David STARBUCK 2, Alexander STRAKEN, Bladen, 1, capt. Edward SMITH 1, Doctor John SIBLEY 3, capt. Samuel SAPER? jun. 1, Joseph STERMY 1, capt. George SAWYER 2, capt. Joseph M. SALTERER?, capt. George STILLMAN 2, Samuel RUSSEL 1, Michael SAMPSON 1, John SWANN 1. T. Rev. Robert TATE, Mount Pleasant 1, William THOMPSON 1, V. Hamon VAWZOYEUR 1. W. Captain Joseph WHITING 1, Durgeon, I. WHITE 1, Monsieur DE WARNIER 1, William WILKINSON 2, Owen WYER 1, Col. William WINGATE, Brunswick 1, Joseph WILTES 1. ... John LORD. April 10.

(463) For Sale, Part of a Lot of Land in Wilmington, situated between Front street and the river..fronting EWEN's alley..and having thereon a dwelling house in tenantable order. Also, A Tract of Land, by three surveys, containing 540 acres, improved with a house and plantation, lying on HARRISON's creek, a branch of the North-east river of Cape-Fear, and within 17 miles of Wilmington... William NUTT. April 4.

(464) Notice. The subscriber having obtained Letters of Administration on the estate of Richard BURDEN, dec. requests those indebted to Richard BURDEN, by specialties or open accounts, to discharge the same without delay..all those that have claims

(464) (Cont.) against Richard BURDEN, dec. on his own private account, are desired to render them to Doctor Daniel M'NEILL, for adjustment... Signed K. BURDEN, Adm'x. Wilmington, March 31.

(465) Notice. The subscriber having obtained Letters of Administration on the estate of John Henry GEE, deceased, requests all persons indebted thereto, to make payment without delay... Sarah GEE, Adm'x. March 27.

(466) Ran away from Fayetteville, sometime since, a Negro Woman named JENNY, the property of the orphan children of Thomas ANDERSON, deceased-she has for some years past lived with Thomas MURPHY of this town, and is well known.. A reward of Five Dollars... Geo. HOOPER, Guardian. April 10.

(467) For Sale, Very Cheap for prompt Payment, Two valuable Plantations on the North east river about 12 miles from Wilmington, situated directly opposite to each other, and well known by the name of The Mulberry and Marle Bluff. Each Plantation contains upwards of a thousand acres of land. They were formerly the property of Benjamin HERON, esquire, and now belong to Mrs. Mary HOOPER. For further particulars enquire of Henry WATTERS, esquire, of Hyrnham, or to the subscriber in Wilmington. A. M. HOOPER, Attorney for Mrs. HOOPER. April 10.

(468) School. The subscriber informs..that on the 7th of April, he expects to resume the business of Teaching, for one year, at the place formerly occupied for that purpose. The terms of Tuition are as follows; viz. for the English language, including reading, writing, grammar and figures, 10 dollars-for the Oriental languages and sciences, 15 dollars per annum. School will be open for the reception of 10 or 12 pupils... Robert TATE. Hanover, March 29.

(469) Charleston, March 15. Circular letter, addressed to the friends and patrons of Medical Science in the United States. Gentlemen: Engaged in an undertaking which has for its objects the promotion of the healing art, the extension of physical Science, and the consequent amelioration of the condition of man, the Philadelphia Medical Society beg leave to solicit your correspondence and aid, in the accomplishment of their design. .. Signed in behalf of the Society, Benj. RUSH, President. Charles CALDWELL, No. 29, Pine-street, John C. COTTON, No. 37, North Fourth-street-Corresponding Secretaries.

Thursday, April 17, 1800. (Vol. IV.-No. 171.

(470) Philadelphia, March 26. In Senate. The following report was made by the Committee of Privileges, viz. The Committee of Privileges who were ordered to prepare and lay before the senate, a form of proceedings in the case of William DUANE .. We yesterday stated that Wm. DUANE, Editor of the Aurora, had refused to attend at the bar of the Senate: We are now furnished with the advice of his lawyers, upon whose authority he has hazarded this daring act of defiance. Mr. DALLAS declined appearing as his counsel from the same motives which are adduced by one COOPER.. whose letter for his impudence we publish... (Copy) To. A. J. DALLAS, Esq. Sir, I enclose you a copy of the resolution the senate passed yesterday, and must request you will favor me, by appearing with Mr. COOPER as my counsel to-morrow at 12 o'clock .. William DUANE. Aurora-Office, March 25, 1800.-A similar letter was addressed to Robert COOPER, Esq. (COOPER's Answer.) Philadelphia, March 25, 1800. Sir, .. I am, sir, your friend and servant, Thomas COOPER.

(471) Wilmington, April 17. Lost at the last fire, in March last, a Mahogany Case of Surgeon's Amputating Instruments, belonging to the estate of Doctor James GEEKIE.

(471) (Cont.) Any person having the same, or will give any information where they can be obtained, will be generously rewarded by Wm. GREEN, Ex'r. April 17.

(472) Married) On Thursday la__ Mr. William BURFORD to Miss C___otte WARD, both of this town.

(473) To Be Let, The brick Tavern belonging to the estate of Mr. H. TOOMER dec'd.. Also the Tenement and Garden lately occupied by Mr. WILKINSON, the mason in Second street. Enquire of Dr. DE ROSSETT or M. M. TOOMER. Wilmington, April 17.

(474) For Sale, At the Stores of John & Samuel SHUTER A neat Assortment of Useful Goods, Among which are Hyson and Hysonskin Tea, Loaf Sugar, Northward Brandy..Paint Oil, Starch, Gun Powder..White Lead, Shot... Wilmington, April 17.

(475) Lost, Out of my pocket, since last Friday was a week, a black Leather Pocket Letter Case, containing sundry papers and accounts..but I cannot at present mention any in particular, except an account of Mr. GABIE, against me for boat hire, amounting to six pounds. It is probable it may have dropped out of my pocket when I was thrown from my Sukey, about 12 or 15 days ago; and having been since ill, I did not miss it 'till yesterday.. Whoever has found the said Letter Case and papers, & will be so good as to deliver them to the subscriber, shall be handsomely rewarded... J. BURGWIN. Hermitage, April 17.

(476) In Senate of the U. States. On Thursday, the second resolution was taken up.. The resolution, as adopted is as follows: "Resolved, That William DUANE, now residing in the city of Philadelphia, the Editor of the said Newspaper, called the General Advertiser, or Aurora, be, and is hereby ordered to attend at the bar of this House on Monday, 24th day of March inst. 12 o'clock, at which time he will have an opportunity to make any proper defence for his conduct in publishing the aforesaid false, defamatory, scandalous and malicious assertions and pretended information and the Senate will then proceed to take further orders on the subject-and a copy of this and the foregoing resolution..and attested as a true copy by James MATHERS, Serjeant at Arms for the Senate and left by said Sergeant of Arms with the said Wm. DUANE..."

(477) Congress of the United States. In Senate, March the 24th 1800. Resolved, That William DUANE..be allowed the assistance of counsel, while personally attending at the bar of the Senate... Attest, Samuel A. OTIS, Secretary.

Thursday, April 24, 1800. (Vol. IV.-No. 172.

(478) Wilmington, April 24. Extract of a letter from William SAVAGE, Esq. Agent of the United States of America at Jamaica, to the Secretary of State, dated Kingston 26th Feb. 1800...

(479) To Be Let, And possession given immediately, The large and commodious Dwelling House on the north side of Princes-street, lately occupied by Monsieur BEAUFORT. There is a good Oven that will contain five dozen loaves and many other conveniences belonging thereto... Wm. CAMPBELL. April 24.

(480) All persons indebted to the estate of John GAILLARD, dec. are requested to make immediate payment... Eliz. SIMPSON, Adm'x. April 24.

(481) Advertisement. Ran Away from his security,..James METCALF, a shoemaker by trade.. He is an Irishman, light complected, wears his hair, which is of a lardy colour, platted and turned up, he is about 5 feet 10 inches high, well set, and ap-

(481)(Cont.) pears to be between 20 and 25 years old... Frederick BUFORD. April 24.

Thursday, May 1, 1800. (Vol. IV.-No. 173.

(482) Wilmington, May 1. We are authorised to say, that General Thomas BROWN, of Bladen county will be a candidate for Elector for Wilmington District, at the ensuing Election to elect a President and Vice-President of the United States.

(483) Last Thursday arrived in this port, in 54 days from Dublin, the Brig Ruthy, captain John GODDARD.. Captain GODDARD sailed from Dublin on the 28th February, in company with the Ship Nancy, Capt. DELANO, of N. York. Left there the Ship Draper, COLLINS, Ship Atlantic, SOWL, and Brig Venus, Joseph DILL, of Philadelphia.

(484) The subscriber has lately imported..a neat Assortment of Drugs and Medicines, Patent Medicines, and Groceries, which he has opened for sale, at the house of Captain Henry HOSKINS, in Market.. Family Receipts and Medical Prescriptions will be also prepared with accuracy. S. HALLING. May 1.

(485) Boarding & Lodging. The subscriber returns thanks to those who have favoured him with their custom, and informs the Gentlemen of Wilmington and others that his house is very convenient for taking in boarders, having a number of private rooms with good locks and keys... Thomas HOWARD. Wilmington, May 1.

(486) T__ subscriber has for sale, a small quantity of Fire Buckets, at the reasonable price of 4½ dollars a pair. Jarrott NOBLE. May 1.

(487) Lost at the last fire in Wilmington, the account Books of James M'ALLISTER, deceased. They were in the house then occupied by Dr. HALLING, and probably were among some other books, &c. that were thrown out of the window in a sheet, which was left. I will be thankful to any person who knows where said book can be found ... Richard QUINCE. May 1.

Thursday, May 29, 1800. (Vol. IV.-No. 177.

(488) List of Acts Passed during the first session of the Sixth Congress of the U. States... 2. An act extending the privilege of franking to William Henry HARRISON, the delegate from the territory of the United States, North west of the Ohio.. ...7. An act for the relief of John VAUGHAN. .. 11. An act for the relief of James YARD.. .. 17. An act for the relief of Campbell SMITH. 18. An act to extend the privilege of franking Letters and packages to Martha WASHINGTON. .. 20. An act to discharge Robert STURGEON from his imprisonment.. .. 44. An act to authorize the allowance of a credit to William TAZEWELL. .. 60. An act directing the payment of a detachment of the militia under the command of Major Thomas JOHNSON, in the year 1794. .. 67. An act to make further provision for the children of Col. John HARDING and Major Alexander TRUEMAN, deceased.

(489) New-York, May 16. The Senate..yesterday afternoon, passed a resolution requesting the President..to direct the Attorney General to institute a process against William DUANE, Editor of the Aurora.

(490) Baltimore, May 10. On the 12th of Jan. about 8 in the morning, several persons in the Southern Prussia saw three suns appear on a sudden. They rose majestically from the horizon. At seven o'clock the sky was clear and serene-a few minutes after it was covered with clouds-and at half past eight there were seen in the east three columns of fire, the middle one of which rose to the height of 45 degrees.

(490) (Cont.) The two others, formed by the two other suns were only a third as big as the middle one.-they seemed to burn in a blazing fire, and as they rose produced a majestic and awful effect.

Another phenomena has occurred in Polish Prussia. Near the village of Labotin, in the district of Pizadesa, is a lake about a league long, and about three quarters of a league broad. A forest of oak is on one side, and the villages of Labotin and Zackrezowo on the other. This lake was all at once covered with red spots.. The peasants from all parts ran to look..& soon saw pieces of red matter float on the water, some of them five inches thick. The lake was frozen, and the red spots remained on the ice. Three members of the administration..remarked that the lake was in reality covered with bloody red, in some places, with red and green spots and with purple and violet spots in others. They caused the ice to be broken one foot from the back, and they found a crust of red and green, three inches deep. Having penetrated to 11 inches depth, they found a red and green substance some of it glutinous. Two of the administrators having resolved to taste it, found it extremely acid. It also produced an immediate and very great pain in the temples & stomach. The melted ice produced a greyish water, which smelled of sulphur. Experiments are now making at Berlin to ascertain what it is, and a quantity of the water has been sent to the royal academy there.

(491) Wilmington, May 29. A ship arrived at Salem, in 26 days from Cadiz, commanded by captain Israel WILLIAMS...

(492) Appoints-by authority. The hon. John MARSHALL, esq. of Virginia, Secretary of State, in the place of the hon. Timothy PICKERING, removed. The hon. Samuel DEXTER, esq. of Massachusetts, Secretary of the Department of War, in the place of the hon. John MARSHALL promoted to the Office of State. Israel WHELEN, esq. of Pennsylvania Purveyor of public supplies for the U. States, in the place of Tench FRANCIS, esq. deceased. William Henry HARRISON, esq. (delegate to Congress from the N. W. territory) to be Governor of the Indian Territory. Gen. John GIBSON of Pennsylvania, Secretary of the Indian Territory. Seth LEWIS, esq. of Tennessee, chief Justice of the Mississippi territory, in the place of William M'GUIRE, esq. resigned. Israel LUDLOW, of the North Western Territory, Register of the Land Office at Cincinnati. Thomas WORTHINGTON, of do. Register of do. at Chilocothe. David HOGE, of Pennsylvania, Register of do. at Steubenville. James FINDLAY, of the North Western Territory, Receiver of public monies for Lands of the United States at Cincinnati. Samuel FIND A , of do. Receiver of do. at Chilocothe. Elijah BACHUS, of do. Receiver of do. Marietta. Zaccheus BIGGS, of Virginia, Receiver of do. Steubenville. John COOPER, of Georgia, Collector of the District of Brunswick, and Inspector of the revenue for that port, in the place of John M'INTOSH, resigned. Jonas CLARK, Esq. of Massachusetts, Collector of the district of Kennebunck.

(493) The subscriber has imported the following articles,..Wines..Bottled Porter.. Ale..French Brandy..Gin..Rum.. A variety of Pickles, & Fish sauces, Stoughton's Bitters..Medicines..Sugar..Coffee.. Also, A large Assortment of Dry Goods... A. T. BROWNE. May 29.

(494) Very Valuable Lands. Will be sold..a number of Very Valuable Tracts of Land, near Nashville, in the State of Tennessee, near which the Lands are now settled. D. WHEATON. May 29.

(495) Notice. The Purchasers at the sale of the estate of Matthew JOHNSTON, dec. are hereby informed, that their bonds and notes are now become payable.. He also requests all persons indebted to the firm of JOHNSTON & CUNNIAM..to make immediate payment... George JENNINGS, Ex'r. May 29.

(496) For Liverpool, The Ship Sally, George CAMERON master.. For freight or passage apply to the master on board, or to John BARCLAY. Wilmington, May 29.

(497) Doctor POISSON Takes this method of informing..that he has removed to Mr. JAMES's plantation, in the vicinity of Wilmington, where he intends practicing Physic, having been regularly bred in France, and practised near 40 years with great success, both in Europe and the West-India islands, particularly in cases of the yellow fever. May 29.

(498) The Subscribers have received..from Europe,..a neat assortment of Dry Goods.. Also, a fresh supply of Groceries... P. VERSCHUUR, & Co. opposite DORSEY's tavern. May 29.

(499) Wanted to Purchase, A Good Female House Servant, for whom a liberal price will be given. F. FONTAINE. May 29.

(500) War Department, March 25, 1800. Sir, The list of licensed traders, schedule H. referred to as accompanying my letter in reply to the enquiries of the Committee being mislaid, I have directed the Agent of War, in Tennessee, Mr. David HENLEY,.to furnish me with a duplicate thereof, which..shall be immediately communicated.. Having understood that incorrect ideas have been entertained relative to the recommendation of John D. CHISHOLM, who has been licensed by the Agent of War, and whose license has been directed to be withdrawn; I think it proper to enclose to the Committee copies of two letters furnished me by the Secretary of State, one from CHISHOLM to the Secretary of State, dated Portsmouth (England) Aug. 15th 1798, the last letter is presumed to have given rise to an idea in Colonel HENLEY, that CHISHOLM was strongly recommended by the Secretary of State and Mr. KING, and may consequently have influenced him to the appointment of CHISHOLM as an Indian trader.. (Copy) Department of State, Trenton, October 29th, 1798. Sir, I have received your letter of August 15th.. As you propose to go to the Indian country, I should advise you first to see Colonel Benjamin HAWKINS, the Superintendant of Indian Affairs for the Southern Department. He is probably some where in the Creek nation... I am, Sir, &c. &c. Timothy PICKERING. (to) Mr. John CHISHOLM.

(501) Notice. All persons indebted to the estate of the late Philip SPAULDING, are requested to make immediate payment... John FERGUS, Adm'r. M. SPAULDING, Adm'x. Wilmington, May 15.

(502) The subscriber wishes to sell or rent his house in this town. The house is about 36 feet long and 30 wide, two story high and a cellar; it hath eight rooms and four fire places-there is a good framed kitchen, a small house, and three acres of ground belonging to it. It is situated on a pleasant eminence, and a good spring very convenient.. For further particulars apply to George LUCAS, Esquire, or at this place to John HENDERSON. Chatham Court House, April 17.

(503) Notice. The subscribers have qualified as administrators upon the estate of John MAGILL, late of Brunswick county, deceased... William MAGILL, Benjamin MILLS, Adm'rs. May 1.

(504) The subscriber has received by the latest arrivals, a large and general Assortment of Goods suitable to the season... Alex'r. Thomas BROWNE. Wilmington, May 7. Wanted a quantity of Red Cedar for ship building. Apply as above.

(505) Forty Dollars Reward. Ran Away on the 27th of Dec. last, in the vicinity of Charleston, my Blacksmith TOM-about 40 years of age-dark complexion, a little pitted

(505) (Cont.) with the small pox, has large full eyes, prominent nose and lips, speaks proper English, but with a tone, about 5 feet 3 or 4 inches high, but is remarkable stout and ethletic built, with an unusual thick neck. TOM was formerly the property of Mr. Charles COGDALE of George Town, where he wroughs some years with James SHACKLEFORD, at the Blacksmith's trade; and was removed from thence to Newbern, N. C. by a person who heired him by legacy from COGDALE, & wrought there at the smith and wheelwright business, until Oct. last, when he was brought away by Major Edward DUDLEY, of Onslow county, New River. JAMES is about 30 years of age, is a small black fellow not exceeding 5 feet 1 or 2 inches high..he was brought from N. Carolina by said DUDLEY at the same time... For Andrew BURNETT, J. MUSE.

(506) U. States of America, N. Carolina District. Court of Admiralty, May 8. Whereas, David WILSON commander of the private armed Brigantine Samuel, of Baltimore, for himself and owners, officers and crew,...heretofore filed his libel..against the schooner Liberty of Norfolk..setting forth that on the high seas, he has recaptured and taken out of the possession of certain people of the French nation, being part of the crew of a French privateer, the said schooner Liberty and cargo, and praying that one half of the said schooner and cargo might be condemned for the use of the libellant, agreeably to the act of Congress.. And his honor, the Judge of said Court did appoint this day for the hearing..now..hath ordered the same..for further consideration at Raleigh on the 4th day of June ensuing... Wm. BLACKLEDGE, Register. May 15.

Thursday, June 5, 1800. (Vol. IV.-No. 178.

(507) Philadelphia, March 24th, 1800. Sir, I have the honour to enclose the copy of a resolution which passed the house of representatives on the 20th instant.. Your obedient servant, (Signed) Roger GRISWOLD. (to) The honourable Mr. WOLCOTT, Secretary of the Treasury. Treasury Department, April 29th, 1800. Sir,.. Your most obedient serv___, Oliver WOLCOTT...

(508) Baltimore, May 16. Brig Littiller, capt. DRISCOLL, from the Havannah, 17 days. Capt. D. on his outward passage to the Havanna, from Baltimore, 3 days from Cape Henry, in lat. 33,44, long. 75, W. 2d of April, at day light saw a sail..and perceived her to be a wreck..came close enough to perceive one boy on board..we hauled him on board, by name George BEACH, 15 years of age, who gives the following account: that on or about the 24th of March, left George-Town (S. C.) on board the schooner Tabitha, of New-Haven, (Conn.) bound to Martinico, laden with plank, shingles, rice and live stock; on the 26th was upset in a gale of wind in the Gulf stream, and..the captain, mate and three men were drowned; one man and the boy held fast by the rigging, two days after the man was washed overboard and drowned. The boy remained on the bowsprit for 8 days, without any subsistance whatever; the schooner belonged to Mess. Giliad KIMBLY, Gideon KIMBLY, Cornelius REYNOLDS and ATWATER, all of New-Haven; captain's name was John RICHARDS; Wilmouth BECKER, mate; seamen, John WARD, David WARD, Jeremiah KIMBLY and Sheale PARKER; on our arrival at the Havanna, the boy took shipping and sailed for Salem.

(509) Norfolk, May 22. The following copy of a circular letter, respecting our connexion with Algiers.. The underwritten consul for the United States will thank you to be informed of what vessels were preparing in Philadelphia, or any of the ports in the United States..destined with stores for Algiers and Tunis... Richard O'BRIEN.

(510) Wilmington, June 5. Various are the reports and conjectures respecting the cause and manner of Mr. PICKERING's dismissal from office..Mr. ADAMS wrote him this laconic epistle-"Sir, you are no longer secretary of state." Alexandria paper.

(511) To the Republican Citizens, resident of Wilmington district-We have the pleasure of announcing that the tried patriot and firm friend of American Liberty, the Hon. Samuel ASHE, will serve, if he should obtain the suffrages, as an Elector of President and Vice-President of the United States.

(512) Wanted Immediately, A Strong serviceable Horse, A liberal price will be given in cash for such a one. T. HILL. June 5.

(513) To be Sold, At the Subscriber's Wharf, On Saturday the 14th of June, The Cargo saved from the wreck of the schooner Pluto, Capt. William COX, consisting of Sugar & Coffee. John MACLELLAN. Wilmington, June 4, 1800.

(514) Sheriff's Sale. Notice is hereby given, that on Monday, the 14th day of July next, will be sold for Cash, at the Court-house in Onslow county..the following lands..or so much thereof as will satisfy the taxes due thereon for the years as is stated.. 49892 acres of land which is said to be the property of Gideon DENNISON, situate on the various branches and head waters of New and White Oak rivers, and the taxes on which is due for the year 1799. 42600 do. do. belonging to Isaac GUION and Co. and is due for..1798 and 1799. 640 do. do. belonging to the heirs of Eli WEST, and due for..1796,'97, '98 & '99. 1300 do. do. belonging to the heirs of John STARKEY, and due for..1797, '98 and '99. 380 do. do. which is said to belong to James RICE, and due for..1796, 1797, 1798 and '99. 640 do. do. which is said to belong to one of the BLOUNTs, and due for the years 1797, 1798 and '99. 300 do. do. belonging to the heirs of Hull JONES, and due for the years 1798 and '99. The above mentioned land was not given in agreeable to law. 46 acres of land belonging to Samuel GARRICK, and due for the years 1796, '97, '98 & '99. 46 do. do. Joseph HILL, do. 250 do. do. Peter ARNOLD, 1798. 100 do. do. Elijah BIDDLE, do. 300 do. do. Shadrach GIBSON, do. 80 co. do. William KELLUM, do. 150 do. do. Peter OLDFIELD, do 40 do. do. Richard OLDFIELD, do. 500 do. do. John SIMMONS, do. 250 do. do. Solomon SIMPSON, do. 75 do. do. Catherine WELLS, do. 100 do. do. Elizabeth BURNS, do. 300 do. do. Frederick BURNS, do. 90 do. do. Thomas PERRY, do. 57 do. do. Francis PERRY do. 250 do. do. Samuel PRICE, do. 30 do. do. James POWERS, do. 113 do. do. Esther PERRY, do. 40 do. do. Solomon RHODES, do. 310 do. do. Robert SAGE, do. 125 do. do. John WHEELER, do. 500 do. do. Robert CUTTLE, do. 200 do. do. Butler COWELL, do. 150 do. do. Barnaby GURGANUS, do. 433 do. do. Abraham GEDDINS, do. 150 do. do. William JINKINS, do. 250 do. do. given in by do. as administrator, 1798. 300 do. do. Obed. JINKINS, do. 225 do. do. Micajah KING, do. 100 do. do. Lord SARY, do. 200 do. do. Lucy LOYD, do. 100? do. do. James WIN, do. 50 do. do. Thomas WIN, do. 200 do. do. Alexander STUART, due for the years 1796, '97, '98 & '99. 50 do. do. Heirs of John CONWAY, due for 1798. 50 do. do. Prudence HICKS, do. 400 do. do. Mason HARVEY, do. 172 do. do. belonging to the heirs of William HOWARD, sen. due for the years 1798 and 1799. 100 do. do. Benjamin HALL, 1798. 100 do. do. Wm. HOWARD, jun. do. 122 do. do. Isaac CHARLESCRAFT, do. 162 do. do. Frederick WOOD, do. 240 do. do. Robert COSTON, do. 273 do. do. John CHAMBERS, do. 100 do. do. Mary YEWELL, do. 825 do. do. Heirs of Elijah NEWTON, 1798. 200 do. do. Shadrach CARY, do. 150 do. do. James BRADY, do. 120 do. do. Thomas J. BRADY, do. 100 do. do. Samuel ARREXON, do. 250 do. do. Brice FONVEILLE, do. 250 do. do. Thomas PEARSON, do. 125 do. do. Elizabeth ROUCKS, do. 100 do. do. John SMITH, do. 50 do. do. Jesse WELLS, '97 & do. 100 do. do. Jacob COSTON, do. 100 do. do. John COSTON, do. 100 do. do. Ahab COSTON, do. 580 do. do. Heirs of Thomas EDENS, 1798. 50 do. do. Wm. FIRFINGER, do. 100 do. do. Henry HANEY, do. 200 do. do. Gabriel HARDISON, do. 50 do. do. John JAMES, do. 250 do. do. Lewis JINKINS, do. 100 do. do. William KING, do. 200 do. do. Sarah LAIN, do. 800 do. do. Samuel LAIN, do. 65 do. do. Elijah NORMAN, do. 1-2 Town Lots in the town of Swansborough, not given in, belonging to the heirs of John STARKEY, and due for 1797, '98 & '99. 1-2 do. belonging to Mar-

(514) (Cont.) garet HUSSEY, due for 1796, 97, '98 & '99. 1 do. given in by Eliz. STEWART, do. 2 do. belonging to the heirs of Eli WEST, due for '96, '97, '98 & '99. 1 do. William FISHER, do. 1-2 do. William DENNIS, do... The Lands are liable for the taxes without attending to those who gave them in.. Lemuel DOTY, Shff. May 27, 1800.

(515) The Copartnership of THURSTON, SMITH & PELHAM Expired on the 14th of April last... Samuel I. THURSTON, Wm. SMITH, Charles PELHAM. Wilmington, June 5.

(516) One Hundred Dollars Will be paid to any person..who will secure in Goal in Wilmington, a certain Negro-fellow named JOHNNY, whom I purchased from John WADDELL, Esq. about 12 months ago. He is of a yellow complexion, about 5 feet 10 or 11 inches high, straight and well made, and has lost some of his fore teeth. Geo: GIBBS. Wilmington, June 3, 1800.

(517) For Sale,..on Monday the 9th June next, Four Petty-Augors belonging to William CAMPBELL, Esquire, and the Estate of John LEVINGSTON, deceased, together with their Sails and Rigging.-Also, at the same time, will be hired out on the usual terms, Eight Negro Men, accustomed to said Boats-and the Hull and Apparel of the Brig-lying on the shore below TELFAIR's wharf. Nath: M: HILL. Wilmington, May 29, 1800.

(518) For Liverpool, The Ship Sally, George CAMERON master.. For freight or passage apply to the master on board, or to John BARCLAY. Wilmington, May 29.

(519) Proposals For Printing and Publishing, by Subscription, Memoirs of the American Revolution, So far as it related to the States of North and South-Carolina and Georgia. By William MOULTRIE, Late Governor of the State of South-Carolina, and Major-General in the Army of the United States, during the American War.. It will form two octavo volumes, of 400 pages each.. The price to subscribers will be Three Dollars per volume. Subscriptions will be taken in by FRENEAU and PAINE, W. P. YOUNG, T. C. COX, and by the Book-sellers in Charleston. Also by A. HALL Printer, Wilmington. May 15.

(520) New-York, April 26. Ship Hope. Thursday morning the following decision took place in the Supreme court.. It was an action by Messrs. ARNOLD and RAMSAY, on a policy of insurance against the United Insurance company, in this city to recover 7,000 dollars, which they had underwrote on the cargo of the good American ship the Hope, from New-York to the island of Cuba.. The Hope was captured, and her cargo condemned at New Providence, "as belonging to Spain, or to persons being subjects, or inhabiting within the territories thereof". It was admitted in the case, that the property belonged to ARNOLD and RAMSAY, and to Daniel HAWLEY, who was also a native American, and at the time of making the insurance resided at the Havanna, in quality of consul from the United States.. Judgment was accordingly given for the defendants.

(521) Augusta, May 7. We learn from captain John M'ALLISTER, who arrived here on Monday last, that previous to his leaving Greensborough, a gentleman..arrived there from the Creek nation who informed that runners had been sent to Colonel HAWKINS, with information that another vessel loaded with arms, ammunition and clothing, had been sent from New-Providence to Augustus BOWLES...

Thursday, June 26, 1800. (Vol. IV.-No. 181.

(522) York, (Penn.) June 4. Thursday last, the President of the United States, attended by his secretary, Mr. SHAW, arrived here on his way to the Federal City.. Next morning the officers of the corporation..waited upon his excellency and presented

(522) (Cont.) the following address: To his Excellency John ADAMS,... John EDDIE, Chief Burgess.

(523) Richmond, June 6. CALLENDER. The trial of James Thompson CALLENDER, for sedition, took place on Tuesday last, in the circuit court of the United States.. The trial was opened at 1 o'clock and continued till six, when the Jury retired, and after some deliberation, brought in a verdict-GUILTY..the determination of the court which was that he be fined..200? dollars, imprisoned nine months, and be bound over in the penalty of 1200 dollars...

(524) Wilmington, June 26. On Tuesday the 10th inst. the Special Court in this state, for trying persons charged with certain ___ (illegible) The trial of John Gray BLOUNT was postponed, but that of Thom__ BLOUNT it was expected would commence the 17th instant.

(525) From an official letter received ___ the office of the Secretary of State from Robert RITCHIE, Consul at Port Republican, it appears that a commercial intercourse has commenced with the port of Petit Guave from Port Republican, which has considerably augmented the prices of American provisions...

(526) Sales at Auction. On Tuesday the 8th July, will be sold opposite the Auction Room of the Subscribers, for the benefit of the underwriters, 12 Hogsheads Sugar, being a part of the cargo of the Brig James, George BOO___, master, from Jamaica... ISAACKS, LEVY & BISHOP. June 26, 1800.

(527) Is Now ___. Smart Active Boy, about 14 years of age, who can be recommended to learn the Watch-Making Business and sundry other Branches in the Gold and Silver Smith's line... John GALE. Wilmington, June 26.

(528) Run-Away from the subscriber, a French negro, named JOE, Taylor by trade, speaks broken English... Peter WISS.

(529) Run-Away from the Subscriber, a Negro-Fellow, about 5 feet 10 inches high, of a yellow complexion, plays on the violin, and it is said that he can read and write; he formerly belonged to Mr. Arthur BAKER, and passes by the name of JOSHUA.. A Reward of 10 Dollars..to any person who will..deliver him to me at my plantation on Black river, or to the Goaler in Wilmington. Alexander STRAHAN. June 9.

(530) To the Freeholders Of New-Hanover County. Having understood that a report prevails of my declining to offer as a Candidate to represent the County of New-Hanover, in Senate, at the next annual session of Assembly, & being called on by a number of respectable characters, it is incumbent on me to declare that the report is without foundation, originating in mistake, or fabricated for the purpose of deceiving my friends, and injuring my election... John HILL. Wilmington, June 19, 1800.

(531) Boarding & Lodging. I Return my sincere thanks to those Gentlemen who have favored me with their Custom, and inform..that my House is open to receive those that please to ca__ me-also, that I have taken the Brick Stable formerly occupied by Mr. DORSEY..apply to the Subscriber, in TOOMER's Alley. Thomas HOWARD. Wilmington, June 19, 1800.

(532) Petty-Augors for Sale. On the first day of the ensuing County Court, will be sold,..in..Wilmington, four valuable Petti Augors with their Tackle &c. Also an old Brig, likewise an old Sloop, as ___ __w lies between Mr. LORCO_ and DEAN's

(532) (Cont.) wharves-being the property of the late Copartnership of CAMPBELL & LEVINGSTON. Wm. CAMPBELL, Surviving Copartner. June 12.

Thursday, July 3, 1800. Vol. IV.-No. 182.

(533) Philadelphia, June 14. Extract of a letter from Mr. David WALKER, Supercargo of the brig Aeriel, of this port, dated Point-Petre, Guadaloupe, 14th May, 1800. (There was a battle between the Aeriel and the French privateer schooner, l'Egypte Conquise.) List of Killed and Wounded, on board the brig Aeriel. Luke FLEVERLY, landsman, killed. ALEXANDER, do. do. J. NEWPORT, seaman, S. KIETLINE, landsman, Died of their wounds. Wounded. Joseph SMITH, boatswain; CHARLES, (blackman) landsman; William ROBINS, landsman; Thomas FOOTE, seaman; _____, cook; John MINK, gunner; Robert GRAHAM, seaman; Benjamin THOMPSON, second mate.

(534) From the log-book of the Iphigenia of New-York, Captain Thomas H. MERRY, from Belfast, bound to Norfolk...

(535) New-York, June 13. On the 2d day of May last the British armed brig Swallow, Stephen BOURDETT, master, sailed from this port for Martinique. After being out 19 days, on the 21st May, in lat. 24,4.N. long. 61,49.W..there came on a sudden gust of wind..which upset the vessel. One of the boats was stove to pieces, the other was fortunately cleared, and 6 persons, consisting of the captain mate, and 4 of the crew got into her.. No prospect of relief had yet presented itself..when on the 9th day after quitting the brig..fell in with the schr. William, Jeremiah GOODRICH master, one of the fleet of American vessels from St. Thomas to New-York, who took them in.. Next morning, Robert DICKIE..died.

(536) Wilmington, July 3. Raleigh, June 24. On Tuesday last John BONDS was tried on the bill..found against him.-The jury found him guilty.. James GLASGOW was tried on a charge of having issued a grant on a duplicate warrant in favour of John Gray BLOUNT and Thomas BLOUNT, for 5000 acres of western lands, and of having afterwards issued a grant on the original warrant, to the said John Gray BLOUNT and Thomas BLOUNT for another tract of 5000 acres of western lands.-The jury retired, and in about one minute returned with their verdict, finding him guilty of the charge. On Wednesday a new trial was moved for on the part of James GLASGOW, in the case in which he had issued two grants for 640 acres each to James MULHERRIN, who by a forged assignment on a duplicate military land warrant claimed to be the assignee of the heir of Elijah ROBERTS, late soldier in the continental line..the motion was rejected.

The court passed the following sentence on Willoughby WILLIAMS, convicted as mentioned in our last..500 pounds, and stand committed to Newbern jail, until he pay the fine and fees..on John BONDS-That he pay a fine of 100 pounds, and..stand committed to Halifax jail..until he pay his fine and costs. The trial of Thomas BLOUNT.. was to have come on and..was postponed, upon his making and filing an affidavit stating that Willie BLOUNT of Tennessee, was a material witness for him..and he and his brother John Gray BLOUNT were bound over to appear at Newbern court on the 15th July next.. The trial of Wynn DIXON was postponed.. He was bound over to Hillsborough Superior Court to be held on the 6th of October next.

(537) Scheme of the Dock Street, Market & Dock Lottery. 600 Tickets, at Three Dols.. A deduction of 15 per cent will be made from all fortunate numbers, to be employed in building a Market and cleaning the Dock in Dock Strett, so that boats may lay safe and dry under the same.. Tickets may be had of H. URQUHART, J. G. WRIGHT, J. ROBERTSON, Jacob HARTMAN, J. CARSON, Managers. Wilmington, July 3, 1800.

(538) List of Letters remaining in the Post-Office at Wilmington, July 1, 1800..
A - Captain Benjamin AYDELOT, 4; Col. Samuel ASHE, 1. B - Capt. Thomas BURTEN, 8; Alexander BUROT, 2; Joshua BABCOCK, 1; Thomas BOARDMAN, 1; Benjamin BRADSHAW, 1; John BURN, 1; Mrs. Mary BLANKS, 1; John BLANKS, 1; Thomas BATEMAN, 1; Captain George BACON, 1; Richard BRADSHAW, 1. C - Henry CUMMINGS, 2; James COXETER, 1; Archibald COOK, 1; William COLLINS, 1; President of the Cincinnati of North Carolina, 2; John COLVIN, Esq. 1; Archibald CRAWFORD, 1; James CLANDER, 1; ____ CALISTA, belonging to Mr. SHAW, 1; Edward CLEAMONS, 1; Robert CHAPMAN, 1; Miss Mary Ann CUMMINGS, 1; Capt. Elkanah COOK, 1; Capt. E. CHANCY, 1. D - Christopher DUDLEY, New-River, 1; Capt. John DRYSDALE, 2; Thomas DRAVES, 1; Wilson DAVIS, 1; Joseph DICKSON, 1. F - James FOY, Onslow, 1; Southy FISHER, Sampson, 1; John FERRELL, 1. G - John GODDARD, 1; Mrs. Sarah GEE, 1; William GREEN, 1. H - Eleazer H. HASTINGS, 2; Levi HORN, 1; Owen HOLMES, Sampson, 1; John HAMMOND; Thomas HUDSON, 1; Jacob HOWLAND, 1; Mrs. HERON, 1; Ned HOLT, 1; Edward HOLT, 1; John HARFORD, 1; Daniel HICKS, Sampson, 1. J - Edward JONES, 1; Captain JODRIE, 1; Wilson JACOBS, 1; William JORDAN, 1. K - Daniel KER, Black River, 1; Michael KENAN, 1. L - Edward LOSING, 2; Mark LAMB, 1; Monsieur LEGROS, 1; Mrs. LASPEYRRE, 1. M - Maj. A. Duncan MOORE, 1; Capt. John MAC FARLANE, 1; Capt. Alexander MORGAN, 1; James MEWS, 1; Messrs. M'CALLUM & PATTERSON, 1; Thomas MALSBY, 1; Col. M'ALLISTER, 1; Mrs. Flora M'ALLISTER, 1; Miss M'ALLISTER, 1; Mrs. Ann MOORE, 1; Doctor E. MORSE, Esq. 1; George M'KAY, 1; The Worshipful Court of New-Hanover, or Peter M'FIELD, 1. P - Richard PARSON, 2. R - John P. REMMINGTON, 2; Thomas ROBINSON, Masonboro, 1; Adjutant General J. T. RHODES, Duplin, 1; Andrew RIGNES, Esq. 1; William RUSSEL, Onslow, 1; Mrs. RICHARDS, 1. S - Alexander SHAW, 2; Capt. Edward SMITH, 1; William SIMPSON, 1; Ephraim SUTTON, 1; William, John or Charles STOCKMAN, 1; Thomas SANDERS, 1; William SNELL, 1; John SIBLEY, 1. T - Thomas TURNER, Bladen, 1; John TAYLOR, Bladen, 1; Rev. Robert TATE, 1; Capt. Isaac TRACEY, 1. V - James VENABLES, 1. W - Captain Thomas WRIGHT, 4; Capt. Sylvester WILLISTON, 1; Mrs. Mary WALKER, 1; William WILKINSON, Federal Point, 1; Capt. John WOOD, 1; John D. WHITE, 1; Timothy WADHAM, 1. John LORD, P. M.

(539) To the Electors Of the County of New-Hanover. Fellow-Citizens, I Take this early opportunity of making known to you my return from the Army.. I have offered as a Candidate in the Commons, and trust at the ensuing Election..I shall meet with your countenance and support. A. Duncan MOORE. Fishing Creek, July 2, 1800.

(540) Notice. The Subscriber intending to set out for Europe in..a few weeks, requests all those to whom he is indebted to call for adjustment of their..accounts... George JENNINGS. Wilmington, July 3, 1800.

(541) To the Freemen Of the Counties of Brunswick, Bladen, Duplin, New-Hanover, Onslow & Sampson. Fellow Citizens, In the month of August next you will be called on, to elect a Representative in the Congress of the United States: having now the honour of representing you in that body, I..declare myself a candidate for your suffrages... W. H. HILL, Wilmington, July 3.

(542) Columbia, (S. C.) May 30. Dying Confession of Willis DANIELS, who was executed at Orangeburg, on the 16th inst. South Carolina, Orangeburg Goal, May 16th, 1800. I, Willis DANIELS, otherwise, by my wickedness, called Richard YOUNG, being at last overtaken by the unerring, though tardy, steps of Justice..do publish the following sketches of my life, as a warning to all others.. I was born on the banks of Little Pee Dee river, in the state of South-Carolina, about the year 1765. My parents were poor. My father was a chair maker by trade; which had he pursued industriously, and been half as vigilant in inculcating the principles of his mystery on my mind, as he was to train..me in the school of vice, I should not..be groaning under the burden of prison chains..which I cannot but reproach him for bringing upon

(542) (Cont.) me. My mother was a pious good woman. At about 12 years of age, I went to live with Mr. John BAXTER, on Waccamaw river..and ran off from him in a short time, and lived a little while with a William MORGAN and James PARKER, but soon left them and returned to my parents. .. Between..12 and 15..I stole for the first time two pen knives from a Mr. DAWSON, and some clothes from a Mr. TINNULY?.. At the age of 15, I went into a kind of shameful co-partnership with my father, in stealing hogs, &c. and lived with him some time, in constant habits of marauding and plundering our neighbors.. I then went to live with a Mr. TIMMONS?, who was an honest man, and tried to reform me.. I left Mr. TIMMONS. I then travelled to Charlestown, and enlisted in the service, under Capt. ROBERTS..about two months and then deserted; was soon taken up and flogged for my desertion 100 lashes.. In a few weeks, I again deserted, and returned to Pee Dee. I then went into North-Carolina..I stole a horse from a Mr. PICKET, was taken up, and put in Wilmington gaol, from which I soon found means to break and escape. I then returned to Pedee.. I stole another horse, from a Mr. M'CRAKAN, and took him off to the mountains, where..I changed my name to Richard BROWN.. My next theft was a horse and some clothing, from one Duncan GRIMES, for which I was apprehended, and tried in Fayette, N. C. .. I enlisted under Robert CRAIG, a recruiting officer in WAYNE's army, where I staid 17 months; but then..deserted. .. I stole no less than five horses, one from a William GOODWIN, on Pedee; one from a Mr. JENKINS, on Santee; one from a Mr. HICKS, near Augusta; one from a Mr. Elijah AXOM..and one from Mr. DOTY, on White Marsh. From a Mr. PARKER, near Augusta, I stole 25 dollars. From this I travelled to Kentucky.. In Virginia I stole one from Mr. Aquila SUGGS, for which I was apprehended and tried in North-Carolina. (I stole) saddles and bridles.. For a theft of this smaller sort, I was next committed to Chester goal, Pinckney district..7 weeks and then escaped.. From Mr. Brian SPRADLEY, of Camden, with whom I some time lived, I stole..clothing, and a pair of saddle bags, and made off..to Statesburg, where I stole a horse, saddle and bridle, from a Mr. WHEELER, for which I was..committed to Camden goal, but broke goal and escaped before trial.. I was tried in Georgetown, by the name of Willis DANIELS..and pardoned ..

I next broke open a house on LYNCH's creek..took clothing, and travelled on to Edisto saw-mills, where I stole a horse from Capt. CAMPBELL..and made for Black river again.. I went to North-Carolina ___ to George town, where I was indicted and tried for stealing the horse of Mr. FAREWELL..and acquitted.. I went to Lenoir county, North Carolina, courted and married a very decent and reputable girl, by the name of Sally KING. With this deluded innocent, I lived one month, wearing the assumed name of James RAMSAY.. I soon exchanged my bridal bed, for a prison couch in Rowan gaol.. sentenced to die, but..pardoned; on a condition of 12 months imprisonment.. On my way home I was recommitted to prison..four months..and was branded with the letter T in the left hand. In Johnson county, I committed other thefts, for which I was imprisoned, but broke out of gaol before trial. On the same night I stole a horse..and in Sampson county another, from a Mrs. CLINTON.. At Waccamaw, in South-Carolina, I stole some clothes, and a gun from a Mr. LOFTON; and a horse.. On him I rode to Orangeburgh district, where I am to terminate my..career of villanies. In this district..before I was arrested, I broke open a house, and stole a watch; stole a horse from Mr. PICKENS, one from a Mrs. DRAPER; last of all one from a Mr. NOBLES, for which I am now to suffer death. .. I have one more crime to add..of a more criminal dye than any yet enumerated. At the last November court, in Orangeburgh, I suffered myself to be suborned as a witness for Silas PEACOCK, on his trial for the murder of his wife... Willis DANIELS.

Thursday, July 10, 1800. (Vol. IV.-No. 183.

(543) From the Aurora. Public Plunder. We have at length so far succeeded as to

(543) (Cont.) possess ourselves of a long and black series of abuse and waste of the public money. We shall..lay before our readers the particulars.. We had some time ago stated, that Timothy PICKERING had drawn on the 18th of April last, the sum of 50,000 dollars from the public treasury.. Judge CHASE has laid down a..doctrine that public records were not to be brought forward in a court of justice, though they were alledged to entertain truths which would benefit the country..or prevent abuses.. On the 24th of February, 1800, the accounts of the late Sharp DELANY, collector of the customs for this port..remained due to the U. States a balance of 86,322 dollars and 80 cents..how is the public to obtain this balance? It will be urged perhaps..and we promised to lay before the public Jonathan DAYTON's account; we shall now do it.. We now refer to the treasury department..to the files in the office of Joseph NOURSE, Esq. register of that department.. To Warrants drawn by Oliver WOLCOTT, secretary of the treasury..in favour of said DAYTON..he appears still to hold in his hands the sum of dollars 18,142 and 52 cents..

Statement of Receipts. At the Treasury of the U. States..28th April, 1800. Extracted from the records... Basil WOOD. A Small Balance. On the 18th of April last..there remained in the hands of Mr. William WINDER? accountant of the navy, a balance of..2,525,201.40.

(544) New-York, June 21. Extract of a letter from Captain Thomas ANDERSON, of the brig Hope arrived at Philadelphia on Monday from Tortola. "I left the island of Tortola on the 1st of June, in company with the brig Telegraph, W. BOOMINS, for Wilmington (Delaware). Coming out, spoke the brig Adventure, captain Samuel STILES, going in, 28 days from Norfolk.. On the 6th spoke the sch'r Biboa of Philadelphia, 15 days out from Baltimore.. Capt. Richard S ILES, of the sch'r Yeatman, was cast away on Crab Island, on the night of 22d of May, his crew and himself..brought up to Tortola by three Anguilsa privateers."

(545) Mr. John DEMAN, of N. Kingston, Rhode Island, informs, that he was one of the hands on board the schooner Abigail, of N. Kingston, bound from Norfolk to Turk's Island..they were boarded by two French privateers...

(546) Wilmington, July 10. On the 5th day of August next, the following lands will be sold at the Court House in Duplin, for the taxes due thereon for the years 1798 and 1799. 330 acres B. EVANS, near Limestone. 250 do. S. WILLIAMS, on the Grove. 100 do. John COOK, Bear Swamp. 1155 do. Needham WHITFIELD, N. E. 1631 do. Stephen BARFIELD, do. 500 do. Martin PHILYAU, do. 375 do. Moses SHOLAR, Cyp. creek. 350 do. Ind. Graves, Th: BURTON. 75 do. Oaky Branch, W. JAMES. 50 do. Pouseman, Amos PILMAN. 273 do. Mohungo, John FLEMING. 113 do. Bear Swamp, W. BLUNT. 455 do. do. James MOORE. 360 do. Panther, Jacob JURNIGAN. 540 do. Rockfish, Wil: CAMPBELL. Lands not given in for 1798 and 1799. 1150 acres Ind. Graves, S. JOHNSTON. 3000 do. N. E. do. 2000 do. joining the above, the heirs of LILLINGTON. 400 do. Cyp. creek, John BURGWIN. 250 do. Persimmon, do. 330 do. Rockfish, do. 150 do. STUART's creek do. 100 do. Cowhole Coshen, do. 200 do. MAXWELL creek, do. 100 do. LUTCHES Branch, I. MURPHY. 400 do. Muddy creek, H. PICKET. 200 do. Limestone, John POISSON, 100 do. N. E. Margaret COX. 12800 do. on Cypress creek and Back Swamp. 5120 joining Jacob MANIER's lines. 3200 do. joining William HALL's line, including good Pocoson. 640 do. joining George SMITH. 1280 do. joining Aaron WILLIAMS. 3200 do. joining James PICKET's line. 640 do. George DOHERTY and William JONES. 640 do. joining Jacob WILLIS's line. The above lands were granted to Roger ALDEN. 381 acres joining Jacob BROWN, John JOHNS. 300 do. joining M'CANE's lines, George HOOPER. Hugh M'CANE, Shff. July 10.

(547) Notice. All Persons to whom the Subscriber is indebted are requested to call on Joseph MILNE, of Wilmington for payment... B. BLANEY. Smithville, 3d July.

(548) (Translation.) Extract from the minutes of the Tribunal of Peace of the Town of Cape Francois. On the 29th Floreal, 8th year of the French Republic, one and indivisible (19th May 1800) at 10 o'clock, A. M. At the request of Citizen Nicholas Ferdinand VIAN, captain of the ship Sandwich, of Nantes, now in the town of Cape Francois. Before me, Charles TELEMAQUE, justice of the peace..appeared Thomas SANDFORD, of Providence, assisted by citizen POLOMY, interpreter to the government for the English language..declare(s) and says..to wit: That his name is Thomas SANDFORD, born in the state of Massachusetts, aged 28 years, a mariner by profession, and master of the American sloop called the Sally, of Providence, in the state of Rhode-Island.. that on the 9th May inst..the barge of the U. S. frigate Constitution, Capt. TALBOT, came with 25 men to Bay Chouchouz?..who went on board the said sloop, cut off the cables and carried her off.. Capt. TALBOT then fitted the said sloop with men and gave them orders to go and take possession of the French ship Sandwich..he was put next day on board the brig Nymph, of Newburyport, Joseph WOODMAN, master, which was going to the Cape...

(549) To Be Let, That commodious new house adjoining the house of the subscriber.. Apply to Jonathan JENNINGS. Wilmington, July 19.

Thursday, July 31, 1800. (Vol. IV.-No. 186.

(550) Wilmington, July 31. Died, On Thursday last, Mr. Jonathan JENNINGS, a citizen of this town.

(551) Mechanical Society. The members thereof are requested to meet at the house of Mr. Jacob HARTMAN, on Thursday the 7th of August next... Richard KELLY, Sec'y. Wilmington, July 3r_.

(552) To the Freemen of Wilmington District & Sampson County. Fellow-Citizens, The day approaches when it will be incumbent on you to elect a Representative in the Congress of the United States and..I do in this public manner announce myself a Candidate... James GILLESPIE. Wilmington, July 28, 1800.

(553) The Subscriber has imported..a very large and general Assortment of European, East & West-India Goods... A. T. BROWNE. Wilmington, July 31, 1800.

(554) Dissolution of Copartnership. The copartnership of ISAACKS, LEVY and BISHOP dissolves this day... Abraham M. ISAACKS, Jacob LEVY, Isaac BISHOP. Wilmington, 31st July, 1800. Their former business will be carried on as usual by the subscribers, under the Firm of ISAACKS and BISHOP... Abraham M. ISAACKS, Isaac BISHOP.

(555) The Subscriber having been appointed by the county court of New-Hanover, to take the list of taxes for the Upper Sound district, for the year 1800, will attend at George HEDGMAN's on the first Monday in August, and at the Court-house in Wilmington, during the election, to receive the same... Thomas BISHOP. July 31.

(556) The Subscriber having administered on the estate of Gooden BOWERS, late of Mount Pleasant, Bladen county, dec. requests all persons indebted to said Estate, to make immediate payment... David ANDERSON. Fayetteville, June 8.

(557) Philadelphia, July 5. We are informed that Thomas FITZSIMONS, Esq. a respectable Merchant of this city has presented to PEALE's Museum an elegant collection of Minerals, Petrefactions of Shells, and a variety of Amethyst Crystals, brought from the river Plata, South-America...

(558) Philadelphia, July 10. We mentioned in our paper of Tuesday, a native of this city named John DUNN, who is detained on board the St. Albans, at New-York. We have since made enquiries, and have found that he has a wife and children now living in Southwark; who had concluded her husband lost, from his long absence.

Thursday, August 14, 1800. (Vol. IV.-No. 188.

(559) To be Sold or Rented, That valuable and convenient Wharf..situated at the lower end of town, formerly possessed by Mr. James HOGG, now the property of WH__-FIELD and BROWN. The terms can be known by applying to Jos. G. WRIGHT. Wilmington, August 7.

(560) To Rent, The house and Lot now occupied by the subscriber, in TOOMER's Alley. For terms apply to Thomas HOWARD.

(561) For Sale, 29 Elegant Looking Glasses, by WILLKINGS & SCOTT. Wilmington, August 14.

(562) Sheriff's Sales. Will be sold, on the 26th day of September next, at the Court-House in Brunswick county, the following Lands for the payment of the Taxes due thereon, viz. 8460 Acres including 17 different tracts, situated on Town-Creek, Mill-Creek, ROGER's Creek and Sturgeon Creek, belonging to the estate, or Widow of the late honorable James HASELL. 3610 Acres, in eight different tracts, seven of them situated on Town-Creek and Mill-Creek, including & adjoining Bill Grange-Plantation, and one of 300 acres on the North side of Town-Creek, on the North-west road, the property of Mrs. WALKER. 18760 Acres situated and adjoining the Green Swamp on the East side, near or including the head of LEVINGSTON's Creek, supposed to be the property of David ROSS. 640 Acres..situated on Dutchman's Creek, taken up by Wm. GOODMAN. 400 Acres..on Cape Fear River, supposed to be taken up by Joseph SHURBERN. 41600 Acres (or part thereof) taken up by David ALLISON, adjoining the waters of LOCKWOOD-Folly, Mill Creek, ORTON Creek, White Spring and Elizabeth River, &c. 1400 acres, situate on Town-Creek and the waters thereof, the property of John HOGG. 400 acres on Town-Creek, the property of Col. OWENS. None of the above lands were entered for taxation, agreeable to law. John BAKER, Shff. Brunswick county. August 12, 1800.

(563) To the Electors of the Town of Wilmington.. I take the opportunity..of declaring that..should you make me the object of your choice at the ensuing election, you may be assured of my endeavours to represent your interests in every thing within the duty of a Representative. Jos. G. WRIGHT. Wilmington, August 7.

(564) To the Public. A Report has..been very industriously and successfully circulated throughout the county of New-Hanover, that I am one of a party which arrogates to itself the appellation of "Republican".. I hereby solemnly protest that the above report is false, scandalous and malicious; that I am, in the fashionable dialect of the day, "A Federalist"... A. M. HOOPER. Wilmington, August 7, 1800.

(565) The Subscriber informs..that he has removed to the store lately occupied by M. SNEED, where he offers for sale a General Assortment of Dry Goods & Groceries... Antonio C. SILVA. Wilmington, August 7.

(566) Ran-away from John BARCLAY (to whom he was hired) a negro fellow named JACK. Pretty stout made, of a yellow complection, a forbidding countenance, and about 5 feet 8 inches high.. For the best part of these 18 months past he has been openly harboured at Mr. John M'KENZIE's plantation, Brunswick county..and frequently at

(566) (Cont.) his kitchen in this town. A Reward of Five Dollars... John BROWN. Wilmington, August 7.

Thursday, August 21, 1800. (Vol. IV.-No. 189.

(567) Philadelphia, July 25. Mr. John SHAW, who is the bearer of dispatches to our government from Tunis, arrived here on Thursday evening last.

(568) Charleston, August 7. Fire. Monday morning about 1/4 before 11 o'clock, the house of Mr. Martin MILLER, on the west side of King street, the third door above Boundary-street, was discovered to be on fire. The reports relative to its origin are..that it was accidentally communicated by the blaze of a candle to a puncheon of rum, in the cellar, from which the unfortunate Mr. MILLER and his wife were drawing off a few gallons in Demijohns. The puncheon exploded immediately and communicated to a keg of gunpowder in the store, which also blew up, and burnt Mr. and Mrs. MILLER in a most shocking manner, so much so that Mrs. MILLER has since died, and there is scarcely a possibility of Mr. MILLER's surviving.. Mr. Samuel WELLS's house was pulled down, to prevent the flames from spreading.

(569) Wilmington, August 21. Return of the Election for a member of Congress for Wilmington District. For W. H. HILL,..1891. For James GILLESPIE,..1008. We hear that William B. GROVE, Esq. is re-elected a member of Congress for Fayetteville district, by a majority of more than 1000 votes.

(570) Return of the Election for Members of the General Assembly. New-Hanover-John HILL, Senate. A. D. MOORE and Col. Sam. ASHE, Commons. Town of Wilmington-Jos. G. WRIGHT. Brunswick-Gen. Benjamin SMITH, Senate. Benjamin MILLS and Abraham BESSENT, Commons. Bladen-Josiah LEWIS, Senate. James BRADLEY and Street ASHFORD, Commons. Onslow-Christopher DUDLEY, Senate. Jesse WILLIAMS and William RUSSEL, Commons. Duplin-Levin WADKINS, Senate. Daniel GLISTON and Charles HOOKS, Commons. Sampson-Josiah BLACKMAN, Senate. Jas. THOMPSON and William CLINTON, Commons. Cumberland-Alex. M'ALLISTER, Senate. John DICKSON and Wm. LORD, Commons. Town of Fayetteville-Thomas DAVIS. Jones-Durant HATCH, Senate. Amos JOHNSTON and John T. BRYAN, Commons.

(571) Notice. The Officers of the late 6th Federal Regiment of Infantry are hereby informed that I am prepared to pay them their arrears of pay &c. and that I shall attend at Raleigh for that purpose... C. WALKER, Pay-master of the 6th Regt. of Infantry. August 21.

(572) Sheriff's Sales. Will Be Sold, on the 20th day of September next, at the Court-house in Brunswick county, the following land for the payment of the taxes due thereon for the year 1799, viz:-640 acres..on or near Indian creek, taken up by Rufus MARSDEN, the property of John LONDON... John C. BAKER, D. Shff. Brunswick county. August 19th, 1800.

(573) Just Imported, by James RICHARD, from London..an Assortment of Goods.. Also A few Cases of Desirabode's Antiscorbutic Decoction.. It cures in four or five days the gums affected by the scurvy..cleans and strengthens the teeth, taking off all the scurf..cures the toothach, renders the breath sweet, and is a perfect cure for the sore throat... Wilmington, August 21.

(574) My Wife, Sarah WHITE, having absented herself from my bed and board, I hereby forwarn all persons from trusting or harbouring her on my account, as I will pay no debts whatever, she may contract from this day. Josiah WHITE. Bladen county, August 18, 1800.

(575) An Oration delivered in Richmond, on the 4th of July 1800..the anniversary of American Independence, by William WIRT...

Thursday, October 23, 1800. (Vol. IV.-No. 198.

(576) Sheriff's Sales. Will be Sold, on Tuesday the 28th day of October next, at the Court-house in Brunswick County, the following Lands for the Taxes due thereon, to wit: 444 acres on Little River, called Cool Spring Plantation, formerly belonging to Francis ALLSTON, and now under mortgage to Joseph BLYTHE, Esq. 200 do..belonging to Samuel DWIGHT, lying on the Sugar Loaf Bay. 200 do. on the west side of Waccamaw river, patented by David SMITH. 16,000 do. in 25 tracts..on the east side of Waccamaw river, patented to David ROSS and Patrick HENRY, Esquires... Wm. WINGATE, Shff. of Brunswick County. September 10.

(577) New-Lon . _____ 17. On Saturday arri___ ___ the United States sloop of war, Trumbull, David JEWETT, esq. commander; brought in with her the French schooner Vengeance...

(578) Charleston, October 6. On Saturday, last a gale of wind came on from the South East..and increased in the evening..when considerable damage was done to a number of wharves, and..small craft.. At 12 o'clock..the gale increased for a few minutes to a species of tornado..most severe in the northwestern part of the town as several houses were blown down.. The house of Mr. CHRISTBURGH, in Cannonsburgh, was amongst the number.. Mrs. CHRISTBURGH was killed in her bed, by the fall of the house and himself and one of his children severely bruised...

(579) From the Aurora, Sept. 26. The Monarchism And the Foreign Devotions of Persons in the Government of the Union, Established on the Testimony of Mr. ADAMS. On Monday evening the 22d of Sept. current, a gentleman of the Presbyterian Church, who is one of their regular Ministers, was in conversation in the borough of Lancaster, in Pennsylvania, with Messrs. William BARTON, Robert DICKSON, and Tench COXE, at the house and in the presence of Mr. Peter GORTON.. The Presbyterian Minister informed that he had seen the address of the Lancaster Republican Committee..and that he knew circumstances, in support of the facts therein..which he would state in writing. In the morning of the 23d inst. he gave to Mr. DICKSON a letter addressed to Mr. COXE, for which the following is a true copy.. "Sir, .. It was currently reported at New-Haven, after President ADAMS had passed through that place, about the 30th of June last, that..he had delivered sentiments to the following effect.. Mr. Pierpoint EDWARDS, Mr. Gideon GRANGER, and the Rev. Dr. DANA, were said to have heard the President avow these sentiments.. Mr. ADAMS says, he has long opposed the anglo-monarchic men in our government." .. Does he mean Mr. HAMILTON, Mr. Charles C. PINCKNEY, Mr. KING, Mr. Wm. SMITH, of South-Carolina, Mr. TRACY, &c.?...

(580) From the Philadelphia Gazette, Sept. 23. We state, upon authority..that John FRIES, who was some time ago reprieved from the gallows by the President of the United States, has been appointed a colonel of militia by his excellency Thomas M'KEAN, the present governor of Pennsylvania!!-And the act has been acknowledged and approved in the Aurora!!!

(581) Twenty Dollars Reward. Ran-Away from the Subscriber, in Fayetteville..two Negro Women; BRUNETTA, about 35 years of age, very stout, remarkably black..and SUCKEY, her daughter, about 17 years of age, well grown and black complected. I bought the above Negroes from Mr. Alexander SHAW, at whose plantation they (from report) are harboured. They are frequently in Wilmington, and have been known to stay at the kitchen of Mrs. HOSTLER... M. MOLTON. Wilmington, August 28.

(582) Wilmington, October 23. A letter from Plymouth to a gentleman in Boston, says, "Arrived this evening, schr. Sally, BARTLET, from Dominica. Capt. B. confirms the New-York account of the French having taken Curracoa, and Massacreeing the Americans, particularly Captain HILLER, of the Pickering, his officers and crew".

(583) GEER & AVERY Have just received a General Assortment of India and European Goods, Suitable for the..season... Wilmington, October 23.

(584) Thirty Dollars Reward. Ran-away from the Subscriber..a Negro Fellow named JACK, of a yellowish complection, about 5 feet 7 or 8 inches high, and well made. He formerly belonged to Mr. John BROWN, of this place, and has a wife at Mrs. M'KINZIE's plantation on Town-Creek, Brunswick county. Also,..a yellow negro called CHRISTIAN, about 20 years of age, a very likely girl, formerly the property of William CAMPBELL, Esq. She has relations in town, and at Mr. Thomas PICKET's, on HARRISON's creek... Holden M'GEE. Wilmington, October 23.

(585) For Sale, Cheap for Cash, That valuable plantation on the sound, right opposite New-Top-Sail Inlet, containing 640 acres..a new Dwelling-House, Kitchen & Barn.. Robert DORSEY, or in his absence, Andrew FULLWOOD. Wilmington, 9th Oct. 1800.

(586) Public Notice. Persons inclined to enter into a contract with the United States, for supplying the Troops..in the state of North-Carolina, during..1801, with rations of provisions, quarter-master's stores..transportation, &c..are invited to send proposals in writing to this office... G. J. M'REE. Custom-House, Wilmington, N. C. October 2, 1800.

(587) Taken Up, And committed to the Jail of this Town,..a negro man named TOM, 5 feet 4 or 5 inches high, about 25 years old, formerly the property of Daniel CARTHY, Esq. of Newbern. He says he now belongs to Mr. Wm. MITCHELL of said Town... Miles KNIGHT, Jailer. Wilmington, October 9th, 1800.

(588) (Top part of column torn away.) _fice, Octobe_..General Post Office as ___. Col. Sam. ASH, 2; ___ John ALLAN; Alex. AN___, ___ ubinaud. ___ Tim. BLOODWORTH, Mer___, Joshua BABCOCK; James BLANEY. ___omas CROSS, 6; Robert CRAIG; Joh___ ONYERS, Smithville; Henry CUMMING; Fred. CRAIG; Eliza. CAMPBELL; Jas. Gold COCHRAN; Thomas DAVIS; Lewis DICKSON, Duplin. E-Rufus ELLIOT. F-Margaret FERGUSON; James FLOWERS; Frances FOSTER, Brunswick county. G-James GARDNER, 2; Captain John GRAY; Mrs. Amey GOODMAN, Brunswick county. H-Lewis HINES; Martha HOLT; Mrs. HERON; James HARPER; John HILL; Mr. HEATLEY, Mr. HOOKS, jun. Duplin. J-Edward JONES, 2. K-Miss Mary KIRKWOOD; Richard KELLY, 3; James KING; John KING; William KEDDIE. L-Judah M. LONG, 3; John LONDON, 2; John LEVINGSTON, 2; Sam. LEVINGSTON, Duncan LEVINGSTON, 2; John LIDDON; Mrs. Sarah LIDDON. M-Alfred MOORE; Mr. M'PHERSON; James D. MAXWELL; Capt. John M. HAND; Murdock M'KAY; Daniel E. MORSE; Thomas MAULSBY; Mr. M'COLLUM; John M'DONALD; Charles M'ALLISTER, South River; Archibald M'NAB, Sampson; George MORRISEY, Sampson. N-Exum NEWBY, Bladen; Abraham NEWKI___; Sam. NORTON; John NICHOLS. P-___ PHILLIPS, Thomas PICKET. R-___ ROSS; Benjamin RHODES, Sampson. S-Wm. SMITH, 2; Jonathan STANDLEY, 2; John STANLEY; Elizabeth SIMPSON; Mary SAMPSON; Mrs. M. SWANN: Alex: SHAW; Mr. SPALDEN; Joseph M. SALTER, 2; Elender SHERRARD; Wm. SNELL; Archibald STEWART. T-John TAYLOR; Charles THOMPSON; Margaret THOMPSON; Clement TOPLIF. W-Benjamin WILLIAMS, Smithville: William W. HOLT; Thomas WOOTEN; Zephaniah WARD; Mary WATTERS; Capt. S. WHITE. John LORD, A. P. M. Wilmington, Oct. 9th, 1800.

(589) Just Imported..And now opening for sale, in Market-Stree_ one door east of Major John WALKER..An Assortment of Dry Goods... Archibald CUTLAR.

(590) For Sale, A Tract of Land, in Bladen county, containing 640 acres, adjoining General Thomas BROWN's plantation, on the northwest branch of Cape-Fear river. Also, a tract of 340 acres, lying on the Sound, 16 miles from Wilmington, on the Newbern road, known by the name of COLLIER's place... Archibald CUTLAR. Wilmington, October 2, 1800.

(591) Fifty Dollars Reward. Ran Away from the Subscriber, about 18 months ago, a Mulatto Lad named HARRY, He is about 20 years of age, 5 feet 8 or 9 inches high, has brown bushy hair, and marked on his right breast, J. W. He is perhaps gone to Caroline county in Virginia, where he was born... John WALKER. Wilmington, N. Carolina. October 2, 1800. N. B. The Reward offered for negro ANTHONY of 40 dollars in last week's paper is inserted for 10 dollars unless he is taken out of this state...

(592) For Sale, A Handsome New Sulkey. Apply to John WILKINGS. Wilmington, October 2.

(593) Notice. The Copartnership between Richard LANGDON & William GILES, under the firm of LANGDON & GILES, was this day dissolved by mutual consent. William GILES, Richard LANGDON. Wilmington, Oct. 23, 1800.

(594) Taken Up, And committed to the gaol of this district on the 17th ultimo, a Negro Fellow, between 5 feet 10 and 11 inches high..about 27 years old.. He calls himself Saul MACCANA, and says he served his time with Reuben BROOKS, of Essex county, Virginia; as a certificate of which he has a pass signed by John EVENS, C. C. bearing date the 16th May, 1794, which is supposed to have been forged; and two papers, one signed by Wm. HATCHETT, of Lunenburg county, the other by Richard HAYLE, of Notaway, setting forth that he is a freeman, and has been in their service as such for upwards of two years, and behaved himself well. It is supposed that the above described Negro is a slave-If so, his owner is requested to come, prove his property, take him away, and pay charges. Miles KNIGHT, Jailer. Wilmington, October 2, 1800.

(595) State of North-Carolina. Wilmington District. Superior Court of law and Equity. Notice is hereby given, that the Rule for the Trial of causes, at the Term ..at the Court-house in Wilmington, on the 13th..of November..is as follows... James MOORE, Clk. Wilmington, Oct. 2.

(596) Advertisement. On Wednesday the 29th instant, will be exposed to public sale, at the Court-house, to pay the Warehouse rent, from 40 to 50 casks of Gunpowder, the property of the United States. John MACAUSLAN, Agent for Edw. JONES. Wilmington, October 16, 1800.

(597) To Let, For one, two, or three years, the house and lot, lately occupied by Samuel MORGAN, in Front-street, Wilmington, the property of Jane JAMES... Wilmington, Sept. 11.

(598) To Be Sold, In South Washington, on the 31st of this inst. by the Executors to the last Will and Testament of John JAMES, dec. that valuable..Dwelling House.. with the lots of ground, in said town... October 2, 1800.

(599) Notice. The Subscriber having administered on the Estate of John R. M'COME, late of this place, dec. requests all persons indebted to said Estate to make immediate payment... Malcolm M'KINZIE. Wilmington, October 1800.

(600) The Subscriber has just received from New-York, by the Three Brothers, Capt.

(600) (Cont.) BELL, an addition to his assortment of Books & Stationary, Which are.. for sale in Front street opposite Mr. BRADLEY's new house..he has also opened a Circulating Library, on the following Conditions:-Each person to pay One Dollar per month, or 10 Dollars per year, in advance... Allmand HALL. Wilmington, September 11, 1800.

Thursday, October 30, 1800. (Vol. IV.-No. 199.

(601) Wilmington, October 30. On Monday next, the Election for Electors of President and Vice-President of the United States, will take place throughout the several districts in this state. His excellency S. ASHE and Gen. T. BROWN, of this district, are candidates for that appointment. The former, if elected, will vote for Thomas JEFFERSON and Aaron BURR.-The latter, for John ADAMS and Mr. PINCKNEY.

(602) Ship News. Port of Portsmouth, Oct. 4. Arrived the ship Mercury, capt. TREADWELL..from St. Bartholomews.. On the 13th September M. John NOYES, of Charlestown (Mass.) died after 7 days illness. On the 17th Sept. at 5 A. M. discovered a wreck to leeward..the ship Hope, commanded by Elijah DOTTE, of New-Bedford, from Wilmington, N. C. bound to Jamaica..dismasted and dismantled in a hurricane. Arrived at Boston, the Swedish brig William, Capt. MOTLEY from St. Batts. Capt. T. BROWN, late of the schooner Aurora, of Portland, came passenger...

(603) New-York, Oct. 1. Arrived ship Russell, GIBBS, in 42 days from Greenock. Sept. 10 fell in with the French frigate Franchise.. She had taken 33 sail,..including the sch. Rambler..from the Pacific Ocean. The Officers of this frigate robbed the ship Russell of about 20000 l. sterling's worth of goods.. This infernal Pirate on the 7th inst..captured the ship Pacific of Portsmouth, N. H. Perkins SALTER, from St. Ubes for Portsmouth; and after plundering her, set her on fire...

(604) To the Ladies of Wilmington and its Vicinity. Mrs. Ann AUSTIN, Midwife, Having served above 20 years, and being generally approved of by those who have been frequent customers in divers places, respectfully informs the Ladies of Wilmington, that she is now ready to wait on all who will want her assistance-living next door to Mr. Robert MUTTER's. Wilmington, October 30, 1800.

(605) ISAACKS & BISHOP Have received..a general..assortment of seasonable Goods, ..for sale on the lowest terms. P. S. Those who are indebted to either of the late firms of ISAACKS & LEVY, or ISAACKS, LEVY & BISHOP, are requested to make payment without delay... Wilmington, October 30, 1800.

(606) Notice. Those who borrowed Guns of the Subscriber, are requested to return the same by the 15th of November next. This being the third time he has advertised for the Guns..on that day a warrant will be put into the hands of Mr. NOBLES, against each person who does not comply with it. C. DUDLEY. Wilmington, October 30, 1800.

(607) WILLKINGS & SCOTT Have received by the schooner Charlotte, Capt. MASTERSON, the following addition to their assortment...

(608) Notice. This is to inform those that may want Boarding & Lodging, that I have taken the new and commodious House, belonging to Mrs. JENNINGS, in Front-street, where Gentlemen may be accomodated... Thomas HOWARD. Wilmington, Oct. 30, 1800.

(609) From the Aurora. To The Public.. The evidence of Mr. DANA, of Connecticut, if correctly reported to the Lancaster Republican Committee is much stronger upon the general ground of a foreign party. The writer of that letter is neither Mr.

(609) (Cont.) OGDEN, who it seems died three days after the real writer penned it, nor is it Mr. GAMBLE.. The real name of the real writer has been given to William RAWLE, Esq. of Philadelphia, General Samuel SMITH of Baltimore, and Tobias LEAR, Esq. of Washington, Potomac, by three letters-also to the Editor of the *Aurora*... Tench COXE.

Thursday, November 6, 1800. (Vol. IV.-No. 200.

(610) Philadelphia, October 15. British Rascallity. Affidavit. City of Philadelphia, to wit. Thomas COATES, mariner, a native of the Township of East Caln?, in the county of Chester, Commonwealth of Pennsylvania; maketh oath and saith, That he was a mariner on board the brig Hope of Charleston, S. C. bound from Greenock to New-Providence, thence to Charleston; that on the 10th day of August, 1799, he was impressed from on board the brig..by a party from..his Brittanic majesty's ship York, of 64 guns, commanded by captain John FARRER, esq..detained..until the 18th March, 1800.. At Port Royal, Jamaica-..about..February, 1800..the following persons, citizens of the United States, excepting only one..who was a foreigner by birth, but had sailed five years out of the United States; swam from..the York, with an intent to return to the United States, and did get on board the American frigate Constellation, commanded by captain TRUXTON to wit: William HARRISON, of Fell's Point, Baltimore; William ROBINSON, of New-Bedford; John COBET, of Boston, and Moses ____, (the latter part of this name this deponent does not recollect).. Captain TRUXTON ordered them on board the British ship of war from which they had escaped, and that they were carried accordingly; that immediately on their arrival on board the York..this deponent saw them tied up to the grating and there each severally flogged on the bare back. Further this deponent saith, that the above named HARRISON and Moses, had been formerly seamen on board the Constellation when captain TRUXTON engaged the Insurgent French frigate; and both of them had on board with them their prize tickets, for their share of the Insurgent prize, and their protections.

That this deponent was on the 13th day of last March, put on board the Mars, of Philadelphia, commanded by captain Richard GEORGE, without receiving any wages or other compensation for the time he was on said British ship of war; and that there were..on board the York..25 others, impressed American seamen, none of whom would enter as seamen, according to the rules of their navy; one person only from Marblehead, having entered on board, of the name of John HIGGINS, a native he believes of that place. Thomas COATES. Sworn and subscribed before me, Oct. 18, 1800. Robert WHARTON, Mayor.

(611) (From the *Aurora*.) Blessings Of A Navy! Borough of Wilmington, ss. Before me James BROBSON, one of the Burgesses of the said Borough, came..Samuel OWENS, master of the sloop Comegrate of Wilmington, and being duly sworn..doth say, That on Tuesday the 20th ult. he sailed from Philadelphia, came up with the launch..belonging to the frigate United States..windward of her..that the officer in said boat hailed him, and bid him for a damn'd rascal to drop his peak and go to leeward of them, which this deponent considering unnecessary, hauled his wind, and passed more than a cable's length to windward of them, for which the officer bestowed on him much illiberal abuse..they got near Fort Mifflin..the said boat came up with him in his wake..the officer (he believes) took the helm and laid the boat along side, giving orders to..jump on board, which they did to the number of 12 or 14.. began beating this deponent and his hands, in a most barbarous and inhuman manner.. threw the anchor overboard..let go the halyards, and cut the boat's moorings and set her adrift. Thus abused and thus situated, they left this deponent and one of his hands bleeding on deck-that capt. ANDERSON, of the brig Hope, of Philadelphia..

(611) (Cont.) witness to this scene..sent his boat, and took up this deponent's boat and brought her on board the said sloop to this deponent. Samuel OWENS. Sworn and subscribed before me, October 4, 1800. James BROBSON.

Borough of Wilmington, ss. Before me James BROBSON, one of the Burgesses of said Borough, came..Johnston OWENS, one of the hands belonging to the said sloop Comegrate, who being duly sworn..saith that he was on board the said sloop at the time, and a witness to the verity of the facts stated in the foregoing declaration.. Johnston OWENS. Sworn and subd. before me, October 4, 1800. James BROBSON.

(612) To be Rented,..that large, convenient and well situated house in Market-street, lately occupied by Mrs. MEEKS.-For terms apply to Dr. HILL, or to T. HILL. November 6.

(613) Isaac TICHENOR, Esq. is elected Governor, and Paul BRIGHAM, Esq. Lieutenant Governor, of the State of Vermont.

(614) Charleston, October 15. On Monday last the Poll was opened in this city, for the election of a Representative in the Congress of the United States, and a Senator and 15 Representatives in the Legislature of this state... Gen. C. C. PINCKNEY-623, Col. Wm. LEE-387.. Mr. Thomas LOWNDES, the candidate for Congress, will, without doubt, be unanimously elected...

(615) Wilmington, November 6. On Monday last, the Election for an Elector of President and Vice-President was held in this town and at Long creek.. For S. ASHE, the republican candidate, 186. For Thomas BROWN, the federal candidate, 182.

(616) A very Great Bargain is now offered for sale.. That valuable Saw-Mill, with the Grist-Mill, on Island-creek.. Enquire of Mr. BLANKS, at Castle Haynes,.. The sale will be made by J. BURGWIN. Hermitage, November 6.

(617) Notice. Those that purchased at the public sale of the estate of Richard BURDEN, are informed that their bonds became due the 8th October, 1800, and it is requested by Mrs. BURDEN, administratrix, that they may be paid immediately, otherwise will be lodged with an attorney at law to recover. D. M'NEILL, Agent for the Administratrix. November 6.

(618) A Bargain. The day formerly advertised for the sale of the Houses and Lots belonging to the estate of the late John JAMES, Esq. in South-Washington, being bad weather, prevented the sale from taking place. The aforesaid property will be sold by private contracts... Benj. LIDDON, John HOLDON, Ex'rs. Alice JAMES, Executrix. South-Washington. Nov. 1, 1800.

(619) Extracts From an Oration on the Extent and Power of Political Delusion. Delivered in New-Haven, on the evening preceeding the public commencement, September, 1800. By Abraham BISHOP...

(620) Extracts from St. Kitt's paper received by the Baltimore. Basseterre, Sept. 30. The Brig Frankland, Mark BLUNT, master, from Portsmouth, New Hampshire, for Tobago, was unfortunately upset by a gale of wind on the 4th inst. in lat. 22.20 long. 57 50. by which accident she lost her masts and deck load of horses; she arrived at Nevis yesterday. The schr. John and Edward, of Bristol, Massachusetts, James SMITHWICK master, for Barbadoes, was also unfortunately upset on the same day, in lat. 22 12 and long. 56..the crew were two hours on the bottom, and without provisions for seven days..she also arrived at Nevis on the 17th.. Yesterday a fleet of

(620) (Cont.) about 20 vessels sailed from hence for America, under convoy of the U. S. ship Connecticut, Moses TRYON, esq. Commander.

(621) The Life Boat. The ingenous artist, the lover of science and the friend of humanity, will be equally gratified with the account of a boat, invented and constructed by Mr. Henry GREATHEAD, of South-Shields, for the preservation of wrecked mariners...

Thursday, December 4, 1800. (Vol. IV.-No. 204.

(622) For Sale, That valuable Plantation on Rockey-Point, known by the name of Strawberry, whereon the late Mrs. George MOORE lived; containing about 500 acres.. R. MOORE. The above Plantation is under a lease to Mr. COBB, for the ensuing year. November 27.

(623) To Masters of Vessels. The subscriber has for sale at his Book and Stationary Store in Front-street, all kinds of Shipping and Custom-House Blanks... A. HALL.

(624) For Sale, The houses and Lot in Fayetteville, possessed by Col. DEKEYSER. The Houses and Lot in do. possessed by Stephen BECK, on the North east corner of the Court-House square. The House and Lot on said square possessed by John O'QUIN. The Houses and Lot on Old-Street, opposite to Mr. ADAM's old store, possessed by Mrs. CRAWFORD. The Houses and Lot on the south side of Kay-street, possessed by James M'CRACKAN. Land & Lots unimproved. One small Lot on the North-west corner of St. John's square. One do. on the Creek.. One do. adjoining James LUNDIE's shop, on the South side of Mason-street. One acre Lot on the Cross-street, below John LAMMON's. One do. behind Mr. WINSLOW's garden. One 1-2 acre on the South side of Grove-street, joining Mrs. VANN's. Five 1-2 acre Lots.. 133 Acres between Grove-street and M. BARGE's brick-yard place. 6 Acres on the South side of the creek, adjoining GROSS's mill place. 120 Acres above Haymount, and towards the race path. 70 Acres above & below James M'CRACAN's old place. 1240 Acres on the drains of Cross Creek. 640 on the East side of the River, below Thomas JONE's. 200 on the back of Thomas JONE's land. 200 on Flat swamp, near Nathaniel HORTON's. 200 on the Brown Marsh in Bladen County. 200 on the Great Marsh in Roberson County. 250 on Waggon branch in Moore County. For particulars apply to James HOGG. Fayetteville, Nov. 10.

(625) Ephraim PABODIE, Boot and Shoe-Maker,..informs..that he has just arrived from New-England, with a complete assortment of Leather and Boot Legs, and has re-commenced his business..in Wilmington, North of the Court-House, and next door south of Mr. A. T. BROWNE's... Nov. 20.

(626) Supervisor's Office, District South-Carolina, Charleston, Nov. 1800. Notice, To Merchants and Masters of Vessels, and to the Pilots. The superintendant of the Light-House establishment at Charleston, South-Carolina, with pleasure announces, that the Charleston Light-House is now completely re-built, having a secure Stair within, built of stone and brick and an iron Lanthern on the top, covered with copper..secure from any accident of fire... Daniel STEVENS, Superintendant.

(627) Wilmington, December 4. On Monday last, about four o'clock..Fire..it was.. the back part of a warehouse behind the store of Messrs. Malcolm M'KENZIE & Co. in Market-street. It was soon extinguished, but..not a doubt can exist..but that it was the effect of intention and design...

(628) Sunday last being St. Andrew's Day the same was observed on Monday, which

(628) (Cont.) the Native and Sons of Native North Britoners, residing in Town..gave a most splendid Ball and Supper..at which Robert MUTER and Henry URQUHART, Esquires, presided.. The whole was so conducted as to reflect the highest honor on the managers, Messrs. BARCLAY, CARSON and M'CAUSLAN.

(629) Governor's Message. "To the Honourable the General Assembly of the State of North-Carolina. Gentlemen,.. The Council were convened in..February and advised the appointing Samuel JOHNSTON, of Martin County, to fill the vacancy on the Bench, occasioned by the resignation of Mr. MOORE... Your obdt. Servant, B. WILLIAMS. Raleigh, November 19, 1800."

(630) His Excellency Benjamin WILLIAMS is re-elected Governor on this date. Joseph GALE is elected Public Printer, by a majority of 24-vice Messrs. HODGE and BOYLAN.

(631) Married-By the Reverend Mr. BAKER, on the 23d ult. Doctor Reuben EVERITT, to Miss Judith F. FLARE, both of Smith-Ville.

(632) Notice. All persons indebted to the estate of Jonathan JENNINGS, deceased, are requested to make immediate payment... Ann JENNINGS, Ex'x. Dec. 4.

(633) Ran Away about two weeks ago, my Apprentice boy, Enoch HINES.. One Cent reward will be paid to the person delivering him to Jacob HARTMAN. Dec. 4.

(634) Received in Wilmington goal, August the 15th, 1800, a negro fellow by the name of MINGO, between 60 & 70 years of age. Said negro was sold by Jonathan STANDLEY of this county, to one MANNING now of Georgia... Miles KNIGHT, Jailer. December 4.

(635) For Liverpool, The American Ship Friendship, Isaac TUBBS, Master.. For Freight or Passage, apply to the Master on board or to R. BRADLEY. Wilmington, Nov. 13.

(636) To Be Let. That pleasant and well known plantation called Castle-Haynes, in New-Hanover County, at present occupied by Mr. BLANKS... J. BURGWIN.. November 27.

(637) Fayetteville Academy. Nov. 12, 1800.. The Rev. Mr. ROBESON is now settled in Fayetteville, and has undertaken the charge of the Academy as principal Teacher... By order of the Board, J. BURKE, Sec'y. Nov. 20, 1800.

(638) Notice. Will be sold at Public Auction..on the third day of January next, in the county of Bladen, 20 miles below Fayetteville, That valuable and well known Plantation, late the property of Daniel WILLIS, dec. with 1000 acres of Land..a very large Plantation Dwelling-House... John THAMES, Thomas BARNES, John ROLAND, Ex'rs. November 27.

(639) WHEELER & CARPENTER, Watch Makers & Silver Smith, Beg leave to inform..that they have commenced business in Front-street, opposite the house formerly occupied by Mr. DORSEY... November 27.

(640) Department Of State, Washington, 30th Oct. 1800. Sir, I enclose a list of men, who alledge they are American citizens, born in the state of Maryland, and who are detained on board of British ships of war, for want of proof of their being such .. (Signed) John MARSHALL. To the Collector of the Customs of Baltimore. State of Maryland. Names. Places of nativity. John DAVIS, Baltimore, (F. P.); William FLOYD, do.; Richard WALKER, do.; Andrew CRAIG, do.; Archibald HUNT; Caesel county, John STAFFORD, Baltimore, (O. T.); William MOORE, Eastern Shore; James SMITH, Baltimore; William FORD, Unknown; Henry CLAY, Baltimore; John SHIELDS, Sussex county, John SOMERS,

(640) (Cont.) Dorset county; John SIMMONDS, Unknown; Thomas BUTTERS, Baltimore; James COOPER, do.; William HULSON, do; Edward CARTER, do.; Benjamin HARRIS, do.; Barney GALEY, do.; Henry LONG, do.; William SCREVERN, Queen Ann's county; John HERNER, Unknown; George RAMSAY, do.; James M'LINNAN, do.; James M'LARING, do.; Horatio GATES, do. William SANDFORD, Caroline county; John M'DONALD, Unknown; Henry CLAY, Harford county.

(641) From the Aurora. It is reported and believed, that the object of Mr. Thomas COOPER's late journey to New-York, was to prosecute Alexander HAMILTON for his highly seditious and incendiary libel against the President of the United States...

END OF VOLUME II

INDEX

As the spelling in this era was phonetic, it is strongly recommended that any surname be checked for all possible spellings.

ONYERS, Joh 588
A KINS, Thomas 288
ABEEL, ___ 462
ABRAMS, ___ 414
  John A. 212
ACADEMY
  Fayetteville 409,637
  Liberty Hall 423
  Lumberton 108
  Pittsburgh 53
ADAM, ___ 624
  Robert 136,213,287
ADAMS, ___ 510,579
  Andrew 12
  John 57,68,160,358,367, 395,411,412,460,522,601
  Joseph 21
  Thomas B. 394
ALCOCK, Solomon 342
ALDEN, Roger 281,546
ALDERMAN, ___ 281
ALEXANDER, ___ 533
  Benj. 404
  Wallace 214
ALLAN, John 165,185,383,588
ALLEN, ___ 111
  Cain 277
  James 410
  Joel 259
  John 195
  Nehemiah 241
  Peggy 120
  Welcome 241
ALLISON, David 103,227,243, 562
ALLSTON, Francis 576
ALSTON, Robert 298
  Titus 120
  Willis 99
ALTON, John 424
ALVES, Walter 214

AMES, Fisher 2
AN___, Alex. 588
ANDERSON, ___ 611
  D. 438
  David 556
  T. 438
  Thomas 466,544
  Wm. 404
ARCHER, John 247
ARMISTEAD, Jordan 255
ARMSTRONG, John 337,342, 357,379
  Martin 21,337
ARNOLD, ___ 520
  Henry 241
  Peter 514
ARREXON, Samuel 514
ARRINGTON, J 255
ASH, ___ 312
  Sam. 588
ASHE, ___ 103,337
  John 29
  S. 601,615
  Samuel 120,185,277,462, 511,538,570
  Samuel, Sr. 462
ASHFORD, Butler 288
  Street 570
ASHTON, Ann 424
ATKINSON, Edward 181,185
ATOTT?, Benj., Jr. 404
ATWATER, ___ 508
AUBINAUD, ___ 12
  Peter 277
AUSTIN, Ann 604
AVERY, ___ 583
  Jonathan 9,19
  Waightstill 244
AXOM, Elijah 542
AYDELOT, Benjamin 12,120, 185,538
AYDETOT, Benjamin 462

B_RN, Nancy 131
B_ARD, Stephen 120
BABCOCK, Joshua 538,588
BACHELOR, ___ 243
BACHUS, Elijah 492
BACON, George 538
BAILY, ___ 250
BAKER, ___ 631
  Abram 396
  Arthur 529
  Blake 337,462
  John 131,562
  John C. 572
  William 298
BALDWIN, Warren 29
BALL, Frances 424
BALLANTINE, Mary 277
BAPTIST, John 433
BARCLAY, ___ 628
  John 55,496,518,566
BARFIELD, Lewis 269
  Stephen 546
BARGE, ___ 624
BARLOW, Thomas 404
BARNES, Thomas 638
BARNEY, Richard 462
BARNUM, Justus 411
BARON, Thomas 44
BARRY, Redmund D. 21
BARTLET, ___ 582
  Amherst 120
BARTLETT, Mary 277
  William 120
BARTON, Benj. S. 450
  William 579
BASDEN, William 185
BATEMAN, Thomas 538
BATTLE, James 298
BAULE?, Jeremiah 298
BAXTER, John 542
BAYARD, ___ 160
BEACH, George 508

BEAMAN, Ozius 269
BEAUFORT, ___ 479
  F. 196
  Francis B. 260
BECK, Henry 243
  John 110
  Stephen 269,624
BECKER, Wilmouth 508
BEE, Thomas 411
BEESELY, Thomas 404
BELCH, Elijah 342
BELL, ___ 600
  Jonathan 433
BELOAT, C. A. 312
BEMBOE, Girsham 312
BENEDICT, Ebenezer 411
BENNER, ___ 192
BENNET, John B. 255
BENTON, Sam. 288
  Samuel 255,336
BERNARD, Isaac 146,288
BESSENT, Abraham 462,570
BETTS, Charles 457
  Sarah 462
BIGGS, Zaccheus 492
BIDDLE, Elijah 514
BINFORD, John M. 255
BISHOP, ___ 255,319,392,
  526,605
  Abraham 619
  Isaac 554
  Isaac, Jr. 339
  Thomas 424,555
BLACKLEDGE, Wm. 506
BLACKMAN, Josiah 570
BLACKMORE, Herral 12
BLAKE, Henry 404
BLAKELY, Johnston 298
BLANCHARD, William 185
BLAND, Joseph 277
BLANEY, ___ 401,408
  B. 90,547
  Benjamin 363
  James 588
BLANKS, ___ 616,636
  John 538
  Mary 538
BLOODWORTH, ___ 84
  Ann 338
  James 338
  James, Sr. 338
  R. 185
  Sam. 234
  Samuel 120
  Tim. 588

BLOODWORTH (Cont.)
  Timothy 277
  Timothy, Jr. 185,277
  William 120
BLOODWOTH, John 234
BLOUNT, ___ 514
  Charles 255
  John, Jr. 255
  John Gray 379,524,536
  Thom 524
  Thomas 214,255,379,536
  William 22,152
  Willie 536
BLUDWORTH, Samuel 462
  Tim., Jr. 240
  Timothy 310
BLUNT, Mark 620
  W. 546
BLYTH, George 11
  Samuel 11
BLYTHE, Joseph 576
BOARDMAN, Offin 120
  Thomas 538
BOISSON, ___ 185
BOITAR, Martial 334
BOLITHA?, Benjamin 120
BOND, J. B. 103,227
BINDIES, ___ 462
BONDS, John 357,536
BOO___, George 526
BOOCOCK, George 185
BOOK, ___ 11
BOOMINS, W. 544
BOOTH, Ben 70
BOSCH, ___ 120
BOURDEAUX, Daniel 404
BOURDETT, Stephen 535
BOWDISH, Asa 92
BOWERS, Barnabas 342
  Gooden 556
  Mary 342
BOWLES, James 342
BOWLY, ___ 192
BOYLAN, ___ 630
BRADFORD, Benjamin 433
BRADLEY, ___ 600
  J. W. 207
  James 53,570
  R. 12,15,120,280,635
  Richard 53
BRADSHAW, Benjamin 462,538
  Richard 462,538
BRADY, James 514
  Thomas J. 514
BRAKE?, Humphrey 424

BRAMAH?, ___ 44
BRANTON, Cader 433
BRECK, Joseph 12
BREER, Canady 120
BRENT, ___ 230
BREWER, Allen 21
  Sterling 21
BRICKELL, ___ 336
BRICKLE, Thomas 185
BRIGHAM, Paul 613
BRIGHT?, Grove 255
BRINSON, Joseph 404
BROBSON, James 611
BROCKETT, Ben. 243
  Benjamin 244
BROKWAY, ___ 44
BROOK, S. B. 247
BROOKS, John 317
  Reuben 594
BROWARD, J. B. 12
BROWN, ___ 18,309,312,
  358,396,559
  A. I. 176
  Jacob 281,546
  Jas. 12
  John 193,235,277,297,
    462,566,584
  John, Jr. 120
  Pearson 462
  Peter 251
  Richard 542
  T. 601,602
  Thomas 462,482,590,
    615
  Thomas, Jr. 462
  Thos. 449
  William 12
BROWNE, A. T. 202,245,
  376,493,553,625
  Alex'r. Thomas 504
  William 120
BRUTON, Simon 255
BRYAN, ___ 255
  Hardy 244
  J. C. 178
  John 342
  John Arthur 342
  John T. 570
  Lewis 178
BUCHANAN, Thomas 251
BUFORD, Frederick 404,
  481
BULKLEY, John 185
BULLOCH, Richard 185
BULOW, C. 44

BULOW (Cont.)
  I. 44
BUNN, Redmund 255
BUNTING, Samuel 11
BUNTON, W. 90
BUONAPARTE, ___ 54
BURCH, ___ 396
BURD, ___ 187
BURDEN, K. 464
  Richard 309,464,616
BURFORD, William 472
BURGWIN, J. 197,223,287,
  475,616,636
  John 6,39,42,86,102,128,
    129,165,232,270,283,312,
    315,356,366,429,434,546
BURKE, J. 637
  John 185
BURN, James 149
  John 538
  William 120
BURNAP, Abram 256
BURNCOAT, ___ 281
BURNET, Andrew 187
BURNETT, Andrew 405,505
BURNS, Ann 131
  Elizabeth 514
  Frederick 514
  John 404
BURNSIDE, Thomas 96
BUROT, Alexander 538
BURR, Aaron 601
  Isaac 12
BURTEN?, ___ 277
  Thomas 538
BURTON, Th. 546
  Thomas 398,456
BURWICK?, White 404
BUTCHER, Thomas 357
BUTTERS, Thomas 640
BUXTON, Wm. 404
BYRD, William 424
C___, Thomas 120
CABAL, Samuel Jordan 230
CABRAL, ___ 287
CAESAR, Peter 404
CAIN, ___ 288
CAINS, John 462
CALDWELL, Charles 469
CALHORDA, John 116,134
CALISTA, ___ 538
CALLENDER, James Thompson
  523
CALLIER, James 255
CALLON, John 185

CALVET, Thomas 317
CAMERON, George 91,120,496,
  518
CAMOCK, John 12
CAMPBEL, William 12
CAMPBELL, ___ 276,542
  Alexander 12
  Archibald 312,342
  C. 462
  Collin 12
  Eliza. 588
  Hugh 29,441
  J. 288
  James 288
  John Ablen 11
  Magdalen 29
  Sarah J. 191
  Wil. 546
  William 166,172,383,517,
    584
  Wm. 479,532
CANBY, Joseph 242
CARD, James 462
CARLIE, Thomas 12
CARMAN, Jesa. 277
CARNEY, Jas. 178
CARODINE, Parker 317
CARPENTER, ___ 639
  Peter 120,182,277
CARR, ___ 1
  Green 342
  James 78
CARRAWAY, I. (or J.) 11
  James 103,227,281
CARSON, ___ 86,628
  George 433
  J. 537
  James 206,292,333
  Miles 269
CARTER, Betty 424
  Charles 424
  Edward 640
  Jas. 433
  William 462
CARTHY, Daniel 587
CARVER, ___ 288,312
CARY, Shadrach 514
CASON, Li ___ 120
CASS, Stephen 185
CASSE, Joseph 185
CASWELL, Richard 8,298
CATE, W. 342
CATHCART, James Leander 395
CEVIL, William 185
CHACE, Gordon 462

CHACE (Cont.)
  Gorton 67
CHADWICK, Joseph 182
  Wm. 12
CHALMERS, Charles 53
CHAMBERS, John 514
CHANCY, E. 538
CHAPMAN, Robert 538
CHARLESCRAFT, Isaac 514
CHASE, ___ 543
  Gorton 277,306
CHASTEN, Richard 281
CHERRY, Jesse 255
  William 298
CHINEY, Ebenezer 185
CHISHOLM, John C. 500
CHRISTBURGH, ___ 578
CHURCH, Rhoda 277
CLAIBORNE, ___ 230
  W. C. 22
CLANDER, James 538
CLARK, ___ 11
  Charles 462
  Gibson 317
  Jonas 492
  Lardner 411
  William 255
CLARKE, ___ 288
CLARY, James 457
CLAY, Henry 640
  Matthew 230
CLAYPOOLE, ___ 12
CLEAMONS, Edward 462,538
CLIFTON, John 120
CLIFTS, ___ 277
CLINTON, ___ 277,542
  George 424
  William 570
CLITHERALL, James 29
  Magdalen 29
CLOPTON, ___ 230
COATES, Thomas 610
COBB, ___ 622
  Tobias 127
COBET, John 610
COCHRAN, ___ 70
  James 154
  Jas. Gold 588
  Thomas 154
COFFIN, James 120
  Weare 120
COGDALE, Charles 505
COHHAM?, Thomas 182
COIT, Wm. 277
COLE, Thomas 185

COLEMAN, Thomas Hereson 277
COLHOUN, Gustavus 22
  Hugh 22
COLLIER, ___ 590
COLLINS, ___ 483
  William 538
COLVIN, John 538
COLVIN?, John 120
CONNER, James 255
CONNOLY, Thomas 12
CONROY, John 21
CONWAY, John 514
CONYERS, John 174
COOK, Archibald 538
  Elkanah 462,538
  John 12,546
  Nathan 404
COOKE, Thomas 277
COOPER, James 640
  John 492
  Robert 470
  Thomas 470,641
  Wm. 97
CORBET, James 404
  John 404
COSTON, Ahab 514
  Jacob 404,514
  John 11,514
  Robert 514
COTTEN, Isaac 404
COTTLE, ___ 397
COTTON, ___ 255
  John C. 469
COWELL, Butler 514
COWPER, Wm. 426
COX, Margaret 546
  T. C. 519
  William 462,513
  Zachariah 137
COXE, Tench 23,579,609
COXETER, James 538
COXETTER, James 365
CR FORD, James 277
CRADDICK, ___ 273
CRAFTS, John Charles 385
CRAI K, ___ 358
CRAIG, Andrew 640
  Benjamin 457
  Elias 457
  Fred. 588
  Henry 457
  Robert 542,588
  Thomas 457
CRAIK, ___ 424
CRAIKE, Thomas 462

CRAVEN, J. 272
CRAWFORD, ___ 624
  Archibald 538
CRAY, Benjamin 457
CRESTON, John 185
CREVILLIER, ___ 3
CREWS, John 120
CROCKER, Nathaniel 363
CROMMARTY, James 312
CROOM, Hardy 255
  R. 255
CROSBY, Richard 462
CROSS, ___omas 588
  Thomas 12
CRUGER, David 187
CRUTCHFIELD, Eusibeus 244
CULLEN, J. 404
CUMMING, Henry 588
CUMMINGS, Henry 538
  Mary Ann 538
CUMMINS, Moses 269
CUNNIAM, ___ 495
  Maurice 171,194
CUNNINGHAM, ___ 258
  Arch. 277
  G. 211
CURRIE, John 120,277
CURRIE?, John 404
CUSTIS, Eleanor Park 424
  George Washington Park 424
  George Washington Parke 424
CUTLAR, A. 90,257,373
  Archibald 146,589,590
  R. Wm. 277
  Roger 334
  Wm. 12,277
CUTTLE, Robert 514
D'VOL, ___ 452
D DLEY, Christopher 185
DABNEY, John 53
DAGGET, John 398
DAILY, Samuel 241
DALLAS, A. J. 470
DANA, ___ 579,609
DANAVON, Jeremiah 12
DANCY, Frank 298
DANDRIDGE, Bartholomew 424
  John 424
  Mary 424
DANIEL, John 312
  Shadrack 312
DANIELS, Willis 542
DARREL, ___ 363

DAVIDSON, Samuel R. 152
DAVIE, ___ (see GAVIE) 274
  W. R. 130,144
  William R. 357
  Wm. R. 272,337,357,379
DAVIS, ___ 32
  Archibald 255
  Bart. 457
  Benjamin 243
  Caleb 457
  George 14,325
  Hezekiah 207
  Isaac 396,457
  John 640
  Joshua 357
  Richard Child 342
  Sarah 342
  Thomas 570,588
  Thomas F. 185
  William 185
  Wilson 457,462,538
DAWNEN, James 120
DAWSON, ___ 542
  John 230
DAY, Ezekiel 185
DAYTON, Jonathan 180,543
DE LA FAYETTE, ___ 424
DE LAMOTHE, ___ 12
DE ROSSET, ___ 414
DE ROSSETT, ___ 473
DE WARNIER, ___ 462
DEALE, Milly 12
DEAN, ___ 532
  Joseph 12,413
DEANE, Joseph 120
DEIST, Emmanuel 433
DEKEYSER, ___ 624
DELANO, ___ 483
DELANY, Sharp 543
DELIHUNTER, Samuel 243
DEMAN, John 545
DENEALE, George 424
DENHURST, Samuel 185
DENNIS, William 514
DENNISON, Gideon 514
DENNY, James 277
DENT, John B. 247
DEPVERDUGON, ___ 462
DESAUSERE, ___ 363
DEVANE, Thomas 45
DEVANNE, James 185
DEXTER, Samuel 59,492
DHERBE, H. 288

DICK, ___ 358
  Catharine 342
  Joseph 342
DICKIE, Robert 535
DICKINSON, Silvanus 462
DICKSON, ___ 336
  James 185,462
  John 269,570
  Joseph 538
  Lewis 588
  Robert 579
DILL, Joseph 483
DIXON, Wynn 357,536
DODD, David 417
DODSWORTH, Ralph 12
DOHERTY, George 546
DOHORTY, George 281
DOLITSON?, Edward 185
DOMNIGO, ___ 185
DONALDSON, J. 276
  R. 276
  Stokeley 21
DONELSON, ___ 379
  Stockly 357,379
DONNEL, Nathaniel 185
DONNELLY, Ross 251
DORSEY, ___ 27,349,498,
  531,639
  L. A., Jr. 393,458
  Laurence A. 458
  Robert 585
DOTTE, Elijah 602
DOTY, ___ 542
  Elihu 277
  Lemuel 405,514
DOUD, Richard 12
DOUGHTY, Ebenezer 131
DOWD, Richard 47
DOWLING, James 277
DRAPER, ___ 542
DRAVES, Thomas 538
DRINKWATER, ___ 344
DRISCOLL, ___ 508
DRY, Virgil 216
DRYSDALE, John 277,462,538
DU PRE, Lewis 187
  Samuel 187
DUANE, William 470,476,
  477,489
DUBOIS, ___ 4
  James 185
DUDLEY, C. 606
  Christopher 120,185,277,
  538,570
  David 407,462

DUDLEY (Cont.)
  Edward 405,505
DUFFEE, Lawyer, Sr. 312
DULUC, A. 185
DUNBIBBIN, Junius 449
DUNBIBIN, ___ 76
DUNCAN, George 33,105,
  288,374
DUNHAM, William R. 312
DUNISON, Gideon 243
DUNKIN, Edmund 120
DUNN, John 558
DUNSCOMB, E. 58
DWAUN, George 404
  James 404
  Wm. 404
DWIGHT, Samuel 576
DYE, Myer 288
  Nimrod 277
EAGLES, ___ 288
EARL, James 182
EASON, Jacob 404
EATON, ___ 43
  John R. 337
  William 395
EDDIE, John 522
EDENS, Jacob 404
  John 404
  Thomas 514
EDWARDS, Charles 312
  James 462
  Mary 185
  Pierpoint 579
EGGLESTON, Joseph 230
EGLESTON, John 462
ELLETSON, Goodwin 27
ELLICOTT, ___ 301
ELLIOT, John 453
  Rufus 185,588
ELLIOTT, ___ 187
ELLIS, Jonathan 462
  Nathaniel 462
ELLSWORTH, Oliver 158,
  337,368
ELMORE, Thomas 137
ELSBEE, Ephraim 342
EMMET, ___ 409
ERWIN, John 404
ETTINGER, M. 263
  Martin 172,233
EVAN, ___ 11
EVANS, B. 546
  Thomas 230
EVENS, John 594
EVERET, ___

EVERITT, Reuben 631
EVERRETT, Reubin 462
EVERTON, ___ 131
EVERTSON, ___ 131
EWEN, ___ 463
FAIRCLOTH, William 357
FAIRFAX, Bryan 424
FAMIN, Joseph Etienne
  395
FAREWELL, ___ 542
FARLEY, Joseph 462
FARLIE, James 381
FARRER, James 610
FARSON, James 277
FATTE, J. 255
FELLOWS, John 404
FELT, John 120
FELTON, Shadrach 255
FENBRACE, John 277
FENNEL, Nicholas 404
FENNO, John Ward 151
FERGUS, ___ 396
  J. 237
  John 277,501
FERGUSON, Margaret 277,
  588
FERREBEE, Joseph 357
FERRELL, John 538
FIND A, Samuel 492
FINDLAY, James 492
FINDLEY, ___ 22
FIRFINGER, Wm. 514
FISHER, George 462
  Southy 538
  William 255,514
FITT, Oliver 255
FITZGERALD, T. 240
  Thomas 35,116,143,
  181,433
  Tho's. 90
  Thos. 449
FITZRANDOLPH, Benjamin
  312
FITZSIMONS, Thomas 557
FLARE, Judith F. 631
FLAVELL, William 29
FLEEMING, Christian 277
FLEMING, James 428
  John 546
FLEVERLY, Luke 533
FLOWERS, James 588
FLOYD, ___ 44
  William 640
FOHEY, Thomas 277
FOLLARSBEE, Thomas 462

FONTAINE, F. 13,499
FONVEILLE, Brice 514
FOOTE, Thomas 533
FORD, William 640
FORFETT, Asa 427
FORSETT, Asa 427
FOSTER, Dwight 22
  Frances 588
  James 433
FOWLLER, John 269
FOY, James 243,538
FRANCIS, Tench 492
FRANKLIN, ___ 424
FRENEAU, ___ 187,519
FRIES, John 231,580
FRYER, Jane 269
FULLER, Edward 462
  Elizabeth 277
  Fen? 404
FULLWOOD, Andrew 585
FURGUS, John 304
FUSSEL, ___ 281
FYETLY, John 367
GABIE, ___ 475
GAGE, Joseph 462
GAILLARD, ___ 187
  John 279,480
GAITHER, Basil 337,357,379
GALBARUSH, M. 185
GALE, John 352,462,527
  Joseph 630
GALEY, Barney 640
GALLATIN, ___ 22
GALLAWAY, Corn's. 457
GALLOWAY, ___ 396
GAMACHE, ___ 120,174
GAMATH, ___ 185
GAMBLE, ___ 609
GARDNER, ___ 62
  James 588
GARETSON, M. 247
GARRICK, Samuel 514
GATES, Horatio 640
GATSON, Peter 404
GAVIE, Wm. R. 286
GAVINO, John 246
GAZZAM, ___ 190
GEBAROCHE, ___ 120
GEDDINS, Abraham 514
GEE, John Henry 465
  Joshua 120
  Sarah 465,538
GEEKIE, James 471
GEER, ___ 135,583
  Henry 462

GEORGE, Richard 610
GERRY, E. 68
GEWELL, William 120
GIBBS, ___ 12,55,74,185, 603
  Geo. 238,422,516
  George 117,125,126,167, 226,277,374,421
  John 215
  Robert 215
GIBSON, John 492
  Shadrach 514
  Walter 312
GIDEON, Benj. 404
  Thomas 404
GILBERT, Clarke 120
GILDEN, James 238
GILDEN?, James 167
GILES, ___ 107,175,397,416
  William 593
GILIARD, John 182
GILLESPIE, James 61,552,569
  Joseph 298
GIPSOM, William 398
GIST, ___ 137
GLASGOW, James 214,357,380,536
GLISTON, Daniel 570
GODDARD, John 483,538
GODKIN, Stephen 120
GOODE, Samuel 230
GOODMAN, Amey 588
  Wm. 562
GOODRICH, Jeremiah 535
GOODWIN, Elias 277
  William 542
GORDON, Samuel 424
GORHAM, James 120
GORTON, Peter 579
GOURLAY, James 131
GOUTIER, Peter 28
GRAHAM, Faithful 312
  Robert 533
GRAINGE, Joshua 288
GRAINGER, ___ 288
  Joshua 288
GRANGE, John Porter? 27
  Mary 120
GRANGER, Gideon 579
GRANT, Stephen 462
GRAVES, Samuel 462
  William 462
GRAY, Edwin 230

GRAY (Cont.)
  John 588
  Sherid 255
  Wm. 342
GRAYHAM, Henry 312
  Thomas 312
GREATHEAD, Henry 621
GREEN, James 185
  Richard 12
  Sarah 424
  Thos. M. 317
  William 234,538
  Wm. 260,471
GREGORY, Owen 269
GRIFFITH, ___ 344
GRIMES, Duncan 542
GRISLET?, William 259
GRISSOM, William 457
GRIST, ___ 337
GRISWOLD, Roger 22,32,507
GROSS, ___ 624
  Jereamiah 277
GROVE, William B. 214,569
GROVES, Richard 96
GROWER, Joseph 433
GUEL, William 185
GUFFORD, James 277
GUION, Isaac 514
GUNNING, James 120
GURGANUS, Barnaby 514
  Samuel 404
  Willie 243
HACKET, James 65
HADDOCK, Drury 312
HADLEY, Joshua 357
HAIL, James 277
HALEY, Edward 462
HALL, ___ 258,275
  A. 201,372,408,419,437,519,623
  Allmand 157,341,600
  Benjamin 514
  David 404
  Edward 342
  John 12,27,179,185,314
  Lazarus 269
  Levi 342
  Priscilla 342
  Roger 314
  William 281,546
  Wm. 277
HALLING, ___ 487

HALLING (Cont.)
　S. 484
HALLMAN, Edward 433
HALSEY, Henry 12,462
HAMILTON, ___ 579
　Alexander 641
　John 214
　Robert 29
HAMMOND, ___ 29
　John 538
　Mildred 424
HAMTRAMMOCK, ___ 137
HANCOCK, George 230
HAND, Jeremiah 120
　John M. 588
　Polly 212
HANEY, Henry 514
HANNAY, Wm. 120
HARDING, John 488
HARDISON, Gabriel 514
HARDY, M___n 120
HARE, Marmaduke 342
　Rachel 342
HARFORD, John 277,462,538
HARGRAVE, John 277
HARGROVE, Britton 312
HARLEY, Robert 118,156
HARPER, ___ 259
　James 12,588
　Jesse 317
HARRINGTON, Job 103,227
HARRIS, ___ 396
　Benjamin 640
　Britain 255
　James 244
　P. 288
　Pat. C. 290
HARRISON, ___ 131;230,
　411,463,584
　E. 288
　James 357
　John 365
　Joshua 120
　R. 247
　William 610
　William Henry 346,488,
　　492
　Wm. H. 394
HARRISS, Pat. C. 297
HARTLEY, Jane 277
HARTMAN, Jacob 12,120,
　277,462,537,551,633
HARTSON?, Rebecca 12
HARVEL, ___ 269
HARVEY, Charles 255

HARVEY (Cont.)
　Edmund 298
　John 269
　Joseph 255
　Mason 514
　T. W. 28
HASELL, James 562
　Zebedee 342
HASKILL, Jonathan 190
HASTINGS, Eleazer H. 538
HATCH, Durant 570
　Ed. 342
　Edmund 112
　Joseph 112
HATCHETT, Wm. 594
HAUSE, George 462
HAWKINS, ___ 250,301,521
　Benjamin 500
HAWKS, Francis 173,188,
　284,334
HAWLEY, Daniel 520
HAY, ___ 337
　James 54
HAYES, ___ 57
　James, Jr. 462
HAYLE, Richard 594
HAYMOND, James 230
HAYNIE, Sally B. 424
HAYWOOD, ___ 298
　John 272,285,298
　S. 21,272
HEARTWELL, Daniel 120,185
HEATLEY, ___ 588
HEATLY, Thomas 12
HEDGMAN, George 555
HENDERSON, James 298
　John 53,298,353,354,
　　459,502
　Robert 354
HENDRICKSON, Isaac 185
HENDRY, Wm. 185
HENLEY, David 500
HENNESSEY, Allan 404
　Wm. 404
HENRY, Francis 404
　Patrick 158,259,367,
　　368,576
　S. M. I. 247
HENSEN, S. George 277
HERNER, John 640
HERON, ___ 366,538,588
　Benjamin 467
HERRINGDINE, Thomas 305,306
HERRINGTON, James 269
HERRITAGE, ___ 243

HICHCOK, Benjamin 411
HICHMAN, Thomas 259
HICKS, ___ 542
　Daniel 538
　Prudence 514
HIGGINGS, John 610
HIGHLAND, John 433
HILL, ___ 127,298,330,
　373,612
　Henry 298
　John 84,420,530,570,
　　588
　Jordan 255
　Joseph 514
　N. 185,454,455
　Nath. M. 517
　Richard 298
　Samuel 243
　T. 51,64,512,612
　Thomas 217
　Thos. 337
　W. H. 67,81,330,541,
　　569
　William H. 25
　Zekiel 277
HILLAR, Benjamin 427
HILLER, ___ 582
HILLSARD, Jeremiah 255
HINDS, ___ 317
HINES, Enoch 633
　Lewis 588
HINTON, ___ 298,337
　William 21
HODGE, ___ 630
　Robert 312
HODGES, Joseph 120
HOGE, David 492
HOGG, ___ 298
　James 559,624
　John 562
　Rob. 288
HOKARD?, J. 342
HOLDON, John 205,618
HOLLADAY, Samuel 357
HOLLY, Henry 404
HOLMES, David 230
　Gabriel 120,185,277
　Hardy 277,417
　Owen 277,538
HOLT, ___ 12
　Cornelius 120,185
　Edward 538
　Martha 588
　Ned 538
　William W. 588

HOMER, Geroham 120
   Gershom 12
HONEYCUT, ___ 269
HOOD, John 424
HOOKER, ___mere 255
HOOKS, ___, Jr. 588
   Charles 570
HOOPER, ___ 311
   A. M. 467,564
   David 120
   Geo. 4,222,277,288,466
   George 110,123,145,161,
     185,546
   James 462
   Mary 467
   William 120,179
   Wm. 327
HORN, Levi 538
HORTON, Nathaniel 624
HOSKINGS, Henry 146
HOSKINS, ___ 78
   Ann 462
   H. 462
   Henry 185,484
HOSMER, Asa 462
HOSTLER, ___ 581
HOUSEMAN, Isaac 277
HOWARD, ___ 312
   Benjamin 462
   C. D. 321,349
   James 11,103,227
   James, Sr. 404
   John 11
   Joseph 28
   Samuel 462
   Thomas 331,485,531,560,
     608
   Thos. 362
   William, Sr. 514
   Wm., Jr. 514
HOWE, ___ 29
   R bert 17
   Robert 77
   Th mas 17
   Thomas 77
HOWEL, William 433
HOWELL, John 27
HOWLAND, Jacob 462,538
HOXSE, John 433
HUDSON, Thomas 277,538
   Wm. 277
HUFFHAM, William 404
HUGHES, Felix 317
   Jas. M. 381
HUGUNIN, C. F. 119

HULET, ___ 185
HULETT, ___ 120
HULINGS, Wm. F. 324
HULL, Henry 120,185
HULSON, William 640
HUMPHRIES, Joseph 396
HUNT, Archibald 640
   J. 21,380
   John 404
   Thomas 298
HUNTER, ___ 243
   Archibald 255
   Catharine 185
HUNTINGTON, Jonathan 277
HURST, Cornelius 185
   Wm. 241
HUSKE, John 277,298
HUSSEY, Margaret 514
   Walter 185
HUTCHENS, Benjamin 185
   William H. 456
HUTCHINS, Benjamin 120,277
   James 277
HUTTON, ___ 199
INDIANS
   BOWLES 140
   BOWLES, Augustus 521
   CHEEHAW MICO 250
   CUSSEITAW MICO 249
   KINNARD, John 302
   METHLOGY 301
INDIAN TOWN
   ? Cusseittaw 249
INDIAN TRIBES
   Cherokees 2,140
   Chickasaw 152
   Creek 250,301,302,500,
     521
   Hitchicaw 302
INGALLS, Daniel 9
INGLES, ___ 336
INNES, James 100
IREDELL, ___ 231
   James 361
IRWIN, Robert 255
ISAACKS, ___ 319,392,526,
   605
   Abraham M. 323,339,554
ISAACS, ___ 300
ISLER, John 243
IVERS, Thomas 131
JABINS, Ephraim 433
JACKSON, ___ 241,250
   John 276,277
   Wm. 303

JACOBS, Wilson 538
JAMES, ___ 27,96,497
   Alice 205,618
   D. 404
   Jane 597
   John 205,514,598,618
   Thomas 288,404
   W. 546
JARMAN, Hall 243
JARVIS, James 432
   Jas. 433
JEFFERSON, Thomas 141,
   460,601
JENK, ___ 344
JENKINS, ___ 542
JENNET, James 27
   Jesse 364
JENNETT, Jesse 277
JENNINGS, ___ 456,608
   Ann 632
   George 318,384,418,
     495,540
   Jonathan 119,549,550,
     632
JEWETT, David 577
JEWKES, Charles 18,182
JEWKS, Charles 312
JINKINS, Lewis 514
   Obed. 514
   William 514
JOCELYN, A. 183
   Fred. J. 82
   S. H. 185
   Sam. R. 96,233,363,
     428
   Samuel R. 18
JODRIE, ___ 538
JOHNS, John 281,546
JOHNSON, ___ 12
   Perigreen 269
   Robert C. 269
   Thomas 12,488
   William 269
JOHNSTON, ___ 495
   Amos 312,570
   Charles 428
   Hollon 255
   Jacob 243
   John 312
   John, Jr. 277
   Jos. 288
   Matthew 194,318,495
   Matthew, Sr. 384
   Proudfoot 377
   S. 336,546

JOHNSTON (Cont.)
  Samuel 214,255,281,629
  Thos. 342
  Wm. 178
JONE, Thomas 624
JONES, ___ 185,190,230, 257,298
  David 127,366,449
  Ed. 73
  Edw. 596
  Edward 12,185,277,462, 538,588
  Frederick 94
  Hull 514
  Jane 94
  John 244
  William 179,234,281,546
  William W. 462
  William Watts 36
  Willie 298
  Wm. 12
JORDAN, Charles 12,24,26
  Dillon 46
  Dilson 12
  Dominick 46,462
  John 255,312
  Joseph 255
  William 462,538
JOSEPH, ___ 243
JURNIGAN, Jacob 546
KAYS, John 185
KEAN, John 453
KEDDIE, William 185,365, 588
KEDDY, William 93,269
KEIGHLOR, ___ 192
KELLUM, William 514
KELLY, H. 240
  Richard 171,551,588
KEMPTON, Ephraim 185
KENAN, James 277
  Michael 538
  Thomas 277
KENNEDY, Charles 462
  John 185,277
KENT, ___ 131,243
KENYON, Henry 355
KER, Daniel 538
  David 108
  Henry 277
KERN, John Frederick 44
KERR, Daniel 404
  James 239
KETCHOM, Conkling 185
KETCHUM, David 277

KEY, Jonathan 243
KIETLINE, S. 533
KILLINGSWORTH, Freeman 342
KIMBLY, Gideon 508
  Giliad 508
  Jeremiah 508
KINBROUGH, Marmaduke 342
KING, ___ 500,579
  James 379,588
  John 588
  Micajah 514
  Rufus 66
  Sally 542
  Thomas 69
  William 514
  Wm. 277
KINGSBURY, Jacob 137
KINNEA, James 404
KINZEY, Daniel 269
KIRKLAND, ___ 44
KIRKWOOD, Mary 588
KITTERA, ___ 411
KNIGHT, ___ 462
  Miles 87,164,587,594,634
KNOWLTON, Joshua 404
LABAZDIER, Papen 430
LACY, ___ 337
LAIN, Samuel 514
  Sarah 514
LAMB, Isaac 404
  Mark 538
LAMBERTOZ, D. 26,85,225
LAMMON, John 624
LANE, Ezekiel 401
  Geo. 59
  J. 186
LANGDON, ___ 18,107,175, 397,416
  Richard 88,593
LANGFORD, Joseph 462
LARKINS, James 185,234
LAROQUE, ___ 12
LASPEYRES, B. 12
LASPEYRRE, ___ 538
LASPEYSE, ___ 185
LASPYRE, Bernard 120
LASSITER, Nathan 357
LATOUR, Lew 185
LAURENCE, Andrew 185
LAW, Elizabeth Park 424
LEAR, Tobias 358,424,609
LEDDON, Thomas 404
LEE, ___ 131
  Charles 436
  George 450

LEE (Cont.)
  Henry 230,382
  James 404
  Jesse 256
  Joel 269
  Sam. 12
  Wm. 614
LEGROS, ___ 538
LEIGH, William 462
LELLY, Stephen 185
LEONARD, Thomas 206,342, 462
  Thos. 259
  Zephaniah 193
LEVINGSTON, ___ 532, 562
  Duncan 588
  John 455,517,588
  Sam. 588
LEVY, ___ 300,319,392, 526,605
  Hart 44
  Jacob 323,339,554
LEWIS, ___ 11,231
  Betty 424
  Charles 433
  Daniel 12
  Eleanor Park 424
  Fielding 424
  George 423,424
  Howel 424
  Josiah 570
  Lawrence 424
  Seth 492
  Thomas 190
  Winslow 345
LIDDON, Benj. 205,618
  John 588
  Sarah 588
LIGHTBOURN, ___ 123
  William 120
LIGHTFOOT, William 433
LILLINGTON, ___ 103, 227,544
  Alexander 182
  Sarah 12
LISTON, Robert 411
LIVINGSTON, ___ 259,411
  Duncan 12,220
LLOYD, David 312
LOCKE, Francis 337
  Moses 298
LOCKWOOD, ___ 259,462, 562
LOFTON, ___ 542

LOGAN, John 433
LOMES, ____ 120
LONDON, John 572, 588
LONG, ____ 396
  Henry 396, 457, 640
  J. 288
  James 255
  Judah M. 588
  R. 337
  Samuel 457
LONGFORD, Joseph 277
LOOMIS, Nathaniel 120
LOPER, Michael 404
  Thomas 377
LORCO, ____ 532
LORD, ____ 18
  J. 455
  John 166, 185, 277, 421, 462, 538, 588
  Peter 288
  Wm. 570
LOSING, Edward 538
LOTT, Abraham 96
LOVE, Amos 11
  Kenan 277, 322
LOVEL, ____ 281
LOWDER, Samuel 413, 439
LOWNDES, Thomas 614
LOYD, Lucy 514
LOYSEL, ____ 49
LOYZELL, ____ 378
LUCAS, Geo. 288
  George 502
  Joseph 120
  Thomas 164, 282
LUDLOW, Israel 492
LUNDIE, James 624
LUTCHES, ____ 546
LUTON, Frederick 255
LYNCH, ____ 542
LYON, Matthew 22, 32, 160, 229, 316
LYTLE, William 21
M'ALLISTER, ____ 538
  Alex. 570
  Charles 588
  Flora 538
  James 487
  John 521
  Mary 7
M'AUSLAN, D. 417
  Duncan 417
M'CALLUM, ____ 538
M'CANE, ____ 546
  Hugh 546

M'CANN, Hugh 462
M'CANNE, Hugh 281
  Nathaniel 281
M'CARTEY, John 416
M'CAULY, James 12
M'CAUSLAN, ____ 628
M'CAY, James 462
M'CLOUD, Roderick 131
M'COLLUM, ____ 588
M'COMB, ____ 12
M'COME, John R. 599
M'CONDRAY, William 12
M'CORMICK, Christopher 433
M'COULSKY, Duncan 312
M'CRACAN, James 624
M'CRACKAN, James 624
M'CRAKAN, ____ 542
M'CREE, ____ 277
M'CULLOCH, Samuel 298
M'CULLOCK, Thomas 12
M'CULLOH, Henry Eustace 342
M'DANIEL, George G. 259
M'DONALD, Geo. 121
  George 12, 210
  John 271, 588, 640
M'DOUGAL, John 142
M'DUGAL, Ronland? 185
M'DUGALL, Ronald 289
M'FARLANE, Andrew 462
M'FEDRAN, John 410
M'FIELD, Peter 538
M'GEE, Holden 303, 584
M'GILL, John 277
  Wm. 277
M'GUFFORD, Nathaniel 11
M'GUIRE, William 492
M'HENRY, James 43, 208, 359, 443
M'INTIRE, Donald 185
M'INTOSH, ____ 250
  John 492
M'KAY, George 462, 538
  Hugh 277
  Murdock 588
M'KEAN, Thomas 387, 580
M'KELLER, Peter 277
M'KENSIE, George 277
M'KENZIE, John 566
  Malcolm 626
M'KERRAL, Wm. 185
M'KERRELL, Wm. 277
M'KINNIE, R. 255
M'KINZIE, ____ 584
  Daniel 12
  George 12

M'KINZIE (Cont.)
  Malcolm 599
M'LAMMY, Joshua 404
  Mark 404
  Mary 404
  Woney 404
M'LARING, James 640
M'LENNON, John 342
M'LEOD, Archibald 12
M'LINNAN, James 640
M'MILLAN, Iver 312
M'NAB, Archibald 588
M'NEES, John 357
M'NEIL, Archibald 462
M'NEILL, D. 617
  Daniel 464
M'PHERSON, ____ 588
M'QUEEN, Alexander 417
M'RAY, John 12
M'REE, G. J. 104, 218, 586
  Griffith J. 161
M____, Griffith J. 188
MC FARLANE, John 120
MAC FARLANE, John 538
MACARIBE?, Archibald 404
MACAUSLAN, John 596
MACAY, James 447
MACBRIDE, Peter 404
MACFARLANE, John 235
MACHIR, ____ 230
MACKENZIE, Malcolm 213
MACKINLAY, Agnes 31
MACKINZIE, M. 332
MACLELLAN, John 211, 326, 415, 513
MACLELLEN, ____ 18
MACNON, Jacob 281
MACPHERSON, ____ 208
MACVURRICH, W. 101
MADEARAS, John 21
MAGILL, John 224, 503
  William 224, 503
MALEY, ____ 442
MALLET, D. 185
  Daniel 270, 315
  Peter 269
MALLETT, ____ 462
  Daniel 103, 227, 462
MALPUS, Henry 404
MALPUS?, John 404
MALPUS, John, Sr. 404
  Simon 404
MALSBY, Thomas 538
MAN, John 138

MANIER, Jacob 546
MANLSLEY?, Basil 342
   Charles 342
MANLY, Basil 342
   Charles 342
MANN, John 21
MANNA, Emmanuel 433
MANNING, ____ 634
MANSDEN?, ____ 87
MANSFIELD, James 277
MARCH, ____ 388
MARGEE, Wm. 1
MARKS, Solomon 243
MARLER, James 237
MARSDEN, Rufus 572
MARSHALL, J. 68
   John 230,404,492,640
   Thomas 462
   William G. 120
   Wm. G. 185
MARTIN, Alexander 298
   Henry 298
   J. P. 108
   John 211,362
   William 298
MASH, John 457
MASON, ____ 229
   Amasa 185
   John 259
   Samuel 12,383
   Thomas 424
MASTERSON, ____ 607
MATHERS, James 476
MATTHERS, James 190
MATTHEW, ____ 281
MATTHEWS, George 433
   M. 369,380
   Mussendine 403
MAULSBY, Thomas 588
MAXWELL, ____ 281,546
   James D. 588
   Peter 234,289,455
MAXWILL, Peter 343
MAY, Wm. 255
MAYER, James 462
MAYO, William 254
MAYORS
   WHARTON, Robert 610
MAZYCK, ____ 187
MEEK, ____ 217
MEEKS, ____ 612
MEL-VILLE, H. 114
MELVILLE, Henry 85
MERCER, John 462
MEREDITH, William 364

MERRICK, ____ 103,227
   George 277
MERRITT, Hezekiah 243
MERRY, Thomas H. 534
METCALF, James 481
MEWS, James 538
MIFFLIN, Thomas 208
MILES, Isaac 462
MILLAR, John 462
MILLER, Ann 277
   Henry 404
   James 336
   John 404
   Martin 568
   William, Jr. 23
MILLINGTON, John 12
MILLS, Benjamin 7,503,570
   John 291
   Robert 317
MILNE, ____ 408
   Joseph 547
MIMS, David, Jr. 275
MINK, John 533
MITCHEL, ____ 120
MITCHELL, George 244
   Robert 150,221
   Wm. 587
MOLTON, M. 581
   Michael 239,314,349
MONROE, ____ 131,361
MONTGOMERY, ____ 337
   A x. 317
MOODY, ____ 446
MOORE, ____ 84,336,404,629
   A. D. 14,325,570
   A. Duncan 83,539
   Alexander D. 37
   Alexander Duncan 277
   Alfred 2,80,120,361,588
   Ann 538
   Duncan 214,538
   Edmond 404
   George 622
   Henry 120,185,277
   James 120,277,299,546, 595
   John 337,450
   John B. 12,163
   Maurice 447
   Moody 120
   R. 622
   Roger 11,185
   Thomas 17,77
   William 640
MOORHEAD, James 312

MORELAND, ____ 250
MORGAN, Alexander 277, 538
   Benjamin 277
   Daniel 198,404
   Elizabeth 277
   Margaret 131
   Samuel 120,288,597
   William 542
   Wm. 243
MORISEY, George 109
MORISON, Duncan 12
MORRIS, R. V. 370
   Richard V. 425
   Thos. 342
MORRISEY, George 588
MORRISON, John 253
MORRISS, John 404
MORSE, D. P. 277
   Daniel E. 588
   E. 312,538
MORTON, Jacob 381
   John 360
MOSEL, Sarah 448
MOSELEY, Maria A. S. 132
   Sampson 132,182
   William 132,165
MOSELY, James 462
   William 462
MOSES, Benjamin 277
MOSLES, Benjamin 185
MOSS, William 317
MOTLEY, ____ 602
MOTTE, Abraham 111
   Edgerton 404
MOULTHROP, ____ 199
MOULTRIE, William 519
MULATTOES
   Allston 67
   Dick 352
   Harry 591
   Isaac 110,419,448
   Will 186
   William 424
   LEE, William 424
MULGROVES, William 433
MULHERRIN, James 536
MULHLAND, Hugh 12
MUMFORD, ____ 462
   James 449
   Robinson 212
MUNIONS, Stephen 252
MUNN, William 12
MURPHY, I. 546
   John 120

MURPHY (Cont.)
  Thomas 120,407,466
MURRAY, _____ 158
  James 120
  Vans 159,337,368
  Wm. 368
  Wm. Vans 368
MURTAUGH, Margaret 47
MUSE, J. 505
MUTER, Robert 264,421,628
MUTTER, Robert 604
MYERS, Fanny 462
MYGOT, Eli 411
NASH, Thomas 411
NEAVES, Thomas 298
NEGROES
  Abraham 182
  Anthony 591
  Apollo 260
  Aston 209
  Bacchus 182
  Bet 164
  Boatswain 96
  Brunetta 581
  Cato 127
  Charles 533
  Christian 584
  Cupid 86
  David 111
  Dick 182
  Elijah 270,315
  Flora 182
  George 182
  Grudge 112
  Harry 86
  Ireland 16
  Isaac 182
  Jack 265,303,448,566,
    584
  Jacob 47
  James 505
  Jem 42
  Jenny 182,466
  Jim 182,448
  Jimmy 224
  Job 182
  Joe 528
  Johnny 516
  Johny 226
  Joshua 529
  Larry 216
  Manuel 366
  Mary 182
  Michael 207
  Mingo 634

NEGROES (Cont.)
  Monimen 47
  Nan 182
  Nan, BLANEY's 401
  Nancy 86
  Nanny 207
  Ned 36
  Peg 182
  Pompey 448
  Prince 112
  Qua 311
  Qua, HOOPER's 311
  Quaco 179
  Quamina 191
  Sally 20,448
  Sambony 325
  Sarah 182
  Suckey 581
  Tom 96,405,505,587
  Toney 132
  Virgil 20
  Will 377
  BACOT, Jack 448
  JONES, Absolesm 394
  MACCANA, Saul 594
  ROUSE, Jack 448
NELSON, _____ 21
  Annanias 342
  John 22
NETTLETON, Oza 120
NEW, Anthony 230
NEWBY, Exum 588
NEWKI__, Abraham 588
NEWLAND, James 459
NEWMAN, _____ 41
NEWPORT, J. 533
NEWTON, Edward 457
  Elijah 514
  George 404
  James 457
  John 457
  Joseph 404
NICHOLAS, _____ 22
  John 230
NICHOLS, _____ 49,199
  Jere. 350,351
  John 153,331,350,351,
    588
  William 48,367
NICHOLSON, Peter 185
NISBETT, Alexander 149
NIXON, George 404
  Richard 185,284,462
NIXSON, Robert 234
NOBLE, Jarrot 185

NOBLE (Cont.)
  Jarrott 486
  Samuel 277,462
NOBLES, _____ 542,606
NORMAN, Elijah 514
  Henry 185
NORMAND, Thomas 277
NORMENT, Thomas 322
NORTON, Sam. 588
  Samuel 462
  W. 288
NOURSE, Joseph 543
NOYES, John 602
  John C. 108
  Lemuel 193
NUTT, _____ 135
  John 5,89
  William 3,38,163,185,
    227,463
  Wm. 4,182,234,282,283,
    288,404
NUYS, John 185
O'BILAN?, Laurence 255
O'BRIAN, Richard 41
O'BRIEN, Richard 395,509
O'ELLER, _____ 371
O'NEIL, John 12,120
O'QUIN, John 624
ODOM, Dempsy 269
  Hallasha 269
  Silas 269
OGDEN, _____ 609
OLDFIELD, Peter 514
  Richard 514
ORCHARD, George 120
ORTON, _____ 562
ORTON?, _____ 259
OTIS, _____ 32
  Harrison G. 443
  Samuel A. 477
OUSSE, _____ 120
OUTLAW, George 255
OWENS, _____ 562
  Johnston 611
  Samuel 611
  Thomas 96
PABODIE, Ephraim 625
PACE, John 404
PAGE, _____ 269
  Robert 230
  Thomas 1
  Wm. 1
PAINE, _____ 187,519
  William 59
PAREMAN, Arthur 185

PARISH, James 120
  Richard 120
PARKER, ___ 32,542
  Hardy 404
  Hyde 411
  Isaac 22
  J. 43
  James 542
  Josiah 230
  Sheale 508
  William 185,312
PARKS, Harriot 424
PARSON, Richard 538
PARVISOL, Isaiah 96
PATTERSON, ___ 538
  William 12
PAUL, Philip 462
PAYNE, Hector 400
  Michael 75
PEABODY, John 120,148,267, 340
PEACOCK, Silas 542
PEALE, ___ 557
PEARCE, Arthur 357
  E. 294
  Nathan 462
PEARSON, Thomas 514
PEASLY, Wm. 342
PELHAM, ___ 162
  Charles 515
PENDALL, ___ 44
PENDLETON, Philip 424
PERENCHIEF, James 462
PERKINS, ___ 40,408
  Jacob 248
PERRY, David 185
  Esther 514
  Francis 514
  Thomas 514
PETER, Martha Park 424
PETERS, Richard 367
PETERSON, Macom 269
PETRIE, Alexander 44
PHIFER?, George 298
PHILIPS, ___ 21
  Calvin 199
  Isaac 98
  Joseph 249
PHILLIPS, ___ 588
  Mann 357
  Samuel 446
PHILYAU, Martin 546
PHOEBUS, James 281
PICKENS, ___ 542
PICKERING, ___ 68,510

PICKERING (Cont.)
  Timothy 252,301,368,395, 436,492,500,543
PICKET, ___ 542
  H. 546
  James 281,546
  Thomas 584,588
PIKE, ___ 312
PILMAN, Amos 546
PINCKAM, Nathaniel 255
PINCKNEY, ___ 601
  C. C. 614
  Charles C. 68,579
PITT, ___ 57
PLAIN, John 120
PLAIR, John 185
PLAYER, Richard 288
PLAYWELL?, ___ 337
PLEASANTS, John P. 291
POINSETT, ___ 44
POISON, John 71
POISSON, ___ 497
  John 546
POLK, ___ 298
  William 12,390
  Wm. 21,272,278
POLOMY, ___ 548
PORTER, ___ 18,312,337, 429
POSTMASTERS
  BRADLEY, R. 12,120
  LORD, John 185,538,588
POTTER, Samuel 457
POTTS, ___ 55,74,126,185
  J. 440
  Joshua 73,125,296,396
POURCENT, John 120
POWEL, Hardy 404
POWELL, Jacob 404
  Leven 230
  Nancy 342
  Nathan 342
  William 433
POWERS, ___ 120
  James 514
POYNTZ, Antonio 433
PRATT, El za 185
PRESCOTT, John 404
PRICE, James 404,462
  John 357
  Samuel 514
PRIDGEON, Matthew 45
PRIDGGN, Francis 404
PRIME, Nathaniel 59
PRINCE, B. 344

PRINCE (Cont.)
  Geo. 427
PRINDLE, Mordicai 462
PULLY, William 185
PUNCHARD, William 277
PURVIANCE, ___ 337
  Samuel B. 337
  Samuel D. 357,379
QUINCE, ___ 12,27
  Ann 20,71
  Richard 14,20,111,155, 206,448,462,487
  Richard, Jr. 103
  Susannah 111
RABINEAU, Francis 52
RAMSAY, ___ 520
  George 640
  James 542
  Wm. H. 404
RAMSEY, John 53
RANDOLPH, John 230
RANKIN, Richard 342
RAWLE, William 609
RAY, David 255
  Duncan 312
READ, George 12
  James 12
REED, George 120
REEVES, Joseph 28
REGISTER, William 312
REGUES, Andrew 462
REID, William 462
REMMINGTON, John P. 538
RETTER, Moses 120
REYNOLDS, Cornelius 508
RHODES, Benjamin 588
  J. T. 538
  Jacob 312
  James Thomas 277
  Joseph 120
  Solomon 514
RICE, James 514
RICH, John 12
RICHARD, ___ 87,243
  James 277,573
RICHARDS, ___ 538
  Elizabeth 312
  John 508
RICHARDSON, Joseph 288
RICKETT, ___ 371
RIGAUD, ___ 461
RIGNES, Andrew 538
RILEY, Patrick 120
RING, ___ 431
RITCHIE, Robert 525

RITTER (see WRITTER),
    Moses 12
ROACH, David 29
ROBBINS, Jonathan 411
    Joseph 185
    Nathan 411
ROBERSON, Alice 329
    B. 269
    Benjamin 329
    John 277
    Joseph 277
    W. 329
ROBERTS, ____ 542
    Elijah 536
ROBERTSON, J. 537
ROBESON, ____ 637
    Edward 120,185
    John 96
    Jonathan 96
    S. 120
    Thomas 120,191
    Thomas, Jr. 96
    Thos. 375
ROBINS, William 533
ROBINSON, ____ 44
    Edward 12
    Jon. 433
    Joseph 12,120
    T. 247
    Thomas 538
    William 610
RODGER, James 12
ROGER, ____ 562
ROGERS, James 404
    John 433
ROLAND, John 638
ROOSAVELT, Nicholas I. 386
ROSE, John 269
ROSS, ____ 588
    David 562,576
ROUCKS, Elizabeth 514
ROUSE, ____ 185
    Alex. 268
    George 120
ROWAN, ____ 239,282
    John 27,282
ROWE, Frederick 404
ROWELL, Benjamin 275,327
    Leeon 275
    Richard 12
ROWLAND, Nelly 462
ROYAL, Hardy 265
ROYSE, John 62
RUFFES, Thomas 277
RUGGLES, Edward 185

RUNDEL, Polly 212
RUSEL, William 120
RUSH, Benj. 469
RUSS, ____ 168
RUSSEL, ____ 22
    Charles G. 451
    Charney 404
    Edward 120
    J. 151
    Samuel 462
    William 538,570
RUSSELL, John 437
    Samuel 12
    Wm. 185
RUSSES, Thomas 277
RUTLEDGE, ____ 386,402
S ILES, Richard 544
SAARS, Jacob 185
SAGE, Robert 11,12,185,514
SAIEL, Peter 427
SALTER, Joseph M. 588
    Perkins 603
SALTERER?, Joseph M. 462
SAMFORD, Samuel 357
SAMPSON, ____ 182
    John 16
    M. 34,293,325
    Mary 588
    Michael 169,277,312,
      462
SANDERS, Thomas 538
SANDERSON, William 312
SANDFORD, Thomas 548
    William 640
SANDS, Comfort 59,190
    David 431
    Juliana-Elmore 431
SAPER?, Samuel
SARY, Lord 514
SASSER, William 342
SAUL, J. 243
SAVAGE, Arther 404
    William 478
SAWYER, George 462
SCALES, Nathaniel 115
SCARBOROUGH, Thos. 404
SCHAW, Robert 283
SCHN?TT, C. C. 70
SCHUYLER, ____ 386
SCOTT, ____ 135,561,607
    James 241
    John 56
SCOTTOW, ____ 44
SCREVERN, William 640
SCURLOCK, John 12

SEAGROVE, James 69,301,
    302
SEARS, ____ 427
SEAWELL, ____ 337
SEDGWICK, Theodore 460
SELLERS, ____ 120
    Simon 120,185
    Sulan 185
SERGEANT, Winthrop 386
SESSIONS, ____ 312
SESSUMS, Mary 269
SEVIER, John 139
SEWALL, ____ 22,386
    Sam. 43
    Samuel 59
SEWELL, Thomas 16,277
SHACKELFORD, F. 352
SHACKLEFORD, James 505
SHAW, ____ 358,394,432,
    522,538
    Alex. 588
    Alexander 538,581
    James 185
    John 567
    Neil 29
SHELBY, Moses 137,357
SHEPPARD, Benjamin 357
    John 357
SHERIFFS
    ALCOCK, Solomon 342
    BAKER, John C. 572
    BOWLES, James 342
    BROCKETT, Ben. 243
        Benjamin 244
    CATE, W. 342
    DOTY, Lemuel 514
    ELSBEE, Ephraim 342
    GREGORY, Owen 269
    HALL, Edward 342
    HARVEY, T. W. 28
    HATCH, Ed. 342
    LEONARD, Thomas 206,
        342
        Thos. 259
    M'CANE, Hugh 546
    M'CANNE, Hugh 281
    MORRIS, Thos. 342
    MORSE, E. 312
    NELSON, Annanias 342
    NUTT, William 163,182,
        227
        Wm. 234,282,283,288,
        404
    O'NEIL, John 120
    RANKIN, Richard 342

SHERIFFS (Cont.)
  SASSER, William 342
  SPEIGHT, Samuel 342
  SPENCER, Zach. 342
  STEPHENS, John 342
  WEATHERLY, Abner 342
  WILLIAMS, Isaac 342
  WILLS, Lewis 342
  WINGATE, Wm. 576
  WRIGHT, Thomas 11,48,103
SHERRARD, Elender 588
SHETO, James 120
SHIELDS, John 640
SHINE, Daniel 243
  J. 243
SHIRLEY, A. 433
  Ambrose 247
SHOALER, Daniel 185
SHOLAR, Moses 546
SHURBERN, Joseph 562
SHUTER, John 204,474
  Samuel 474
SIBLEY, John 406,462,538
SILBY, Henry 255
SILVA, A. C. 392
  Antonio C. 391,565
  Joze Roiz 391,392
SIMMONDS, John 640
SIMMONS, Green 342
  John 514
  Thomas 404
SIMONS, Maurice 187
SIMPSON, ____ 241
  Charles 189
  Eliz. 480
  Eliza. 279
  Elizabeth 120,189,277,588
  John 404
  Solomon 514
  William 538
SIMS, Isaac 12
SINGLETARY, ____ 29
SITGREAVES, Samuel 436
SKINNER, John 21
SLADE, Thomas 277
SLOAN, Daniel 12
  John 169,312
SMALL, Gamalu 185
  William 433
SMEETON, William 50
  Wm. 262
SMELLEY, Frances 342
  John 342
SMITH, ____ 162,363,411
  Benj. 21,369,380

SMITH (Cont.)
  Benjamin 27,29,87,147,161,
    170,174,216,274,403,570
  Campbell 488
  Curling 103,227
  David 576
  Duncan 120
  Eben. 317
  Edward 462,538
  Eli 312
  George 281,546
  J. 445
  James 404,640
  John 433,514
  Joseph 533
  Obrien 149
  Philip 433
  Robert 337,433
  Samuel 609
  Wm. 515,579,588
SMITHWICK, James 620
SMYTH, Stephen 120
SMYTHE, Samuel 192
SNARES, Jacob 277
SNEAD, H. M. 320
  Harriet M. 335
  R. W. 320
  Robert W. 335
  Thomas 418
SNEED, M. 565
SNELL, ____ 396
  William 185,538
  Wm. 588
SNOW, Jonathan 12
SOMERS, John 640
SOTLOR, George 317
SOWL, ____ 483
SPAIGHT, Richard D. 394
SPALDEN, ____ 588
SPAULDING, ____ 24
  M. 501
  Marg't 304
  Philip 295,304,501
SPEARMAN, Edward 404
SPEED, John 342
SPEIGHT, Samuel 342
SPENCER, Zach. 342
SPENDLOVE, Jannet 277
  Jennet 120,179
SPILLER, James 334,417
SPOTSWOOD, Elizabeth 424
SPRADLEY, Brian 542
SPRING, S. 288
SPRUILL, Charles 255
  Samuel 255

STACKS, Levisa 113
  William 113
STAFFORD, John 640
STAGG, John, Jr. 381
STALLINGS, Hugh 240
  Shadrick 209
STANDLEY, James 404
  Jonathan 404,588,634
STANLEY, ____ 337
  John 588
  Catharine 277
STANTON, John 120,185
STANWOOD, Lemuel 251
STARBUCK, David 462
STARKEY, John 514
STAUNTON, Peter 120
STEELE, George 12,120
STEMUR, Geo. 185
STEPHENS, John 342
STERMY, Joseph 462
STERRET, Andrew 247
STEVENS, Daniel 626
  Ebenezer 381
  Edward 442
STEVENSON, Thomas 433
STEWART, Archibald 588
  Eliz. 514
  James 185
  William 120
STILES, Samuel 544
STILLMAN, George 462
STOCKING, Samuel 12
STOCKMAN, Charles 538
  John 538
  William 538
STODDART, ____ 432
  Benjamin 259
STOKELY, John 404
STOKES, ____ 452
  M. 380
STOLEY, Henry 12
STONE, ____ 99
STORIE, John 120
STRAHAN, Alexander 529
STRAKEN, Alexander 462
STREET, ____ 199
STRUDWICK, Wm. F. 255
STUART, ____ 546
  Alexander 514
  David 424
  Eleanor 424
STUCKEY, Arthur 404
STUDWICK, William 120
STURGEON, Robert 488
SUGGS, Aquila 542

SULLIVAN, Edward 120
  Selah 120
SUTTON, Bailey 312
  C. 28
  Ephraim 538
SWAIN, Luke 396
SWAN, John 94
SWANN, ___ 291
  John 120,462
  M. 120,588
  Samuel 11
  Thomas 277
SWINSON, John, Sr. 404
SWORDS, J. 228
  T. 228
SYKES, John 45
SYM NS, John Cleves 411
TALBOT, ___ 548
  Silas 442,461
TANCY, Francis Lewis 103, 227,259
TATE, Jas. 11
  Robert 462,468,538
TATOM, Absalom 255
TAYLOR, ___ 108,190
  Absalom 404
  Geo. 277
  James 53,244
  Joel 269
  John 538,588
  Major 411
  W. 404
  William 121,255
  Wm. 291
TAZEWELL, William 488
TEACHY, Jacob 281
TELEMAQUE, Charles 548
TELFAIR, ___ 233,517
  John 93,235,261,315
THACKER, ___ 150
  Barker W. 277
THALLY, John 281
THAMES, John 638
THOMAS, Caleb 12
  Charles 342
  Francis 29
  James 404
  Jenny Jarrett 342
THOMPSON, ___ 250
  Benjamin 533
  Charles 120,185,588
  Jas. 570
  John 120,185
  Jon. 258
  Jonathan 162,376

THOMPSON (Cont.)
  Margaret 588
  Thomas 65
  William 462
THOMSON, Charles 12
THORNTON, George 298
  Jane 424
  T. 243
THURSTON, ___ 162
  Sam. I. 9
  Samuel I. 187,515
TICHENOR, Isaac 316,613
TIFFIN, Edward 412
TILSON, ___ 12
TIMMONS, ___ 542
TINNULY, ___ 542
TODD, William 457
TOLMAN, William 185
TOOLE, Henry Irwin 342
  Lawrence 342
TOOMER, ___ 153,300,356, 414,531,560
  A. B. 90,184,308,311, 328
  Anthony B. 106,120,183, 219,448
  H. 473
  Henry 87,182-184,219, 328,334
  John 298
  M. M. 473
TOPLIF, Clement 588
TOWERS, James 31
TOWKES, ___ 312
TOWNING, James 120,404
TRACEY, Isaac 538
TRACY, ___ 579
TRASH, Robert 120
TREADWELL, ___ 602
TRIGG, ___ 230
TRUEMAN, Alexander 488
TRULY, James 317
TRUXTON, ___ 610
  Thomas 247,432,433
TRYON, Moses 444,620
TUBBS, Isaac 635
TUCKER, Mary 195
TUFTON, John Mason 446
TULON, Wm. 277
TUNSTALL, James 255
TURNER, Amey 185
  James 255
  Thomas 538
  Wm. 120,185
TYRREL, Wm. 21

TYRRELL, ___ 379
  William 21,357
UHTHOFF, Hero Antonio 422
URE, ___ 185
  Andrew 449
URQUHART, H. 185,537
  Henry 185,277,628
VALENTINE, ___ 367
VALLEAD, William 131
VANDEPUT, ___ 452
VANDERBURGH, H. 412
VANN, ___ 624
VAUGHAN, ___ 327
  John 488
VAWZOYEUR, Hamon 462
VENABLE, ___ 230
VENABLES, James 538
VENTERS, Arthur 447
VERSCHUUR, P. 498
VIAN, Nicholas Ferdinand 548
VOSBURGH, H. 76
WADDEL, Hugh 288
WADDELL, ___ 429
  John 226,516
WADE, John 457
WADHAM, Timothy 538
WADKINS, Levin 570
WALDERMAN, William 277
WALDREN, ___ 250
WALKER, ___ 562
  Ann 424
  C. 571
  David 533
  James 12,79,185,288
  James W. 124,200
  Joel 250
  John 79,334,404,448, 589,591
  Mary 538
  Richard 640
  Wm. 404
WALLIS, John 404
WALN, ___ 394
WALSH, Michael 12,120
WARD, ___ 18
  C___otte 472
  David 508
  John 508
  Zephaniah 588
WARDEN, William 53
WARE, Geo. 28
WARKINS, John 185
WARNER, George 40

WARREN, Jonas 300
  R. 433
WARSTER?, Martin 244
WASHINGTON, ___ 381,423
  Augustine 424
  Bushrod 2,423,424
  Charles 424
  Charles Augustine 424
  Corbin 424
  Elizabeth 424
  Geo. 348,382,390,424
  George 358,359,373,383,
    396,424
  George Augustine 424
  George Fayette 424
  George Steptoe 423,424
  Hannah 424
  Jane 424
  John Augustine 424
  Lawrence 424
  Lawrence Augustine 424
  Maria 424
  Martha 424,488
  Mildred 424
  Robert 424
  Samuel 424
  Thornton 424
  William Augustine 423,424
WATT, Samuel 190
WATTERS, Henry 185,467
  Joseph 29
  Mary 588
WATTON?, David, Sr. 435
WATTS, Richard 185
WAYNE, ___ 288,542
WEAR, James 185
WEARE, George 28
WEATHERLY, Abner 342
WEBB, ___ 117
  William E. 214
WEDERSTRANT, P. C. 433
WEEKS, Levi 431
WELL, Jacob 281
WELLS, Catherine 514
  Jesse 514
  John 399
  Lewis 342
  Samuel 568
WELSBY, Wm. 277
WESSINGER, ___ 44
WEST, ___ 317
  Eli 243,514
  John 437
  John S. 203
WESTBROOK, James 243

WH FIELD, ___ 559
WHARTON, Robert 610
WHEATON, D. 494
  Daniel 11,103,122,227
  Joseph 180
  Starling 103,227
WHEELER, ___ 542,639
  John 514
  William 312
WHELEN, Israel 492
WHITE, ___ 29,312
  Bishop 367,382
  Burgwin I. 277
  George 404
  Hays G. 12
  I. 462
  John 404
  John D. 538
  Josiah 574
  Luke 404
  S. 588
  Sarah 574
  Thos. 317
  William 154,357,403
  Wm. 236,272,379
WHITFIELD, ___ 309
  Joseph 12
  Needham 255,546
WHITING, Joseph 462
WHITTY, Edward 244
WI ___, Peter 245
WICK, James 243
WIGGENNS, Elisha 277
WIGGINS, Thomas 255
WILKINGS, John 592
  Marshall R. 404
WILKINSON, ___ 473
  Rebecca 185
  William 312,462,538
WILLESTON, Sylvester 277
WILLIAMS, ___ 120
  Aaron 281,546
  B. 629
  Benjamin 588,630
  Edward 401
  Henry 385
  Isaac 342
  Israel 491
  Jesse 570
  John 433
  John P. 234,277
  John Pugh 120
  Jonathan 404
  Mary 269
  Philip 95

WILLIAMS (Cont.)
  Robert 286,390
  Robert, Jr. 130
  S. 546
  Samuel 120
  Solomon 298
  Thomas 244
  William 12,120
  Willoughby 357,536
  Wm. 336
WILLIE, William 424
WILLIS, Daniel 638
  J? 266
  Jacob 546
  John 108,337
WILLISTON, Sylvester 538
WILLKINGS, ___ 135,561,
  607
  M. R. 56,177
  Marshall R. 63
  Robert 168
WILLS, James 244
  Lewis 342
WILMERDING, William 58
WILSON, ___ 291
  David 506
  David, Jr. 435
  Gilbert 120,185
  James 404
  John 433
  Joshua 290
  Thomas 424
WILTES, Joseph 462
WIMBLE, ___ 288
  James 73
  William 73
WIN, James 514
  Thomas 514
WINDER?, William 543
WINGATE, William 462
  Wm. 576
WINSLOW, ___ 624
  John 389
  Joshua 276
WIRT, William 575
WISS, ___ 12,120
  Peter 528
WITHERSPOON, David 243
WOLCOTT, Oliver 436,
  507,543
WOOD, ___ 27
  Basil 543
  Frederick 514
  John 185,538
WOODCOCK, Joseph 169

WOODEN, Thomas 457
WOODMAN, Joseph 548
   Joseph H. 388
WOODS, Benjamin 173,188
WOODSIDES, Thomas 404
WOODYEAR, Edward 192
WOOTEN, Thomas 588
WORTHINGTON, Thomas 492
WRIGHT, David 322
   Howel E. 120
   Isaac 120
   J. G. 537
   James 322
   John Storie 120
   Jos. G. 24,72,168,177,
     313,559,563,570
   Joshua G. 439,441
   Thomas 11,48,103,177,
     322,538
WRITTER, Mores 404
WYER, Owen 462
WYNNS, Thos. 380
YANCEY, ___ 337
YARD, James 411,488
YEWELL, Mary 514
YOUNG, Elizabeth 334
   Henry 11
   Richard 542
   Robert 21
   Thomas 334
   W. P. 519
YZNARDI, Joseph 252

LOCATION INDEX

Only those areas included within the continental limits of the United States have been indexed. Locations that are preceeded by a question mark indicate some doubt as to their exact nature, as it is not specified in the text.

BAR
  Cape Fear 62
BAY
  Sugar Loaf 576
BLUFF
  Indian Grave 281
BOROUGHS
  Lancaster 579
  Wilmington 611
BRANCHES
  Broad 281
  Burncoat 281
  Cherrytree 281
  Lutches 546
  Matthew's 281
  Oaky 546
  Plumb 29
  Pometer 243
  Rattlesnake 243
? Tar-kiln 312
  Tuckahoe 243
  Waggon 624
CITIES
  Alexandria 291
  Baltimore 30,98,140,192,
    241,291,294,348,423,435,
    452,461,490,506,508,544,
    609,610,640
  Boston 30,57,97,151,188,
    344,345,582,602,610
  Charleston 22,44,70,111,
    149,154,187,253,300,
    402,452,469,505,519,
    568,578,610,614,626
  New-York 40,58,108,131,
    152,158,181,201,228,
    238,241,251,253,254,
    345,355,370,376,381,
    391,392,427,431,432,
    444,456,483,489,520,
    534,535,544,558,582,
    600,603,641

CITIES (Cont.)
  Norfolk 43,139,242,435,
    506,509,534,544,545
  Philadelphia 61,100,103,
    138,142,151,159,190,199,
    227,231,238,243,246,251,
    252,254,272,301,359,368,
    371,382,394,395,432,442,
    443,450,460,469,470,476,
    483,507,509,533,544,557,
    558,567,580,609-611
  Raleigh 21,130,144,201,
    236,272,274,278,286,
    298,336,337,357,390,
    506,536,571
  Richmond 66,424,523
  Washington 424,609,640
COUNTIES
  Berkely (Va.) 424
  Bertie 255
  Bladen 18,27-29,81,96,
    124,164,169,179,259,
    269,277,288,312,429,
    462,482,538,541,556,
    570,574,588,590,624,
    638
  Brunswick 27,28,81,124,
    154,224,259,277,342,
    462,503,541,562,566,
    570,572,576,584,588
  Bucks (Pa.) 208
  Caesel (Md.) 640
  Camden (S.C.) 237
  Caroline (Md.) 640
  Caroline (Va.) 591
  Carteret 255,342
  Chatham 47,342
  Chester (Pa.) 208,610
  Chowan 255
  Craven 243
  Cumberland 4,570
  Cumberland (Eng.) 290

COUNTIES (Cont.)
  Currituck 342
  Davidson (Tenn.) 8
  Dorset (Md.) 640
  Duplin 81,96,120,121,
    124,185,209,277,281,
    322,462,538,541,546,
    588
  Edgecombe 255
  Essex (Va.) 594
  Fairfax (Va.) 424
  Franklin 255
  Frederick (Va.) 198
  Glasgow 255,342,357
  Gloucester (Va?.) 424
  Green (Ga?.) 249
  Guilford 342
  Hanover 468
  Harford (Md.) 640
  Hyde 255,342
  Iredell 342
  Johnson 342,542
  Johnston 342
  Jones 112,242-244,281,
    342,570
  Knox (Tenn.) 152
  Lancaster (Pa.) 208,
    609
  Lenoir 243,255,281,542
  Lincoln 342
  Loudon (Va.) 424
  Lunenburg 594
  M'Intosh (Ky?.) 250
  Martin 255,336,629
  Mecklenburg 255,342
  Montgomery (Pa.) 208
  Moore 342,624
  Nash 255,342
  New-Hanover 4,11,27,
    81,83,90,103,113,124,
    128,169,189,227,264,
    281,282,284,343,373,

COUNTIES (Cont.)
  New Hanover (Cont.) 404, 448,449,458,530,538, 539,541,555,564,570, 636
  Northampton 255
  Northampton (Pa.) 208, 367
  Notaway (Va.) 594
  Onslow 11,12,81,120,124, 185,243,277,281,320, 335,342,405,447,505, 514,538,541,570
  Orange 255
  Pasquotank 337
  Perquimans 255,342
  Philadelphia (Pa.) 208, 394
  Pickering (Miss.) 317
  Pitt 255
  Prince George 424
  Princess Anne (Va.) 447
  Queen Ann's (Md.) 640
  Randolph 342
  Richmond 342
  Roberson 624
  Robeson 312
  Rockbridge (Va.) 423
  Rockingham 115
  Rowan 212,542
  Rutherford 342
  Sampson 16,80,81,109, 110,265,269,277,318, 329,462,538,541,542, 552,570,588
  Surry 342
  Sussex (Md.) 640
  Tyrrel 255
  Wake 209
  Warren 255
  Wayne 255
COURT HOUSES
  Chatham 353,459,502
  Onslow 405
COWHOLE COSHEN 546
CREEKS
  Ashe's Mill 103,227
  Bachelor's 243
  ? Bigg-Harpoth 8
  Carver's 312
  Cross 624
  Cypress 281,546
  Doctor's 103,269
  Dogue 424
  Dutchman's 562

CREEKS (Cont.)
  Fishing 539
  Fussel's 281
  Governour's 259
  Hammond's 29
  Harrison's 463,584
  Holly Shelter 11,103, 227,325
  Hunter's 243
  Indian 27,572
  Island 48,163,232,243, 244,616
  Levingston's 562
  Lillington 103,227
  Lilliput 259
  Little Hunting 424
  Little Rockfish 281
  Livingston's 259
  Long 11,185,277,462, 615
  Lynch's 542
  Maxwell 546
  Merrick's 103,227
  Mill 8,562
  Moore's 11,169,404
  Muddy 546
  Orton 562
  Orton? 259
  Persimmon 546
  Prince George's 39,128
  Quewhistle 269
  Rockfish 96,103,209, 227,281,546
  Roger's 562
  Smith's 184
  Stuart's 546
  Sturgeon 562
  Town 259,562,584
  Tuckahoe 243
  Vaughan's 327
  White's 29,312
  Wood's 27
DISTRICTS
  Brunswick 492
  Columbia, of 423
  Fayetteville 569
  Hillsborough 21
  Kennebunck 492
  Mero (Tenn.) 266
  North Carolina 75,173, 188,278,284,506
  Orangeburgh 542
  Pennsylvania 367
  Pinckney 542
  South Carolina 411,626

DISTRICTS (Cont.)
  Upper Sound 555
  Washington (Tenn.) 139
  Wilmington 80,96,104, 124,185,200,280,299, 363,428,482,552,569, 595
EASTERN SHORE 640
FOLLY
  Lockwood 562
  Lockwood's 259,462
FORTS
  James 250
  Johnston 218,237,290, 295,297,396,462
  Massac 137
  Mifflin 611
GROVE 546
GULLEY, Deep 244
HAMPTON ROADS 452
HILLS, Walnut 152
HOLE, Muddy 424
HOOK, Marcus 432
IND. GRAVES (see BLUFF) 546
INLETS
  Barron? 415
  New-Topsail 284,585
ISLAND, Snake 259
LIMESTONE 546
  Beaverdam of, 281
LINE, State 259
MARSHES
  Brown 624
  Great 624
  White 29,312,542
MILLS, Sampson's 182
MOHUNGO 546
N. E. 546
NATCHEZ 317
NECKS
  Eaton's 43
  Porter's 18,429
NEW-ENGLAND 625
NEWTOPSAIL 462
OCCACOCK 218
OCEAN, Pacific 603
PANTHER 546
PECOSON/PERCOSON/POCOSON
  Alderman's Great Bay 281
  Black Swamp 243
  Dover 243
  Good 546
  Harvel's 269

PECOSON/PERCOSON/POCOSON (Cont.)
  Herrington's, James 269
  Herritage's 243
  Holley-Shelter 103,227, 281
  Lovel's 281
  Whiteoak 244

PLANTATIONS
  Ashton Barn 28
  Barn, The 184
  Bill Grange 562
  Castle-Haynes 39,86,128, 616,636
  ? Cedar Grove 77
  Cool Spring 576
  ? Forceput 51,64
  Greenfields 260
  ? Haymount 624
  Hermitage 39,42,86,102, 128,129,223,232,475, 616
  ? Hyrnham 467
  Marle Bluff 467
  Moorfields 20,155
  Moseley Hall 127
  ? Mount Pleasant 556
  Mount Vernon 358,424
  Mulberry, The 467
  Myrtle-Grove 165
  Newfields 28
  Poplar Grove 48
  Porter's Neck 18
  Rowan 27
  Spring-Hill 4
  S̄rawberry 17
  S̄trawberry 622
  Vinyard, The 165
  Westmoreland 27
  ? White Rock 244

POINTS
  Federal 4,538
  Fell's 610
  Old Point Consort 43
  Peter 349
  Repose 27
  Rockey 127,132,185,186, 622
  Rocky 17,330

POUSEMAN 546

RIVERS
  Black 4,269,349,529,538, 542
  Black? 182
  Cape-Fear 11,174,289,292,

RIVERS (Cont.)
  Cape-Fear (Cont.) 319 396,562
  Cape-Fear, North East Branch of 39,103,227, 420
  Cape-Fear, North west Branch of 590
  Cashy 342
  Deep 353,459
  ? Edisto saw-mills 542
  Elizabeth 259,562
  ? Great Kenhawa 424
  Haw 353,459
  James 423
  Little 576
  Little Miami 411
  Little Pee Dee 542
  Mississippi 152
  Neuse 342
  New 505,514,538
  North-East 11,64,128, 179,281,467
  North-east of Cape-Fear 463
  North-west 18,27,28,185, 282,312
  Ohio 8,137,346,394,488
  Patapsco 30
  Piscataqua 41
  Potomac 423,424,609
  Santee 542
  Shallott 259
  South 28,45,269,588
  Trent 243,244
  Waccamaw 29,169,259,312, 542,576
  White-oak 243,244,514

ROADS
  Newbern 590
  North-west 562

RUNS
  Difficult 424
  Dogue 424
  Four Mile 424
  Six 269,318

SOUNDS
  Sound, ____ 48,185,343, 377,455,585,590
  Cabbage-Inlet 96
  Masonboro 4
  Stump 11

SPRINGS
  Gum 424
  White 562

STATES
  Connecticut 158,411, 508,609
  Delaware 544
  Florida 445
  Georgia 59,237,352, 436,492,519,634
  Kentucky 137,229,542
  Maryland 640
  Massachusetts 188,199, 492,548,602,620
  New Hampshire 41,65, 603,620
  New-Jersey 386
  New-York 424
  Pennsylvania 190,208, 367,387,424,460,492, 522,579,580,610
  Rhode-Island 545,548
  South Carolina 111, 149,161,187,300,405, 508,519,542,579,610
  Tennessee 2,8,122, 139,266,337,492,494, 500,536
  Vermont 22,160,229, 316,613
  Virginia 43,158,199, 229,230,259,291,361, 368,382,423,424,447, 492,542,591,594

SWAMPS
  Back 281,546
  Bear 546
  Bearskin 269
  ? Beaver dam 269
  Big Colley 312
  ? Blackmingo 269
  Colley 28,312
  Flat 624
  Goshon 269
  Great 96
  Great Cohery 269
  Great Dismal 424
  Green 259,562
  Gum 243,312
  James' 96
  Little Coherry 269
  Little Colley 312
  Maxwell 281
  Panther 281
  Porter's 312
  Raft 266
  Roan 269
  Starling 269

SWAMPS (Cont.)
  White Oak 11
TERRITORIES
  Indian 492
  Mississippi 317,386,492
  N. W. of the Ohio 346,394,
    412,488
  North-West 411,492
TOPSAIL 185,462
TOWNS
  Albany 271
  Alexandria 141,358,424,
    453
  Augusta 249,521,542
  Belvedere 27,29,87,216
  Bridge-Water 199
  Bristol 620
  Brunswick 11,289
  Brunswick Old-Town 207
  Camden 542
? Cannonsburgh 578
  Charlestown 542,602
  Charlotte 218
  Chester 542
  Chilocothe 492
? Chotauck 424
  Cincinnati 492
  Columbia 542
? Combahee 187
  Cooperstown 271
  Cumberland 241
  Danbury 411
  Edenton 99,214,255
  Edinburgh 424
  Fairfield 424
  Fayette 542
  Fayetteville 4,96,212,214,
    218,239,256,314,349,352,
    389,400,406,409,417,466,
    556,569,570,581,624,637,
    638
  Fredericksburg 291,424
  Georgetown 103,187,227,
    505,508,542
  Gloucester 54,57
  Greensborough 521
  Halifax 99,214,298,536
  Hawwood 353
  Hayfield 424
  Hillsborough 96,214,255,
    298,336,536
  Kinnard 250
  Knoxville 137,152
  Lexington 317
? Little-Bridge 303

TOWNS (Cont.)
  Louisville 69,250
  Lumberton 108,266
  Malo 250
  Manchester 424
  Manhattan 431
  Marblehead 610
  Marietta 492
  Masonboro 538
  Middletown 444
  Morgan 214
? Mount Pleasant 462
  Mulberry 154
  N. Kingston 545
  Nashville 8,122,337,494
  New-Bedford 602,610
  New-Haven 508,579,619
  New-Lon___ 577
  New-London 456
  New-Orleans 324,453
  Newbern 49,52,62,178,214,
    273,284,427,505,536,586
  Newburyport 248,388,548
  Old Town 86,224,292,319
  Orangeburg 542
  Plymouth 582
  Port Tobacco 358
  Portland 344,602
  Portsmouth 41,65,602,603,
    620
  Providence 1,241,548
  Salem 54,491,508
  Salisbury 214,218
  Savannah 69,427,446
  Smith-Ville 631
  Smithland 137
  Smithville 95,147,174,296,
    396,440,547,588
  South-Shields 621
  South-Washington 103,121,205,
    210,598,618
  Southwark 558
  St. James' Santee 187
  St. Mary's 69,237,301
  Statesburg 542
  Steubenville 492
  Swansborough 256,514
  Trenton 243,500
  Vergennes 229
  Washington 185
  Wilmington (Del.) 544
  Woodbridge 131
  York 522
TOWNSHIP
  East Caln? 610

TREE
  Royal Oak 243
UNIVERSITY
  North-Carolina, of 28,
    144,214,298,313,342
WAM SQUAM 312

www.ingramcontent.com/pod-product-compliance
Lightning Source LLC
Chambersburg PA
CBHW042353070526
44585CB00028B/2910